ERIC BERNE:
Master Gamesman
A TRANSACTIONAL BIOGRAPHY

ERIC BERNE:
Master Gamesman
A TRANSACTIONAL BIOGRAPHY

Ω

*By Elizabeth Watkins Jorgensen
and Henry Irvin Jorgensen*

GROVE PRESS, INC./NEW YORK

Copyright © 1984 by Elizabeth Watkins Jorgensen
and Henry Irvin Jorgensen

All rights reserved

No part of this book may be reproduced, stored in a retrieval system, or transmitted in any form, by any means, including mechanical, electronic, photocopying, recording, or otherwise, without the prior written permission of the publisher.

First Hardcover Edition, 1984
First Printing 1984
ISBN:0-394-53846-3
Library of Congress Catalog Card Number: 83-49369

First Evergreen Edition, 1984
First Printing 1984
ISBN:0-394-62124-7
Library of Congress Catalog Number: 83-49369

Library of Congress Cataloging in Publication Data
Jorgensen, Elizabeth Watkins.
  Eric Berne, master gamesman.

  Includes bibliographical references.
  1. Berne, Eric. 2. Psychiatrists—Biography.
3. Transactional Analysis. I. Jorgensen, Henry Irvin
II. Title
R C339.52.B48J67   1984   150.19'5 [B]   83-49369
ISBN 0-394-53846-3
ISBN 0-394-62124-7 (pbk.)

Printed in the United States of America

Grove Press, Inc., 196 West Houston Street,
New York, N.Y., 10014

5 4 3 2 1

DEDICATED

To the late FRANK LLOYD, a true friend of Eric Berne,

whose friendship to us was an inspiration,

a *sine qua non* for this biography

ACKNOWLEDGEMENTS

The authors are grateful to the following publishers for permission to reprint from previously copyrighted materials:

Dover Publications, Inc., and the James Branch/Margaret Cabell Estate for excerpts from *Jurgen* by James Branch Cabell, 1977 edition, copyright © 1970, by James Branch Cabell.

Grove Press, Inc., for excerpts from *The Happy Valley*, by Eric Berne, copyright © 1968 by Eric Berne; for excerpts from *Transactional Analysis in Psychotherapy*, by Eric Berne, copyright © 1961 and *What Do You Say After You Say Hello?* by Eric Berne, copyright © 1972 by City National Bank, Los Angeles, Robin Way, and Janice Way Farlinger.

McGraw Hill, Inc., for excerpts from *Laughter on the Hill* by Margaret Parton, copyright © 1945.

Real People Press, Inc. for excerpts from *In and Out of the Garbage Pail*, by Fritz Perls, copyright © 1969 by Real People Press.

Simon & Schuster, Inc., for excerpts from *Sex in Human Loving* by Eric Berne, M.D., copyright © 1970, by the City National Bank of Los Angeles.

Contents

Preface	ix
Introduction	xv
1. Scattering Golden Apples	1
2. The Blonde Princess	12
Counterpoint 1	23
3. Moral Fibre	24
Counterpoint 2	38
4. An "H" Marriage	39
5. The Happy Days Lie Ahead	49
6. Forever May Last as Long as Seven Years	60
Counterpoint 3	66
7. Prince Lennie	68
8. "Crazy" Lennie	79
9. There's Only Room for One	91
10. The Martian Finds a Haven	100
11. Jack in the Beanstalk Meets Cinderella	119
12. Poker	133
13. The Dorothy Who Did Not Understand	138
14. The Unsinkable Dr. Berne	152
15. Go Ahead! You Can Do It! It's Easy!	166
16. The Outsider on the Inside Track	185
17. A Boys' Club	199
18. A Maserati, a Best-Seller and a Young, Blonde Wife	215
19. Farewell to Queen Helen	225
20. Stopped Running	241
Coda	252
Notes	254
Index	269

Ω

Preface

This is the story of a psychiatrist, a genius with an IQ close to 200, who founded a new school of quick-cure psychology called Transactional Analysis (or TA), wrote a best-seller that was the rage of the sixties, and was successful in everything he set out to do, except that he was "powerless in the face of beauty."

How should a great man's life be told?

Veterans of more than one TA group, we set out to write a book about this larger-than-life individual who had lived in a town near us (Carmel, California), about his deep respect for the mental abilities of his humblest patients, insistence on honesty in communications with them, and his "demystification of psychiatric cant."

He wrote like a god and he developed Transactional Analysis. Even now, TA still is not a household word. It may be some time before its full impact hits the mental health world. But TA does for psychoanalysis what mass production did for the automobile—makes it possible for large numbers of people to live at their optimum, a feat formerly achievable by only a few. Transactional Analysis does not necessarily supplant conventional psychotherapy, but it is steadily making progress as an effective means of marriage and family counseling, reforming criminals, treating mental breakdowns, and improving communications between people. The directness of the TA approach now makes much of dream analysis as a therapeutic technique appear awkward and lumbering.

So that's what we should have written about. There is a great deal of exciting material there, *but* the story of Berne's life took over, and it turned out that we were powerless in the face of that life.

Berne was a master at making the complexities of the human

brain comprehensible to the people most disturbed by its tricks. He was also a master at wrapping himself in a cloak of mystery, in keeping his personal life guarded and compartmentalized so that when he shifted from one of his compartments to another, he appeared an entirely different person. Even after working for eight years on his biography and uncovering a score of "secrets," we do not pretend to know the ultimate secret.

Berne wrote: "The destiny of every human being is decided by what goes on inside his skull when he is confronted by what goes on outside his skull. Each person designs his own life. Freedom gives him the power to carry out his own designs, and power gives him the freedom to interfere with the designs of others. Even if the outcome is decided by men he has never met or germs he will never see, his last words and words on his gravestone will cry out his striving."

We uncovered no dramatic last words on his gravestone. However, we followed Berne's own recipe for seeking the essence of a man, for in the remainder of this quotation he says: "If by great misfortune he dies in dust and silence, only those who know him best will get the slogan right, and all outside the private chambers of friendship, marriage and medicine will see him wrong. In most cases he has spent his life deceiving the world, and usually himself as well."

Did Berne spend his life "deceiving the world"? Some thought so. TA's Claude Steiner said: "Eric was in hiding. I told him that. I think it very important that you find out what he was hiding. Something was going on. People in TA were hiding for Eric, too. The charade is continuing."

The doctor who knew him best in the private chambers of medicine thought of Berne as a "bright kind of madman." Those who knew him best in the private chambers of friendship and marriage have many intriguing stories to tell. A few of these stories are beautiful, and most of them seem to say that here was a wizard who liked secrets. His intimates did not "see him wrong," but they saw him only as he related to them personally. They saw him out of the context of the overall picture, tangents of the whirling dervish in his spin cycle.

When he was still in college, Lennie Bernstein, as he was then called, wrote in the college literary magazine, *The McGil-*

Iiad, an observation which gives a clue to some of the aspects of Berne's personality treated in this book. He said that there are emotions which society "considers it desirable to repress—some forms of sexual desire, some fears, some forms of egotism. . . ." People must use large amounts of energy keeping forbidden desires suppressed into the subconscious by "sheer strength," he said, and so it follows: ". . . the less repressed we are, the more alive we will be since we will have additional energy to put to useful ends—both the energy of repression and the latent emotional energy. This obvious conclusion will be offensive to many of the more conservative minds among us."

For Berne this conclusion was not offensive, because something had preserved in him the unprogrammed thinking of his childhood. Berne was the person most likely to see that the emperor had no clothes or, if he had clothes, to wonder about why he was wearing them that particular way. He didn't accept the conventional explanations of why people behaved as they did. He determined to find out for himself, as not all of civilization made a great deal of sense when viewed with uncorrupted thoughts. He decided to use himself as a guinea pig to see what would happen if he didn't use large amounts of energy keeping forbidden desires suppressed by sheer strength.

So the less repressed he was the more alive he was. But few could understand what he was up to. His actions, like his conclusions, quite frequently turned out to be offensive to others.

One TA leader told us the following anecdote: Berne arrived at one of his concepts about the way people behave by an experiment at his home town post office. In Carmel there is no home mail delivery because the residents take pride in refusing to number their houses, the result being a daily parade to the post office.

Berne analyzed the reactions of those he met, coming and going, and decided that there was a fairly rigid behavioral formula involved. If a person knew another well, a simple "How are you?" was deemed inadequate, and further remarks of a meaningless but honorific nature were usually pursued. On the other hand, if the two people were only slightly acquainted, an answer to the question "How are you?" was not expected to involve a description of body temperature, pulse rate, or a catalog of other vital signs. Berne wanted to switch the formulae around a bit and got Fort Ord colleague Dave Kupfer to help him.

The two of them behaved perversely contrary to the norm, "So that to the man with whom they had a cordial relationship they would say: 'Hello,' and then turn their backs, and to the men with whom they had a routine relationship they would start saying: 'How's your wife? How's your child?' (What have you been doing lately? Have you seen any good movies, etc.?) Naturally, the latter thought they were crazy, and the former thought they were rude, and before long everybody they knew who went to the post office hated them."

The post office experiment served a scientific purpose, but Berne's acquaintances who were not in on the game found the quixotic behavior hard to fathom. He was planets away from the usual "earthian" thinking. This was just one of those compartments of his personality that was striking. Even more striking was his energy-crackling refusal to repress himself when confronting that romantic aspect of his being where he was so much alive to female beauty that "it cut through him like a knife." This is the compartment that keeps trying to take over this book.

At the same time he seemed relentlessly driven to ferret out every possible variation and quirk in human behavior—so much so that many people felt he was ignoring them as persons and treating them like rats in a psychologist's maze. So in one area he was largely defenseless, in another a wizard, always in control.

In *What Do You Say After You Say Hello?* he indicated that the TA way to look at life was to think "Martian"—in other words, we weren't to be hornswoggled by the conventionalities. Unhornswoggled Berne was able to spend 80 percent of the time "in his Adult," looking at the results of people's misconceptions, the payoffs—the transactions.

But he spent a certain percentage of his time in the quest for intimacy. Here he seemed at his most Martian. The conventional ways of looking for intimacy weren't for him. He reasoned that a controlled experiment in which games were eliminated would be the yellow brick road to that desired state which people rarely achieved. (Claude Steiner says: "Berne believed that intimacy was a generally unattainable state, and . . . [people] could consider themselves lucky if they experienced 15 minutes of intimacy in their lifetimes.") Was he speaking here more from his own experience than from observation of people in general? He defined intimacy as the state where there were no games, but his first wife, Elinor, identified him as a Master Gamesman in two senses: "of all the people she ever knew 'Eric was the games player to end all games [players].'" On the other hand, "He knew all about games. So he was the logical person to present the subject, as he did, for a very useful purpose."

Since Berne was continually looking at things not as they *ought* to look but as they really did look, we have taken the same approach in this biography—looking at Berne's transactions as they really took place, not as they "should have been" for someone who wrote like a god, had an IQ nudging 200, etc.

As biographers we have been obliged to include the violent reactions of some of those who knew this Martian in his private chambers, some who resented being treated like statistics, and others who couldn't understand his obsession with having "secrets." Their comments were at times acid; but nonetheless they seem to us like vivid shards that contribute to a brilliant mosaic.

Before we completed the manuscript, and with some trepidation, we showed parts of it to selected leaders of the TA movement. They could have told us that we were playing a game called "Blemish" and that we should burn the book. We were surprised by their largeness of spirit. Although some people have criticized the ITAA for elevating Berne to sainthood, we have been assured by Norman James, at that time president of the ITAA, and by a number of other prominent members of that organization, of their support in our endeavor. Several of them have given generously of their time in critiquing parts of the manuscript.

Berne is not here to explain himself and people see reality in different ways. Our viewpoint may have caused us to distort, change, or magnify the reality as seen by another. We can't know the absolute truth of any incident, but we have tried to avoid untruth. One early adherent to TA commented that she was sorry that Eric didn't make his discoveries in time to cure himself but felt, as we do, that the contributions he made to society were so significant that they overshadowed personal drawbacks.

Actually it is probably one of the best arguments for the effectiveness of Transactional Analysis that many of Berne's closest TA disciples have reacted so positively to this "warts and all" story of this eccentric genius. Those who were close to him say that they knew Eric had some quirks, though they didn't see the full panoply. They loved him at the time, love him still, and say it seems good to have him back again, even if only within the covers of a book.

Ω

Introduction
What Is Transactional Analysis?

Transactional Analysis is a system for treating mental or emotional problems. Emotionally charged exchanges between people, called "transactions," are analyzed, often in a group setting, and these give clues to what is really going on in a person's thinking processes.

Instead of putting a patient on a couch, or asking him to say anything that comes into his mind, or getting him to tell about his dreams or malfunctionings of the day, the transactional analyst watches the person in action in group therapy. She also hears about the patient's adventures outside of therapy and shows him what "games" he is playing. The games the TA therapist is concerned about are the ones that end up in "bad payoffs"—negative feelings, put-downs, and estrangement between people.

Some critics contend that TA is "shallow," because patients often come out of therapy with the wrong attitude—instead of being festooned with guilt for failing to produce analyzable material for the therapist, they burst out of their sessions chortling, chuckling, and hugging each other. Furthermore, critics can't understand why, when there is such a deal of sin and shame in the world, the usual TA practitioner seems to exude an inner radiance and a sense of well-being. These are considered out of place in a world where everyone should be waiting for Godot.

Another thing incomprehensible to many is that TA maintains that a person can change and change fast. There is no anabolic-catabolic struggle going on in her cellular structure that keeps her from living a full life. If a person in the past has cultivated repeatedly the art of making messes, there is not some inherited or archetypal compulsion that will keep her making them forever. TA says she formulated her script when she was too young to know better. At the time she made this script decision (perhaps at age five) it may have represented a reasonable way of coping with life-threatening elements in her environment. Now that she is older, she can know better. She can reassess the original response and decide whether her present-day behavior is still reasonable.

People sometimes chuckle after their TA groups or individual sessions because they have stumbled onto exciting secrets about themselves and the significant figures in their lives. They have realized that their mothers and fathers have been giving them double messages from birth. Early on they didn't know what these unformulated messages meant, but they sensed an emotional undercurrent of fear, anger, love, or hatred all mixed up together. In TA groups these mixed messages finally get sorted out amid cries of "aha!" from here and there about the room. The great phallic snake in the Garden of Eden bedevilled Adam and Eve into tasting the ovum-like apple, and ever since, passive consumerism has lost out to the excitement of finding out *what is really going on*. Since that time some sort of linkage has existed between knowledge and sexiness.

Some people believe that the "Parent," "Adult", and "Child" concepts used so much in TA are merely Berne's way of making the Freudian Superego, Ego, and Id more palatable to the general public. But there really is a difference, as Berne explains in several of his books. For one thing, Parent, Adult, and Child are all in the conscious mind, and the Id is not.

TA therapists and even many group members can recognize that a person is reacting like a stern Parent when he beetles his brow and shakes his finger at a bumptious teenager, just as own parent did when he was a child. The same person may exhibit a wheedling Child when he's seeking a favor from someone else in the group. Communications often break down when a straight inquiry for facts coming from a person's Adult is interpreted by another as coming from her Parent, as when a wife's question to her husband—"Have you taken out the garbage yet?"—is interpreted by him as a Parental criticism for not having already performed this function.

> Berne says: "Some professionals earn a living by the public exhibition of a constant ego state: clergymen, the Parent; diagnosticians, the Adult; and clowns, the Child."

The Child ego state is considered the source of intuition, joy, creative masterpieces, and playfulness. If stifled by an overcontrolling Parent, the person goes through his life like a joyless automaton. On the other hand, if the person has no Parental programming to restrain a rambunctious Child, he may "act-out" wildly in ways that harm himself or others.

The Adult part of the personality is the fact-processor; it checks out what is real or not real in the impressions received. It is the Adult that monitors the messages flying back and forth from the Child to the Parent, and which makes the decision as to what is appropriate in light of the available facts. The use of the Adult, therefore, requires more energy because it must make comparisons and decisions, whereas the other two ego states generally function with automatic reactions. Also, as the semanticists tell us, the world of facts can be very tricky and the sorting out process is not easy.

Other aspects of the TA theory: complimenting or giving friendly attention to another person is called a positive stroke. Blasting another person is called a negative stroke. Because a baby needs stimulation it will learn to call forth negative strokes if it can't get positive ones; any attention is better than none at all. Games are devices by which a person ends up with negative strokes. Bad scripts are those which produce ugly results or recurring negative pay-offs over a life-time.

For a more detailed explanation of TA principles, the reader is referred to Berne's own books, particularly *Transactional Analysis in Psychotherapy*; Claude Steiner's *Scripts People Live*; Tom Harris's *I'm OK—You're OK*, which Berne called "the first real Layman's Guide [to TA];" Muriel James and Dorothy Jongward's *Born To Win: Transactional Analysis with Gestalt Experiments*; and *The Power Is in The Patient* and

Changing Lives Through Redecision Therapy by Mary McClure Goulding and Robert L. Goulding.

1

Scattering Golden Apples

What to do about death? Finish everything and then wait for it like a rotting log? Or leave some things unfinished and die with regrets? The art of living is to walk the earth like a prince, scattering apples wherever you go. The art of dying is to finish your own apple just at the right moment to say, "I am content, the rest are for you to enjoy at my wake."

Eric Berne, Sex in Human Loving

Eric Berne, creator of Transactional Analysis, psychiatrist, author of *Games People Play*, and originator of the *I'm OK—You're OK* concept, after walking the earth like a prince, scattering good feelings to right and left amongst his thousands of admiring followers, died at the early age of sixty. He was working on an unfinished "apple," *What Do You Say After You Say Hello?* in his room at Monterey Hospital near Carmel-by-the-Sea, California, his home and haven for many years, when he suffered his fatal heart attack on July 15, 1970.

Legend has it that just before he died Berne quoted to his doctors a statement from his last book, that it is difficult for a man to live past the age at which his father died but doubly difficult to live past the age at which his mother died. Berne believed his mother to have died at sixty; he had survived his sixtieth birthday by only a little over two months.

Unfortunately, biographical research ruins many a good legend. Berne's doctors had never heard him talk about surviving his mother's age at death. His most significant last words may have been those he uttered over the telephone to his former secretary, Anne Morse, the morning of the day he died. He told her, "I have accomplished everything I set out to do and I have finished everything."

Simple graveside rites were arranged with care. Berne's youngest sons were then fifteen and eighteen. Their mother, Dorothy Berne, and their aunt, Grace Berne Rose, sister of Eric, had determined that it be a quiet family leave-taking. Torre, the "blonde Venus," twenty-seven years Berne's junior, whom he had married after his divorce from Dorothy and who was being divorced from Eric, was specifically asked not to come. Claude Steiner, author of *Scripts People Live*, and felt by some people to be Berne's spiritual descendant and chief disciple in the Transactional Analysis movement, was also specifically asked not to come.

As a matter of fact, no one in the TA movement was asked to come. Dorothy and Grace did not want the TA aspect of Berne's life to overshadow the family mourning, nor did they want the type of funeral that might be turned into a media event.

As the black limousine slowly approached the grave, however, the family saw by the coffin none other than Torre, weeping uncontrollably. Shielded by one of the majestic Monterey pines, which look so much like the *pini parasole* of Rome, were Frank Lloyd and Nadya and Valerio Giusi, dear but uninvited friends.

According to Viola Litt Callaghan, long time member and first secretary-treasurer of the TA seminar, the only TA member present was Dr. Franklin Ernst from Vallejo, who had reportedly said, "I don't care what they say—I'm going!" Viola told us: "I wish I had known Frank was going; I would have gone. It was terrible! Why did they keep us all out? We weren't connected with the family, but we loved Eric and he loved us." (Dr. Ernst, though, reported to us that he had not been at the cemetery but had paid his respects at the funeral parlor.)

The rabbi, who had come from San Jose to conduct the services, said that although he had not personally known the deceased, he had known of him as a great man. The only absent widow was Elinor, who had married Eric in the 1940s and lived in Connecticut. Ellen, the daughter of Elinor and Eric, was there, but their son was in Europe.

A day or so after the ceremonies were concluded, Claude Steiner drove down to the little wind-swept cemetery near the ocean where he "wailed and wet the ground with his tears."

In Marion, Illinois, Dr. Martin Groder took a hammer and chisel, went outside his house, and furiously attacked a stone wall for about an hour. Gradually the word *Eric* could be seen taking shape. Groder was not impressed by the crispness of the image, but he had been in a rage because he felt that Eric had let himself die and "it helped to get the anger out."

On the other side of the Monterey Peninsula, some of the uninvited held a Carmel-type of ceremonial near the mouth of the Carmel River. Here a stretch of white sandy beach curves southward from Carmel toward the river. *The Carmel Pine Cone*, from time to time, publishes stories of beachcombers who have ventured along this dangerous strand only to be pulled into the surf by an unexpected surge, never to be seen again.

Still, it was along this beautiful but unpredictable shore that Eric used to jog on Sundays. There he and his young son were once scooped out of the boiling surf by artist Valerio Giusi, after they had been knocked down by a great wave. On the other side of the river, in a small clump of trees, a tribe of Costonoan Indians roasted one of its members over a fire around 1910. Toward the Pebble Beach side, poet Robinson Jeffers built his Tor House, stone by stone, as a refuge from the "thickening center" of vulgarity and corruption of what he called our "Perishing Republic."

A little north of this wave-washed crescent lay Stewart's Cove and Reamer's Point, where Berne and his friends used to gather every Sunday to jog, gossip, get their sun-tans or fog-tans, as the case might be—and eye the pretty girls (the pretty girls also eyeing the personable men). Berne came here on Sundays with his children. He would do his constitutional up and back several times, pull his insubordinate Charlie Brown cap over his eyes, and begin to take a nap, after remarking, "If anybody says anything funny, wake me up."

From Stewart's Cove one can see the tower of the Carmelite

Monastery across the bay, a scene which Berne said flashed into his mind's eye even when he was half-way around the world—a symbol of peace, home, and the rare acceptance and camaraderie he felt there.

It was in this spot, at eight in the morning, that the rump funeral was held. His Carmel friends, left out of the family ceremony, felt the need for some form of leave-taking. Eric Berne, a man who had drastically altered many of their lives, had suddenly been taken from them. Later a rumor was circulated that this was some form of witches' mass organized by enemies of Berne, with lighted candles and incantations raised to Beelzebub. But such was not the case. The event was not even organized, exactly ("organized" is not a Carmel-type of word). It arose mostly out of need, the need of beach friends, neighbors, and former patients.

There were memories to run through. Frank Lloyd, a former editor of the weekly *Pine Cone*, stood there in the swirling mists that blanket the Carmel area of a summer morning. He was remembering the scrawny, funny-looking kid who'd opened the ceremonies every day at Montreal High School with his bugle, and who had worked with him on the McGill college newspaper.

Marjory, Frank's wife, remembered the time Berne had come to their house, glowing with childlike enthusiasm and pride because his publisher had sent him news that *Games People Play* had outsold *Lady Chatterley's Lover* in England.

Dorothy Smythe remembered looking for a psychiatrist in the yellow pages of the phone book and calling the one first listed (Berne). She expected his secretary would be able to squeeze in an appointment in three months at the earliest. Instead Berne himself answered the phone. He asked her where she lived, and when he found it was nearby, said she could be there in twenty minutes. Arriving breathless, she was then struck by the cramped office shared by no noticeable secretary, and wondered if he were some unsuccessful alcoholic, with little practice and no prospects—until he began to talk, and then she was startled by his wit, his brilliance, and the exciting quality of his mind.

Jerry Barron, a lawyer and local political figure, was asked to say a few words of farewell. Noting his diffidence about beginning, Dorothy Smythe passed him a copy of *Games People Play*, opened to the back of the book. There Berne was concluding his message by pointing out that there are alternatives to the self-defeating games that most people engage in.

Barron read:

> Awareness means the capacity to see a coffeepot and hear the birds sing in one's own way and not the way one was taught. . . . Awareness requires living in the here and now, and not in the elsewhere, the past or the future. . . .
>
> . . . the person who is aware . . . will not hurry because he is living in the present moment with the environment which is here: the sky and the trees as well as the feeling of motion . . . The aware person is alive because he knows how he feels, where he is and when it is. He knows that after he dies the trees will still be there, but he will not be there to look at them again, so he wants to see them now with as much poignancy as possible.
>
> The somber picture presented . . . in which human life is mainly a process of filling in time until the arrival of death, or Santa Claus, with very little choice, if any, of what kind of business one is going to transact during the long wait, is a commonplace, but not the final answer. For certain fortunate people there is something which transcends all classifications of behavior, and that is awareness; something which rises above the programming of the past, and that is spontaneity; and something that is more rewarding than games, and that is intimacy.

At this point, Louis Conlan said something like: "What is more rewarding is to have more wine and less bullshit." Everyone dove for the bread, cheese, and wine. Even the fortunate few who are aware of coffeepots and trees can sense when they are getting too close to cracking up, and it is one thing to sniffle uncontrollably in the programmed setting of a funeral parlor, but around a campfire at the beach?

A third memorial service was held at Dr. John Dusay's house in San Francisco. Viola Litt Callaghan set it up—about forty people were there, those who had regularly attended the Tuesday night TA seminars at Berne's house in San Francisco. Vi said: "I put on a little thing—a long scarf—like a rabbi wears and I read from a Hebrew prayer book and Ray Poindexter brought a big bowl of plums. I passed around plums so everyone would eat them as part of the ceremony."

In Berne's *The Structure and Dynamics of Organizations and Groups* he had told the story of his first attempt to form a club when he was a small boy in Montreal. As an inducement to membership, he'd promised refreshments at the end of the meeting, but the big boys stole the plums he had bought, and Berne's first "group" fell apart.

Also in San Francisco, a fourth memorial service was hastily arranged in a more formal setting. The highly esteemed Rabbi Joseph Asher was prevailed upon to mention Berne in his regular Friday night service at the imposing Temple Emanu-El in San Francisco. The candlelit chapel was always fairly well attended for 5:30 P.M. services, but this week it was crowded with fifty or sixty of Eric's friends. Rabbi Asher wove an appreciation of Berne into his Sabbath "sermonette." He had admired Eric's work but had not known him personally.

The gist of his message was this: History was said to repeat itself. Dr. Berne had been an advocate of candor as opposed to games. Asher told his congregation: "If we could break the cycle of games played among nations as well as people and get back to candor we could assure ourselves that history need not always repeat itself."

After the services, the TA members drove over to Berne's house on Collins Street, where the Tuesday night seminars had been held in recent years. Memories were swapped, but nobody felt that he was at a wake enjoying golden apples left him by his prince. The members were stunned and rudderless. The makeshift memorials seemed to emphasize the fact that they had never been able to get close to Berne, but rather had been shut out by the heavy curtain that surrounded Berne's private life.

Some TA members felt there had been no final sign on the part of the master that their relationship with him had meant anything. Claude Steiner, for one, told us: "There are a lot of things Berne didn't do. I find it inconceivable that he should g write a will and not mention in some way—just something— about his most devoted disciples. It's impossible for me to understand. I'm not saying that he should have left anything valuable, but some remembrance, something that connects you up."

Steiner felt that while the great TA leader was alive he did give out "loving vibes and if you were willing to leave it at that—you were loved by him and you knew it. But he never put it into words or gave a sign of affection. That was unlike him at least with men." Later in *Scripts People Live* Steiner was to write: ". . . when I think of [Berne] today, three years after he died, tears still well up in my eyes." When Steiner moved away from his house in Kensington, California, he ripped out a section of plaster wall (on which Berne had scribbled during his sixtieth birthday party: "Eric—Dad—The Great Pyramid") and took it with him.

Shortly after Berne's death another of his earliest disciples, ex-ITAA president Dave Kupfer, succumbed to cancer. One of his last requests was that his ashes be buried at Eric's feet.

TA's Dr. John Dusay rescued from Collins Street the chair with the green vinyl cushion that Berne used to sit in for the seminars. It wasn't "worth anything but . . . it had sentimental value for us." The chair, with a brass plaque, now is the symbolic "empty chair" at the Tuesday night seminar meetings which still go on at ITAA headquarters.

TA's Pam Levin told us: "He got us all traveling ninety miles an hour down the freeway, and then all of a sudden he was no longer there driving the machine. We were left with bits and pieces. We all had relationships to him and we all had minor (in comparison) relationships to each other. I think he kind of fostered that separateness." Pam said several of the TA regulars went into therapy as a result of Berne's sudden death.

When Fritz Perls died, TA-trained lay analyst and teacher Carolyn Crane had asked Berne: "What happens to the followers of a great man who dies?" Eric had replied bluntly: "They always get screwed. Either way they get screwed. If they go on believing in the system it becomes a dead end, and if they go out on their own in reaction to the death of the leader they get equally lost."

Berne had been the heart and soul of the TA movement, editing the *Transactional Analysis Bulletin* single-handedly, although both Dave Kupfer and Dr. Stephen B. Karpman had suggested that it might be good for the movement if Eric stepped down to let the younger members get some experience.

Berne responded by carefully picking others to take the top official positions in the International Transactional Analysis Association and SAFTAS (San Francisco Transactional Analysis Seminar) and eventually, in the last year of his life, giving up the editorship of the *Bulletin*. But he was still the power behind the throne.

After his death the members wondered, according to Herbert Courland, whether they should disband the organization entirely. How could they continue by themselves? No matter who the nominal head of the organization was, everybody knew that what held things together was the group's excitement over the thoughts that crackled out of the self-regenerating Berne dynamo.

Berne's charisma is shown in Steve Karpman's statement about the impression the TA leader made on him when, as a young psychiatrist teaching at the Langley-Porter Neuropsychiatric Institute, he first saw Berne's leadership in action. Fellow psychiatrist John Dusay had suggested that he and Karpman attend one of Berne's seminars together. (Dusay had first attended when he'd noticed Berne's flyer posted on the bulletin board of the University of California Medical School. Berne had put these up at several clinics in the area.)

Karpman said:

> I went into the room and it was almost like some Hollywood biblical movie I think, where Barabbas meets Christ, or in the movie *Quo Vadis*? . . . I went into this horse-shoe shaped apartment on Washington Street where there was supposed to be this great man . . . Berne was actually sitting in the other room out of sight

of me. It was crowded and I . . . sat at a work table right in the middle of the floor in the front room. And I could hear the voice of this master talking. It was like in *Quo Vadis* where a follower first met Christ way up on the hill a thousand yards away. I'm not saying it was a religious experience; I'm not that way. It was sort of amusing, though, all those people sitting around hanging on the words of "The Master." He definitely was "The Master" at this point, although *Games* hadn't come out, or if it had, it hadn't become well-known yet.

Collins Street was a lot more informal [Berne moved there subsequently] and he picked a place that had sufficient parking spaces nearby. At Collins Street there were also crowds of people sitting on the floor at his feet, listening. His wasn't an ordinary voice; it was a very full voice, like an announcer's. He spoke in chopped, clipped phrases, with pauses, and dry, understated wit, and you always heard a new idea.

Then I went five consecutive years without missing a Tuesday night. . . . I liked the humor and I liked the brains.

Luckily, the great mind had attracted bright people. After a brief period of reorganization, instead of falling apart, the international organization grew like wildfire.

Not so quick to recover were Berne's close friends, especially his women friends. The man, who for much of his life had been considered an ugly, inept oddball, developed from mid life on a number of relationships with women, some of whom were madly devoted to him.

Immediately after Berne's death, his dear friend Nadya Giusi, accompanied by Berne's wife, Torre, visited the funeral parlor. She entered the room where Eric's body lay in the casket, hoping to put a small and exquisite seashell in his inert hand as a token of happy days on the Carmel beach and the affection felt for him by his "sand-between-the-toes" friends. She was overwhelmed at the last moment, however, and dropped the "tiny, perfect shell" into the coffin and fled; she later told us that it took her ten years to get over Berne's death. He was not only her friend but her mentor—the first person who convinced her she was beautiful and made her feel OK about herself.

A woman who had had a relationship with Berne before he developed TA still dreams of him and that "they have made it together." She feels that Berne is telling her that he is sad because biographers are writing about him and because of this "a cloud is hanging over Carmel." He is asking her not to reveal anything about him to us. According to her, Berne had no faults and was perfect in every respect.

A teacher and therapist trained in TA principles was his last amour. Ten years after his death she, too, felt that he was keeping her from talking freely about their relationship. The night before he died, she dreamed that she was searching for him in the basement of his hospital. She realized upon awakening that the back door in the basement was where they wheeled out the corpses.

A vital contributor to cardinal TA theory dreamed soon after his death that she and Berne had taken off their Mickey Mouse masks and were finally able to make love. Her affair with him in the sixties came close to wrecking her life, but she feels that in spite of "all the rottenness and unfairness of Eric—there was magnificence there somehow."

The sadness over his death goes on and on. We received a letter from a non-TA social worker who was supervised by Berne in 1951-55. She told us that upon reading part of our manuscript she "had been having a full-blown grief reaction over his death even though [she] cried at the time and went to his funeral in San Francisco. . . ."

Berne burned up his sixty years too fast, but that was part of the excitement of the man. He accomplished extraordinary things in those sixty years but failed to accomplish a number of things that are par for the course for many ordinary mortals.

But then the deeper the vales the higher the mountains.

So a basic unevenness exists here. He was magnificent in extemporaneous exposition, possessing an amazing vitality and unceasing creativity. He was superlative at teaching other therapists to do what he did. He planned his TA international organization "so it would be a world-beater from the beginning." On the other hand, he appeared confused and awkward in human relationships, sometimes even shockingly crass in his approach to those who wanted to be close to him.

One of his colleagues remarked that he "was never able to love." Certainly he seemed unable to love a woman in a long-term relationship as an equal human being. Wives and most of his lovers he treated as commodities and "kicked [women therapists] out of his life" after his affairs with them were over.

But it also seems clear that some of his children, stepchildren, most TA disciples, and some of his friends and colleagues felt that they had been touched by his love.

Our feelings toward Berne during the years we have worked on this book have swung from fervent admiration to rage and pity at his failure to be as marvelous in private life as he was in his writings. We have known wild curiosity about the secrets he kept. We have wept over the way he short-circuited himself so that he could not receive affection from others. And our dream has been that, through the chinks and interstices of the fence of silence and isolation that has surrounded him, enough has filtered through to make this biography take on some of the fascination of the enigmatic man himself.

2

The Blonde Princess

If you don't know which girl to choose, let someone else choose and then choose the same one.
                                     Eric Berne, *Sex in Human Loving*

When a man meets a married couple he too often asks, "What could she do for me?" Instead of "What is she doing for him?"
                                     Eric Berne, *Sex in Human Loving*

In 1941 when Elinor and Ian McRae met some New Haven Trotskyist friends of theirs, who were passing through the small Connecticut village where they lived, they were told, "Hey, we know a guy, really a very interesting guy, but kind of a nutty guy—who's the junior psychiatrist at the sanitarium located here. You really ought to look him up. He's lonely because he doesn't know anybody in town."

This nutty but interesting guy was Eric L. Bernstein, who had finished his two years' psychiatric residency at Yale in 1938. After a brief sojourn at Ring Sanitarium in Arlington, Massachusetts, and two trips studying mental institutions in Syria, Lebanon, and Turkey, Bernstein had obtained in late 1939 or early 1940 a post as a psychiatrist on the staff of a sanitarium in Connecticut. This institution was located in a village (which shall remain unnamed) on the Long Island Sound between New York and New Haven, a community with a population of less than 5000.

The local stores extended credit to all the residents. The

quaint frame salt-box houses surrounded by enormous, tree-studded lawns, the winding river, and the New England-style churches and public buildings made the village a magnet later on for artists, movie stars and TV personalities. In the thirties, however, this spot was undiscovered and unappreciated except by people of perception like Eric L. Bernstein and the Ian McRaes.

Lonely Eric hung around with Trotskyists and Socialists and was interested in their ideas, but he kept to his usual role of observer. He was liberal but he was no activist, whereas the McRaes were right in the thick of things.

Not long after Ian and Elinor got to know young Dr. Bernstein, he gave a party in New York. His mother, Sara, had an apartment on West Seventy-Second Street for which he paid the rent. She worked days building up an advertising business, leaving the apartment free for Eric when he came to town in connection with his work at Mt. Sinai Hospital, where he was a clinical assistant in psychiatry. That way they saved the cost of two establishments. When social gatherings such as this were scheduled, his mother could stay overnight with her married daughter, Grace, in New Jersey.

Perhaps in Eric's mind this party was to be the first in a series; he was launching a "salon," just like the one his mother had had when he was growing up in Montreal. He invited everyone he knew who was "interesting"—even a stationmaster from Damascus he had met on his trip to the Levant and somebody from Smyrna, who was eagerly expected but didn't show up. Among those who did show up were Dr. Houze, the director of the sanitarium where Eric was employed, and Dr. Gerow, also on the staff, who was not on speaking terms with Dr. Houze.

Also included was an old Montreal medical school acquaintance who wrote us in detail about this party. The guest list appeared to be aimed at bringing together people of opposing views and interweaving irascibilities. About fifty people crammed into the tiny smoke-filled rooms, all "drinking and babbling," voices raised. Through it all Eric stood in the doorway to the kitchenette observing everyone with a "glint in his eye" or alternately "sitting on the floor paying no attention to his guests."

Dr. Gabriel Yelin said a "more bizarre assemblage of people has seldom been encountered."

Afterwards Eric told the McRaes, "I knew a lot of those people would just hate each other, and it was such fun watching them!" Two weeks later he gave the second (and the last) in the "series": nobody came. Eric was puzzled. He couldn't understand what went wrong, as he "certainly had had good liquor."

Eric abandoned the salon. He had found a new kitchenette to observe from. No need to spread himself thin watching the interweaving hostilities of a multitude of acquaintances. He had a gold mine of medical problems and vivid personalities to explore right at hand in the Ian McRaes. He took to dropping in frequently on the McRaes. The second time he called on them, the young doctor abruptly opened the front door and marched across the living room floor. Pulling down Elinor's lower eyelid, he said, "Hmmm—I see—anemia. Better come round to the sanitarium for tests tomorrow."

Ian had been hospitalized for ulcers and arthritis, and still lounged around a lot in his bathrobe. In the early part of his marriage to Elinor, he had had a touch of tuberculosis. An alumnus of the WPA art project in Chicago (one of Roosevelt's New Deal innovations which supported artists during the Great Depression), he was a landscape architect and a painter of beautiful, gloomy landscapes. He was excellent at both, but Elinor had to eke out their income with piano lessons.

Ian and Eric never did hit it off, but they respected each other's abilities. And the late night discussions got a bit much even for this frail veteran of University of Illinois and WPA bull sessions, as the emphasis seemed inevitably and enthusiastically to shift to Elinor's activities.

Elinor was not just a lovely young piano teacher. She was a firebrand, a visionary, a fascinating mixture of beauty, ferocity, and purity. She carried banners in peace parades, wearing a peaked cap and looking like some historic French Revolutionary storming the Bastille. She was, besides, a pianist of concert calibre and was quite used to playing before admiring groups. She had studied music for years in and around Chicago and at the

American Conservatory there. She had always been something of a musical prodigy. At the age of three she was already forming harmonies and playing the piano by ear.

She and Ian were also card-carrying members of the Socialist Workers' Party. Eric associated with their friends and seemed to agree with their political stands but would not support them in any way in public. He wouldn't go to a Trotskyist meeting.

Her mother was a Christian Science practitioner, and Elinor still hewed strongly to principle, mind over matter, high moral purpose, etc., although the religious aspects of her mother's indoctrination had long since sloughed off.

One time, while marching along with a workers' parade for peace, she made a vow that if she saw one Christian Scientist among the bystanders lining the road, she would continue playing the organ in their church. But she saw none, and she quit. She had never had any close friends among the local "Scientists," who were not attuned to the artistic-Bohemian approach to life nor to rattling the economic cage, and, besides, she didn't like their attitude toward animals.

According to them, she felt, animals were put on earth just to be used by man, but she disagreed. No matter how pinched her budget might be, she found ways to feed the raccoons, squirrels, and birds in her garden. A quasi-vegetarian (who eschewed red meat), she had never become convinced that the human race had achieved the state of grace which entitled it to lord it over the creatures of the wild.

Now what would a scientifically trained M.D. find of interest in a quasi-vegetarian, quasi-Christian Scientist, who was, after all, married already and to a "friend" of his?

She was fair. She was not fairly beautiful. She was beautifully fair.

Elinor had a haunting sort of beauty that Hollywood might overlook, finding it lacking in blue collar box-office appeal. But a discerning theater director might have found her suitable for Joan of Arc or Anna Karenina.

Tall, slender, curvaceous, and blonde, with a fragile, spiritual look, Elinor was (Eric told her later) "the epitome of his adolescent dream." He couldn't take his eyes off her. He followed her around, listening to her spirited discourses on Wagner the genius, Wagner the monster, Wagner the superman. Among the composers Wagner was her star, a vital, energetic, bombastic, self-centered man.

Eric knew very little about music. He had "mastered" the flute in his youth, but he had difficulty with his bar mitzvah because he couldn't carry a tune. No matter, he hung around Elinor, music or no music, even though Elinor contended, later on, he was the only person she had ever met whose face remained a complete blank, whose eyes didn't light up, when music was played. Music may have had no effect on him, but Elinor certainly did. He was determined to become her Wagner.

In *The Mythology of Dark and Fair* (written long before the days of *Black Is Beautiful*), Eric contended that there seemed to be a "universal" association of light complexion with holiness, angelic manifestations, shining purity, nobility, cleanliness, good, and truth." He spoke of the stereotyped characters in women's magazines, "the ethereal blonde, who is fearful, pure, innocent, frigid, ignorant of sex and evil, and easily exploited by the dark villain." The "ideal type" of the "blonde princess" is generally conceived of as receiving unconditional love and protection from society at large.

And ignorant of sex Elinor was.

Ian and Elinor had had nine years of the most beautiful brother and sister relationship ever, "just like Hansel and Gretel." They had married impulsively when they were students; they were intellectual soul mates; their marriage was a buffer for them against the buffetings of the ever-impinging Philistines. They shared a secret which no one in their lusty, arty, hedonistic circle of friends would have guessed—they had never consummated their marriage. Elinor remained a married virgin, not consciously missing sex, having never acquired the taste; she did, however, look with a pang of envy now and then at other couples who had children. She was thirty-one when she met Eric and saw no prospects of starting a family.

Frail Ian worked when he could and contributed what he could to the household, but it wasn't enough. They were close to starving. They visited Elinor's Aunt Alice in Connecticut in 1938, were taken with the place where she lived, and decided to move there.

Elinor was both fascinated and repelled by Dr. Bernstein, and she was interested in his mind. Though he would not attend left-wing meetings or man any barricades, he said such outrageous, spunky things. And she was attracted by the fact that he was Jewish. She thought, "Gee! a young Jewish psychiatrist, a great brain, maybe another Freud!" And he was a *character,* a very interesting character.

She couldn't help thinking what a jolt he would give her mother (against whom she had rebelled all her life), her Christian Scientist practitioner mother in that proper little suburban town of Wheaton on the Illinois prairie where she had grown up.

The young doctor's effervescent shock system was always in gear. One time he read her a short story he had written called *The Smyrna Embrace,* and it turned out to be about necrophilia. Another time he told her about a trip he had taken on a steamer through the Bosporus. The steamer had no staterooms; everybody slept on the open deck under the stars. "It was very informal; people urinated on the deck and everything." At the crack of dawn Eric had awakened to see a beautiful woman lying asleep nearby, with abundant, glossy hair spread out fan-shaped around her. With each roll of the boat a small stream of urine was inching its way toward her hair. Eric was in a quandary. "When in Rome do as the Romans do" seemed a good rule to follow in this situation, as did "Let George (or Kismet) do it." But finally, as the boat gave a particularly significant roll, he could stand it no longer and woke her up.

Also in appearance Dr. Bernstein was "a little unusual," according to Dr. Moses Margolick (who had gone through medical school with Eric). "He was tall and sort of droopy, with a hawklike nose and tight, curly [reddish-blonde] hair." "He used to stick it down with hair-dressing and try to make it look straight, but as it dried, it would spring up and stick out," Elinor said. "He never had a good haircut. It was very unbecoming. He used to hate his hair because it made him look Jewish—you know: tight curls. And I thought, Why doesn't he sit up straight? Why didn't his mother make him sit up straight? He'd be so much more distinguished looking. His shoulders were very hunched over."

A waspish ex-patient of Eric's once described him as being

"so unattractive as to be physically handicapped," but when we mentioned this to Elinor she was shocked. She thought carefully and then said, "He was arresting-looking, startling-looking. When you first saw Eric you were struck by the crazy, grotesque combination of potential great beauty and awful ugliness. That beautiful, curly, golden hair—so much of it—just rioting over his head—God, what hair! It was marvelous! And very white skin, and if you could look through those glasses, very blue eyes!"

She continued: "He was tall and he had beautiful hands, beautiful surgeon's hands. He dressed rather interestingly—not necessarily becomingly, but it was kind of interesting. He chose funny suits and funny jackets and ascot ties [the kind of clothes that used to embarrass some of his McGill chums, Albert Lapin, for example], and once in a while he'd put on a beret and look awful in it. But you were struck most of all by the grotesqueness. Because you were conscious of the fact that if he'd done something about his nose and stood up straight and if he hadn't acted vulgarly—if he'd lowered his voice—he would have been a stunning man.

"When he was embarrassed or felt people were looking down on him," Elinor said, "he would walk with his feet turned out like Charlie Chaplin. And he made an elaborate ritual out of lighting his pipe when he felt that people might be critical. And then he would puff! puff! puff! And then, just as your heart was melting toward him, feeling that here was a poor guy, just churning inside, wanting to be loved—and trying so hard to be nonchalant," he would do something contrary—"make some abrasive or cocky or insulting remark that bothered people and made them stiffen against him."

Elinor concluded: "I felt some awful things must have happened to him in Montreal when he was growing up. He seemed so insecure. . . . He appealed to my protective instincts, my championship of the underdog."

So he was not handsome in the conventional sense, but he was born with "ten extra ounces of energy." He was able to burn the candle at both ends and get away with it, not for weeks or months but for years and decades. From college on, he made do with four or five hours of sleep a night. He practically always carried on two or more jobs simultaneously, usually commuting between different cities, and he didn't ever seem to get tired. In a place packed with people he would slash through the crowd to get to his objective immediately. This was not the sort of time-lapsed life of actionless vistas that Elinor was accustomed to see in a man.

Although he was friendly with Ian as well as Elinor, Dr. Bernstein was indignant about the position in which Ian had placed Elinor, and told her so, on repeated drives about the nearby countryside. In Eric's view, Ian was "weak" and "parasitical" and Elinor shouldn't have to put up with it. Later on in life he fulminated against artists who sacrificed others in order to pursue their muse, artists who couldn't manage to support their families adequately and "create" on the side, as he did (at considerable cost, however, in emotional support both to himself and his families).

He referred to Ian as "that sick fellow" and talked about Elinor's "wasting her life's blood on him instead of having children." Elinor listened noncommittally.

Eric's attentions did something for Elinor's ego. She was rather flattered when he would pop in and sit up half the night talking to her, although she knew it irritated Ian. She knew it was not the height of propriety to go riding around the countryside in this eccentric young psychiatrist's La Salle convertible, but then neither she nor any of her unconventional friends were bucking for the Good Housekeeping Seal of Approval. Besides, what harm could come from parking in Eric's impressive (although secondhand) car in broad daylight under the shade of the immense trees on the grounds of the sanitarium where Eric worked? What harm from the two of them watching the fitful waves of the Sound lap the nearby beach? How could she forswear the titillating unexpectedness of Eric's sallies:

"I just fell in love with your teeth!"

"What?"

"You know, ever since I met you, I've been falling in love with you little by little: your eyes, your hair, your neck, your legs, your ankles—and now, your teeth!"

Another time, learning that her middle name was Helen, he asked her if he could call her that instead of Elinor.

"Why?"

"Because I want to have a name that no one else uses, a name just for me alone."

Elinor didn't know it, but it was all very much in the James Branch Cabell tradition of urbane and witty love patter. Helen was also the name of one of the lovely ladies Jurgen longed for, but Elinor hadn't been "commanded" to read *Jurgen* at this time, nor did she know that the switching of names was in Eric's family tradition.

Name switching was also one of the notable features of *Jurgen*. A fantasy by James Branch Cabell, *Jurgen* was the bible of "wild-hairs" at McGill with whom Lennard (as Eric was then called) associated. Several of his classmates have emphasized the importance of this book in Lennard's life and in their own. Much of the literary style E. Lennard Bernstein adopted when writing his columns for the McGill daily seems to have come straight out of *Jurgen*.

But there was more to it than that. Jurgen was a seducer of fair ladies (a half dozen of whom he probably married), mostly queens and countesses, who would often play hard to get but would eventually succumb to his animal magnetism and guile. Once he had had his way with them, he would quickly grow tired and begin to scorn them for having been "too easy." The book is laid in a kaleidoscope of mythical kingdoms, salted with fanciful names of fake Latin or medieval French flavor. There is much coyness about Jurgen's stout sword being in or out of the scabbard, or sheath, which only the densest reader would fail to recognize as phallic symbolism.

For 1919, when it was published, it was totally scabrous. The pubescent males of Montreal were doubly delighted with this picaresque novel because it was targeted by the New York Society for the Suppression of Vice, and hence they could read it with a sense of supreme wickedness. "You should have read it in 1923!" exclaimed a fellow McGill student and close friend of Eric's, when we commented that we weren't much taken by *Jurgen*.

If Lennard or Leonard (he was actually named the latter, but changed the spelling himself) read it in 1923, he would have been about thirteen at the time—it being the sort of book that a boy of the twenties must have sneaked out of the library and read under the covers with a flashlight.

But is it the sort of book that one would remember at age thirty-one? Eric did. In 1941 he told Elinor that *Jurgen* and *The Store* by A.T. Stribling were his favorite novels, and he did not urge but "ordered" her to read them. (In fact, he was still using unusual words he had discovered in these two books when he was forty-one and even fifty-one, *cantrap* and *palimpsest* among them.) But Elinor tried them both and didn't like them. *The Store* tells of a Southern colonel, picking up the pieces after the Civil War, who by artifice and guile manages to achieve some semblance of the status he knew before the war. Both books seemed cynical and Machiavellian to Elinor.

Idealistic Elinor was a great reader, but her favorites were books by such authors as Tolstoi, Chekov, Gorki, and Sigrid Undset. She didn't care a whit about psychology or psychiatry but was interested only in the soul.

Given these facts, a beginning Transactional Analysis therapist these days would easily be able to predict that a relationship between these two highly charged individuals of intense but opposite polarities wouldn't last. He might say that Eric had a Sleeping Beauty Rescuer Script, that he was unable to look upon desirable women as real people; he might talk about women placed on pedestals, the Beautiful Woman Syndrome, and he would certainly hit hard on Karpman's Drama Triangle, with the drama coming from the breath taking reversals as the two players alternately switch from persecutor to rescuer, victim, and back again.

But would it have made a difference to their relationship if there had been a TA therapist available, since Eric was "powerless in the face of beauty"?

Eric said to Elinor in wonder, "Elinor, you're an amazing person! You're beautiful, you're intelligent, you're charming, you're talented—but you don't throw your weight around!" And she didn't. She appeared to have no vanity, kept no snapshots of herself, seldom looked in the mirror. Not only that, she seemed "just right" to Eric in that she was domestic. She baked bread, antiqued furniture, loved to work in the garden, and hungered after babies.

Relatives or the canniest of therapists could not have dissuaded him. She was a challenge. Like the men who had to climb Annapurna because "it was there," he had to have her. When he was in close proximity to this shapely, blue-eyed goddess with waist-length blonde hair twisted up in an "Ann Harding" knot, all the intricate psychiatric "beware" circuits he had so carefully cultivated blew, and he was in overdrive, on autopilot—unarmed, and dangerous.

What would Jurgen have done? He would have used his wits. Eric used his wits, but should one challenge Annapurna in ballet slippers instead of boots?

The "eyeball encounter" had been an opener.

Ω

Counterpoint 1

He started his seminars in '58 and there were not a lot of therapists who came to listen to him at that time—there was only a very small group who could tolerate, I have to say, his personality. His approach was to shock and startle people and see what they would do. That, in a sense, was a good diagnostic opening, but it was one of the reasons why he was misunderstood in his lifetime. He antagonized people. People didn't see—they couldn't with that approach—that the man underneath was a very loving, human (in a humanistic sense), human being, that underneath this abrasive exterior was a man who cared about humanity.

Fanita English

3

Moral Fibre

The man who is loved by a woman is lucky indeed, but the one to be envied is he who loves, however little he gets in return. How much greater is Dante gazing at Beatrice than Beatrice walking by him in apparent disdain.
Eric Berne, *Sex in Human Loving*

One day Eric suggested to Ian that Elinor needed some relief from her nursing and teaching chores. She was anemic; tests showed that she too was developing T.B. (they were startled to hear). As her doctor, Eric felt it was necessary for her to have more amusement. In fact, he claimed, her life depended on her being placed in his care. He said, "If Ellie is going to have to carry the financial burden here, Ian, she's got to be built up. She needs to get out. She needs better food. She can't keep nursing you without a break."

Eric was prepared to take Elinor to the city on Thursdays, her day off from music lessons, give her a good dinner, treat her to a concert or two, and, besides, place her under his complete medical care, with medicines and treatment gratis.

This was the free and easy style the McRaes were accustomed to among their friends, and Ian greeted this proposal with moderate enthusiasm or, at least, resignation. Elinor looked forward to the concerts, which she couldn't afford otherwise.

Both Ian and Elinor were impressed by the concern of their doctor friend. His remarks about Elinor's health troubled them. She had always been so energetic, the dynamic force in the marriage.

"Eric appeared to us as invincibly strong and decisive. It never occurred to us to question his motives, and we naively equated intellectual brilliance with ethically principled actions," Elinor said.

So, in June 1941, Eric and Elinor began their in-town Thursdays. Often they would go to the Fleur de Lis for dinner. ("It was so wonderful," Elinor said, "every time I hear the name Fleur de Lis I can still taste their French bread.") And then Eric and Elinor got in the habit of dropping in at his mother's empty apartment after the concert. In TA terms, Elinor might have been playing a hard game of "Little Red Riding Hood," pretending to herself that the wolf was, after all, only her grandmother.

In *Sex in Human Loving* Berne set down these words:

> These, then, are the stages of sexual bliss.
> First looking and hoping sweet hopes.
> Then seeing and testing in delicious anticipation.
> Then the conquest with its glorious sighs.
> After that comes certainty and confidence, with its smug feelings of superiority when other men throw her admiring glances, or even more perceptive strangers bow to her or tip their hats in her direction.
> The final stage of paradise, unknown even to Dante, is when there is not only certainty, but a guarantee from what has gone on previously, of the highest possible degree of sensuousness, response, and surrender, the attainment of the unattainable. This guarantee gives such ineffable splendor of anticipation to whatever goes before, the dinner, the concert, or the starlight by the sea, that even the admiring glances of other men become irrelevant, and the whole evening is like a warm and gentle flight toward the interior of a golden magnet where you will be borne high over the earth on blue flames of pleasure.

In telling us about this period Elinor said, "After a few weeks we made love. It was the first time I had ever really made love. The first night it happened I was worried. I said to Eric, 'Is this safe? Is this all right? Couldn't I have a baby?'

"And Eric answered, 'My dear girl, I'm a doctor. Do you

think I'm not thinking of all these things? I'll take care of you. It'll be perfectly safe. Leave everything to me.'

"And I thought, 'Well, fine.'"

After this evening, Eric and Elinor didn't go to the city again for two weeks.

Along about the middle of October, Elinor began to feel peculiar. They were still going to the Fleur de Lis; they were still having those "divine shrimp cocktails." They were still coming home in the wee hours of the morning. Sometimes Ian would be sitting up waiting for them. Elinor wondered if he suspected something. She felt nauseated and mentioned it to Eric, but Eric said that pregnancy was out of the question. So Elinor sneaked off to a gynecologist, who confirmed her suspicion. Their first night together had resulted in her pregnancy. She informed Eric, who said, "Well, you can marry me now."

Elinor replied, "Why? I'm already married."

Eric countered, "Well, you're certainly not going to stay with Ian and have my baby."

Elinor didn't want to leave Ian. Ian was sick and needed her badly. She cared deeply for him and wanted to go on living with him. Eric replied that if that were the case, he could arrange an abortion.

Elinor went along for about a month not knowing quite what to do. She managed to hide her nausea and vomiting from Ian and keep on with her schedule of nursing him, cooking the meals, and giving music lessons. What a quandary! She didn't want an abortion; she wanted her baby. She didn't want to hurt Ian. If Ian found out, would his indignation at Eric's and her deception provoke some incident? Sick as Ian was, his sense of outrage might force him to try to take Eric apart, and with those "great, big, powerful hands" he could do it. He had the "moral fibre" for it, even though it wouldn't do his fight against arthritis and ulcers any good.

Eric was in the middle of his didactic analysis with the distinguished Dr. Paul Federn, one of Freud's inner circle who had recently come to the United States from Vienna. Dr. Federn had told Eric that he didn't want him to make any major changes or marry while he was in analysis, and Elinor knew that, but she decided to go to Dr. Federn and get his advice.

Federn at this point was about seventy, and Elinor said he was "lovely" to her. He was a "wonderful looking man with a beard which made him look stern and fierce," but actually (according to Edoardo Weiss) he was a ". . . melancholy, romantic, and exceedingly mild man."

He had his office in a cluttered apartment in New York. "It was filled with furniture from an old, big Viennese residence—dark, oversized pieces that filled the room and overpowered you—an interesting atmosphere, but kind of gloomy. There were dark rugs and a huge desk. He had an impressive beard, very red lips, and very kind-looking eyes." Somewhere in the background dishes were rattling and the smell of cooking cabbage filled the apartment. His elderly wife also occasionally scuttled in and out.

Elinor told Federn the whole story. "I told him that Eric had said that I would have to have an abortion if I didn't marry him, and he said, 'These are not the only choices you have, my dear. It's your baby. Now you make up your mind as to what you want to do.'"

Ever since meeting Elinor, Eric had been having a difficult time with his analysis. He was in so much turmoil over the Ian-Elinor situation—and having to verbalize it for Dr. Federn—that he sometimes sat the whole hour without uttering a word. Then he would "worry terribly" about "wasting money" and would come home from New York "in a rotten mood."

After mulling over Dr. Federn's advice, Elinor wrote Eric a letter implying she had lost the baby and saying she would no longer need his "care." She had decided to keep the baby, keep Ian, and write Eric off.

At first Eric apparently believed the miscarriage story, but she "got plump very quickly." Then he took to following her around. He would hide behind bushes and jump out at her when she walked down the street. "He watched me! Wherever I went I would see his car parked and he would show up. I couldn't be free of him. It was a nightmare! And I still didn't dare tell Ian about the baby."

In a desperate move, Elinor told Ian that she "had had enough of this ridiculous marriage. Unless he would be a husband to me, I was going to leave him. So he exerted himself and we had one night together which was very unsatisfactory. It was awful, horrible, but anyway that gave me my one trump card."

A few days later Elinor said to Ian, "I feel funny; I think I'm pregnant." Ian appeared to accept this. "At last," she told us, " I could relax and throw up in peace." But Elinor wasn't certain that Ian was thoroughly convinced.

Eric wrote letters every day, begging her to see him, sometimes only one line, but always disturbing. Aunt Alice used to notice the young psychiatrist pacing back and forth, back and forth, across from Elinor and Ian's house. She wondered, as she drove by, what he was doing out there. And Elinor was worried that other people would also wonder.

Elinor countered by informing young doctor Bernstein that she was pregnant again—this time by Ian. Eric appeared to accept this revelation but continued writing alarming letters. There were prophecies that horrible things might befall Elinor and those she loved—that Eric might not be able to control his rage. The letters were full of deletions—sentences and whole paragraphs ominously cut out with a razor. The single sheets were full of holes, and Elinor shuddered to think what ideas could have been so controversial that he didn't dare send them: the words that survived the razor were bad enough.

"He threatened to denounce me on the street corners, to put a sign on my front door saying I was a whore. A whore! Yet he knew better than anyone that I was a virgin until my encounter with him. He wrote dreadful letters to my mother and father, too. I became afraid to take the mail out of the box. On the other hand, I had to be sure to get to the mailbox first. I was a nervous wreck all through my pregnancy.

"He kept away from Ian, though. He didn't bother him—because he was afraid of Ian. Although Ian was a frail guy in a bathrobe, Eric was afraid of Ian's moral strength. He was trying to browbeat me into marrying him. I couldn't see it at the time, but he was genuinely suffering."

Elinor represented to him a means of emancipation from his constricted past. She was "everything he wanted to escape from the stigma of being a Jew, everything he wanted in a wife.

". . . Now I grieve for him. This was a kid who became convinced early in life that no one was ever going to love him.

But he was going to dominate others through sheer brains and will, as if he were saying: 'I'll show them who has power!' "

One day the young psychiatrist met Elinor's Aunt Alice on the street and they carried on a polite conversation. The doctor asked after Elinor, and Aunt Alice said she was pretty well, considering—"She's expecting, you know."

"Ah, and when is the baby expected?" he asked.

Aunt Alice told him the correct due date, and the cat was out of the bag. Eric's suspicions were now confirmed—Elinor was still carrying his baby! He wrote her saying he had "the right that transcends all other rights, the right of a prospective father." Elinor agreed to see him at the sanitarium. To the meeting she wore a very becoming peasant dress made out of an India-print bedspread. He placed his hand on her stomach and called her "his little pregnant peasant."

Elinor remained unmoved. She looked on Eric as a willful seducer who would stoop to any wickedness to get his way. She was not going to let him profit from what seemed to be unethical conduct.

Later on in the pregnancy, Eric announced that since she was unavailable to him, he had taken on another mistress. Eric felt, à la Jurgen, that it would damage a man's health if he didn't have a sexual outlet at least every ten days. He had met a suitable outlet in a New Haven bar, and he assured Elinor that there was no emotional attachment on his part.

While she was still in the hospital with her new baby, Ellen, Ian, who up until this time had been cast in the role of the innocent and invalided husband, announced that he had fallen in love with an attractive young woman, a writer named Betty. Ian wanted to marry Betty, brought her with him to sit on Elinor's hospital bed. At this point, Elinor was too stunned to do otherwise than accept the ultimatum.

Ian's involvement with the pretty young writer completely undid Elinor's hope that she could bless her marriage with the child of a brilliant outsider but keep the core of her soulful relationship with Ian intact. Now she was the mother of a small baby, and adrift. Her own family had become alienated by Eric's letters—afterwards he confessed that he had gone so far as to write, "Someone has to save Elinor from the wild, promiscuous kind of life she is leading—that's why I want to marry her."

He didn't want her to have anyone to turn to but himself. One letter had purported Elinor to be "so weak and easily influenced that any degenerate might get ahold of her and ruin her." Elinor's mother wasn't on speaking terms with her daughter for quite a while after receiving that letter.

Her "lying-in" having become an emotional nightmare, Elinor tried to convince herself that Eric might have some redeeming qualities after all.

"I used to be very easily pushed around. I didn't have much sense of my own worth. When a stronger, more aggressive person took a deep interest in me, I was flattered. It never dawned on me that I was just as strong, just as impressive as that person might be, especially if that person were a man. My mother said that for a woman not to be married was the most terrible thing that could happen to a woman and that any man was better than no man at all. She despised women who weren't married, just despised them. My sister and I were taught right from the beginning that that was our goal. Get married! To whom? No matter. Get married!

"Besides, Eric was so desperate for me. . .

"I felt as if I might as well give in to Eric, or he'd make the rest of my life miserable, dogging my footsteps, and that the whole thing might blow up in my face one day if I didn't . . . I was terrified . . . I never knew what was going to happen next. I was in a panic, so I married him. And I tried very hard to make my admiration for his brightness compensate for the fact that he wasn't nice, that he wasn't decent, that he wasn't kind, that he wasn't honorable."

So Elinor left for Las Vegas for the divorce. Ian paid her fare out there, but Eric was to take over her support once she arrived. Elinor packed off with her red-haired baby Ellen. Luckily there was a goodly amount of red hair among Ian's and Elinor's forebears, as well as Eric's.

During the six-weeks' residency necessary for the divorce, Elinor received $20 a week to live on for herself and the baby. (It certainly wasn't much, but Eric wasn't earning much, and he also had to contribute to his mother's support.) Ellen and Elinor had quarters in a rooming house in a run-down neighborhood. She bought her food at a grocery store nearby and kept it on the window ledge, boiling a dozen eggs at a time on a hot plate and losing a painful amount of eggs and milk to spoilage in the heat.

"I couldn't afford to eat in restaurants. Six dreadful weeks! It was his way of bringing me to my knees. It was his way of showing his power. He always used money or lack of money as a weapon, at least with me . . . always tried to force me to beg for more. I never begged for it; I just made do."

After six weeks Eric came out and they were married by a Mormon bishop. The date was October 24, 1942.

The wedding picture shows a radiantly smiling Elinor in a black dress. Was the dress Elinor's way of predicting disaster for the marriage? "No," Elinor says. By this time she was anxious to make it work. She had picked out a dress that seemed right for the occasion, but Eric's mother, Sara, had sent the black one, which she had bought on sale and which may have expressed some of her feelings about her son's marriage. The color was not the only ominous note; the style was elaborate, overelegant, and too citified for Elinor. It depressed her, but she wore it anyway.

Sara Bernstein couldn't understand why Eric didn't marry someone more suitable for him. She believed that Elinor didn't really care for him and that they had little in common. Sara discussed it with him quite openly, and so did sister Grace. When Eric told Sara that Elinor was the embodiment of his "wildest adolescent longings," his mother said, "You musn't marry a girl like that. You must marry someone who is more your type."

Grace and Sara thought this marriage was slated for failure. They knew of Eric's ambition. They were proud of his abrasive wit, his raucous camaraderie. When they were together they snickered and guffawed as they roundly insulted each other. This was their style of family intimacy. But Elinor, who in their eyes tended to be entirely too prim and proper, looked bleak and disapproving. She winced at people who roared and brayed in public. She was shocked at their callous disregard for each other's feelings.

Sara thought he should have married someone who would be

proud to be the wife of a doctor, who would serve him as a handmaiden, create a nest, and take care of his every need. She would have liked someone who believed the world was waiting for his creativity, who would understand that he had no time to indulge in the companionship and co-operation expected of the conventional American husband.

Why did he have to marry a spoiled blonde princess who acted as if she were doing him a favor to put up with him? Elinor was already nagging him before they were married, Grace said. Why, Mrs. Bernstein thought, couldn't he have married a "nice Central Park West girl," who would be as ambitious for him as he was for himself? His sister Grace wished he'd married the "good egg" psychiatric nurse he had palled around with in his Yale days.

In *Sex in Human Loving*, Eric wrote:

> Marriage is six days of excitement and the world's record for sex.
>
> Five weeks more of getting to know each other, fencing, lunging, and pulling back, finding each other's weaknesses, and then the games begin.
>
> After six months, each one has made a decision. The honeymoon is over and marriage or divorce begins—until further notice.

After they were married, "it was immediately horrible," according to Elinor. Eric objected to Elinor's nursing two-month-old Ellen in the middle of the night. "He was jealous of the attention I paid her. He said she could wait until morning."

He also objected to Elinor's "faithful mommie dog" (an English Springer Spaniel named Janie) sleeping in the bed with them. Elinor dutifully shut her out, but she whined all night on the stairs, and when Eric was sleeping particularly deeply, Elinor tiptoed out and let her in again. Janie snuggled down cozily in the covers, was completely contented, and would have remained so all night, but Eric awoke and protested vigorously. In fact, he got out and lay on the floor, stating that Elinor should choose between Janie and himself. Elinor refused to choose, and Eric lay on the floor uncovered the rest of the night.

When they had been married a few weeks, Eric confided in Elinor: "I'd like to be married to about six different women, and have children by them all!"

The return to their home town had done nothing to solidify the relationship. They took up battle stations immediately as they were given the "no room at the inn" message.

While Elinor was in Las Vegas, Eric had obtained a new post at a sanitarium not far away. Although his work at the previous sanitarium had been interesting, and he had made a statistical study about the shock treatment employed there—the new place had offered him the princely salary of $400 a month. Living quarters were included—an apartment in a tower at the rear of the grounds. Eric was pleased that it would have plenty of room for the little family of three.

However, he had left for his trip to Nevada without discussing his prospective marriage with his employers. At the end of his week's honeymoon in La Vegas, he sent officials at the new post a telegram that he was bringing a new wife and baby back.

On their arrival they found the apartment doors locked against them. Their attempts to persuade those in authority to relent were unsuccessful. Off the weary travelers went to Ian's house. Ian was civilized about the matter and moved out shortly thereafter. He had been sharing his quarters with a number of dogs who were poor housekeeping risks.

The gay return in triumph that Eric had anticipated turned into an Augean-stable–Old-Dutch-Cleanser encounter for Elinor and ruffled feathers at the sanitarium for Eric. If his contract hadn't been already signed, Elinor said, he might have been dismissed. The administration raised its collective eyebrows. One did not acquire instant families from Nevada if one were a true New Englander, and if one intended to, one needed to approach the situation with long months of explanation.

They lived on in their little shingled house, Eric working at the sanitarium days and coming home nights, until he went into the army several months later.

Elinor labored over a nice note to Mrs. Bernstein, thanking her for the wedding dress; she was trying to be the "perfect daughter-in-law." Mrs. Bernstein wrote back to Eric instead of to Elinor, saying, "I got a sensational letter from Helen! I was surprised that her letter showed so much personality! She's such a little mouse!"

Elinor, enraged at being taken for a mouse, was further enraged at being renamed Helen by Mrs. Bernstein. No one had ever called her that except Eric, and he now adopted this as her regular name. "They rejected my real name and self," Elinor felt. And not long after that, on one snowy day around New Year's, 1943, Eric L. Bernstein shortened his last name and became Eric Berne at the County Courthouse in Bridgeport.

On the same day he was naturalized as an American citizen. He said, "Creeping Jesus [one of his favorite expressions of the time], I've never been a flag waver or patriotic particularly, but I was really moved by that ceremony, Helen."

"Helen" didn't care one way or another about changing their last name. Six or seven years earlier Eric's mother—tentatively, at least—had changed hers to Byrne. Grace and Eric had also been thinking about formalizing a name change for a long time; they had had family conferences about it. Eric said, "The choice is whether to keep the name and make it illustrious like the conductor, Leonard Bernstein [who pronounced the final syllable *steyn*, whereas Eric pronounced his *steen*], or to change it altogether and turn one's back on the Semitic factor."

Sara's parents had modified the family name from *Astrovsky* to *Astroff* to *Astor*, and Sara had gone under her middle name of *Gordon* for many years and taught under that name after her marriage. Grace remembered a joke that went around Montreal about the man who changed his name to Smith. Somebody asked him: "What was your name before you changed it to Smith?"

Answer: "Jones."

"Well, why did you change it?"

"So when people ask me what my name was before I changed it to Smith, I can say 'Jones.' "

Mark Twain tells the story of how many painfully absurd names were foisted on unfortunate Austrian and German Jews. The governments decided that everyone had to go by Germanic names, so that people with Jewish surnames or Jews without surnames (there were many of these, a holdover, perhaps, from medieval times when nobody had surnames) had to be renamed. This was done by minor civilian or military functionaries who went from door to door looking for payoffs.

Those who paid well got the names of precious stones, metals, or flowers (Goldstein for gold stone, Blumenthal for flower vale, or Rosenthal for rose vale); and others who could not pay, had to make do with names such as Abraham Bellyache or Samuel Godbedamned. One of the pretexts for the renaming program was that the officials claimed that Jewish people changed their names too often and it was difficult to keep track of them.

The fact that Eric Berne had originally been Leonard, then E. Lennard Bernstein, or Eric L. Bernstein (after his Yale years) came as a surprise to many who had been closely associated with him in the TA movement. They first heard about it in Warren Cheney's biographical sketch in the Eric Berne memorial issue of the *TA Journal*, January 1971. Berne himself felt, according to his sister Grace, that the name Bernstein was "no name to make a name for himself with."

He saw no reason to keep a name that might cause him to be discounted on his way to the top. At any rate, he was in the practice of making many names for himself. During his days as a contributor to the *McGill Daily* and the *McGilliad,* he had used a variety of pseudonyms such as Ramsbottom Horseley, Lennard Gandalac, Cynical St. Cyr (in TA days changed to Cyprian St. Cyr), Peter Pinto, and Count Gandalac (absurd pseudonyms were very big with James Branch Cabell as well).

Some of Berne's McGill colleagues who retained their Jewish names and have had illustrious careers in their own medical specialties have inferred that we have exaggerated the academic anti-Semitism in Montreal, and by implication have questioned the necessity for Berne to have changed his name. We do not doubt that Berne would have achieved a startling success as a psychiatric innovator under the name of Bernstein.

The more interesting question is the significance of Berne's turning his back on his father's strongly held convictions. Dr. David Bernstein had named his Montreal clinic after Theodor Herzl, the founder of modern Zionism. Also his middle name was Hillel, a memorialization of the name of the great Hebrew sage, who said: "If I am not for myself, who will be for me? But if I am for myself only, what then am I? And if not now, when?"

All of Eric's wives got the impression that he had suffered some devastating blows in his childhood, and that anti-Semitism had contributed to a goodly portion of those blows. Some of his close friends offered the same opinion. Discrimination has varying effects on different people. To some it may present a challenge—to others it may be crippling. Each person copes with such problems in his own way. After all, Herzl himself, at one point was considering the possibility of having his son Hans baptized as a Christian and asked himself ". . . if I have the right to sour and blacken his life [by not so doing] as mine has been soured and blackened."

Changing his name may have brought minor inconveniences to Berne when he stumbled upon old Montreal friends who knew him only by his original surname; some were undoubtedly unsympathetic to name changes. But he was adroit at handling difficult situations. For instance, in *Who's Who in America* he listed his parents as "Dr. David B." and "Sara B.," but in the Canadian *Who's Who* he gave their names as "Dr. David Bernstein" and "Sara Bernstein."

Berne didn't wish to have his children feel that they were persecutees. His second wife, Dorothy, said his children didn't look upon themselves as bearing any particular label. On the other hand, Eric didn't ignore Jewish culture entirely; his daughter Ellen remembers hearing him teaching her half-brothers Jewish prayers. Virginia Mitchell also remembers "receiving a letter from Berne saying he was teaching his two sons the same prayers he had been taught as a boy."

And so the *Vita Nuova* of the star-crossed lovers began. It may be that the sufferings of our modern Dante were, indeed, nobler than the reflections on the "whole catastrophe" by our "disdainful" Beatrice. And we don't have the measured cadences of the *terza rima* to tell us the other side of the story. However, our Beatrice is also of a heroic strain. She has had the courage to tell us a tale devoid of self-aggrandizement, a story that is very real. She looked at our Dante with dread, wonderment, pity, and pure unalloyed fear, and she has given us a vivid impression of a courtship and capture as strange as any of the wildest fantasies in *Jurgen*.

But do dread, wonderment, pity, and pure unalloyed fear form an enduring foundation for a marriage?

Lennie Bernstein.

Eric's childhood home,
73 Sainte Famille St., Montreal.

Lennie Bernstein and his sister Grace.

Eric's father Dr. David Hillel Bernstein.

Eric's mother Sara Gordon Bernstein.

Eric Berne, McGill graduate, 1931.

Eric carrying his six-month-old nephew, 1939.

Eric, Elinor and Ellen on trip west, June, 1943.

Eric and Elinor on their wedding day, October 24, 1942.

Elinor at World War II anti-war parade.

Elinor and Ellen, 1944.

Captain Eric Berne, U.S. Army.

Ω

Counterpoint 2

What I feel you should emphasize is, that as a result of this man's influence, important changes took place in individuals and in society. That Eric dared and sometimes dared clumsily and stupidly, and out of his own compulsions (not always necessarily because of Adult decisions). It may be that, thanks to his crazy, compulsive daring, some of us did things and changed situations, systems, people, in a way that couldn't have been done otherwise. I want you to say this, not only from the perspective of "Oh, Eric was so wonderful!" but also from the perspective of someone like me who occasionally said: "Damn the guy!" Sometimes he was a bastard! He may have irritated people; he irritated me. However, without him hundreds of thousands of people would not have benefitted from what he had to teach.

Fanita Engish

4

An "H" Marriage

> . . . all men [are] bizarre and inexplicable composites of contraries; that is what those fellows who turn out novels and plays refuse to understand. Their men are all of one piece. There are no such creatures. There are ten men in one man, and often they all show themselves within one hour, under certain circumstances.
>
> Eugene Delacroix, *Journal*

What was the foundation on which this marriage was built? Eric's Child probably believed that all you did with princesses was to capture them and put them in a castle.

In *Jurgen* none of the princesses played the piano or marched in anti-war parades. They minded their own business and lived happily ever after. So superior strategy had snared Berne a princess, and would no doubt be sufficient to keep her at his side, urging him on to preeminence in the battles of the mind, their golden-haired children a symbol of the beauty of their relationship. Elinor, on her part, despite her misgivings, no doubt felt that Eric was well-endowed with the raw stuff of all that it takes to be a hero. There was much to work on here, and she was sure that her energy and perseverance would succeed.

Eric thoroughly frustrated the hero-polishing scenario Elinor had devised for herself. She was prepared to *épater les bourgeois*, but she wasn't able to cope with his energetic goofiness.

They had invited a group of friends over to their little house one evening. Eric was proud of his wife and wanted to show her off. Elinor played a particularly exciting "showpiece" on the piano. Arpeggio followed arpeggio, and Elinor was the center of the admiring attention of all their guests. But when she happened to look up, Eric was standing on his head in the middle of the room.

Afterward, she asked him what was the meaning of his Father William caper. He replied that things had seemed too stiff, and the party needed livening up. Elinor noticed, after that, that the parties always seemed in need of livening up when the attention of a group was on her—and she felt it was part of some long-range tactic on his part to keep her from fulfilling herself as a person. His idea of a good party was having a group of male psychiatrists over who would look at Elinor lecherously for a brief period, then huddle near the fireplace comparing the quality of their patients' positive and negative transferences. Meanwhile the ladies at the other end of the room talked about their children.

Even his standing on his head at the beach down near the Sound seemed out of place. There was something awkward and inept about it. "I never could make up my mind as to whether he knew he looked absurd and reveled in it, or whether he just thought he was attracting attention to himself and didn't realize the ridiculousness of it," Elinor said.

Later on, as well, when he became successful and appeared on television, she winced at the strange straw hat he wore—it made him look more like a musical comedy hayseed than a psychiatrist.

The first few months they were married, Elinor tried hard to mold Eric into a person she could look up to. She worried over his posture, stealing the two fat pillows he insisted on sleeping on every night and hiding them. She endeavored subtly to get him to improve his table manners by talking loudly to drown out the roar of his eating. She tempted his palate with exciting vegetable arrangements, but he preferred his diet of plain meat and bread, which he would liberally dose with salt.

And then there was his cornflakes mania. The nightly ritual was to soak the Kellogg's variety in cream for a suitable period (say, about fifteen minutes) until the flakes were the consistency of wallpaper paste, and then, after liberally seasoning them with sugar, ingest them as a bedtime snack. Efforts on Elinor's part to vary this routine were resisted with all suitable force. Nothing else that snapped, crackled, or popped would do. Other brands besides Kellogg's were scorned. If she forgot to get them, or the store was out of them that day, he pouted and called her "mean."

Eric would not be changed. Years later he wrote in the *TA Bulletin* one of his cryptic humorous articles about the hillbilly who escaped the dominance of the female sex by refusing to eat the last morsel on his plate.

Elinor went again to Dr. Federn. She felt her marriage had been a mistake. But Federn was "not so nice as the time before." He seemed impatient and indicated he thought Elinor was behaving in a "queenly" manner toward Eric.

Eric, on his part, would often spend his whole analytic hour raging impotently against Elinor's "wickedness." Women were baffling creatures; after enchaining "men in eight ways: [by their] Dancing, Singing, Playing, Laughing, Weeping, and by their Appearance, their Touch and their Questions," they left a man nervous and uneasy.

Marriage counseling wasn't, however, what kept the newlyweds from separating at this point—it was the beneficent intervention of the United States Army. Eric joined up in the spring of 1943, and the army shipped him to an indoctrination center at Carlisle, Pennsylvania.

"It was so nice not having him at home!" Elinor said. "So nice just getting letters and phone calls. When he would come home on leave it was as tough as ever."

Elinor couldn't figure out the role she was supposed to be playing. At first there was the goddess role, then there was the household slavey role. She had hardly any time for practicing her piano. It was not that Elinor minded work. When Eric's mother visited, she noticed that Elinor was doing the washing, ironing, cooking, dishes, cleaning, gardening, mending, and baby tending. "You shouldn't have to to do all that, Helen; you're a doctor's wife," Sara said. Elinor insisted she liked to do her own work but was finally persuaded to get a woman to come in once a week. When Sara found out that Elinor was paying her cleaning woman the same wages for one day that the French-Canadian girls used to be paid for a whole week, however, she objected that "Helen" was being cheated.

Elinor was getting a message: she was no longer center stage, her music didn't matter, she didn't exist as her own self but only as the "straight man" for Father William out there in the spotlight.

In addition, she couldn't get over her fear that at any time Eric might pull some trick on her, particularly after she had learned she had never really had T.B.—Eric's diagnosis had just been part of his campaign to take her away from her husband. She discovered his deception when she asked him one day how she could have brought forth such a sturdy baby when she had been "consumptive." He laughed and said, "Oh, there was nothing wrong with you; I had to get you away from Ian!" It was at this point, too, that Eric confessed to the outrageous letter he had sent her family, in which he had said that if he couldn't rescue Elinor by marrying her, "sooner or later she would get mixed up with some filthy old man with a venereal disease and it would just ruin her life."

Despite their difficulties, after Eric's weeks of basic training were over, the Berne family headed West together for an assignment at the army's Baxter General Hospital in Spokane, Washington. Lieutenant Berne had turned in his La Salle for a secondhand Packard convertible. So off they went: Eric, baby Ellen, Elinor, collapsible crib, bathinette, diapers, picnic basket, bottles, thermoses of water, and the indomitable Janie and her favorite dog dish.

Eric had always hated dogs and he had a particular grudge against Janie now. Spoken in his Canadian accent, the word dog sounded like dahg to Elinor and the accent seemed to lend an added fillip to his loathing. "Ugh," he would say, "they're so hairy, and they smell!"

Nevertheless, after they had driven a little way on the Merritt Parkway, Eric pulled into a turnout, took a deep breath, and said, "Creepin' Jesus! What a picture we must make! We've got all the right ingredients: a soldier, a blonde, a baby, a 'dahg,' and a convertible!"

Elinor's thoughts were: He doesn't really care about any of us; it's only the "picture" we make. "He was like the character 'Popeye' in Faulkner's *Sanctuary,* who couldn't feel for himself, but only watch others and try to get excited over what they felt."

However, he certainly was completely devoted to Nellie (his

pet name for Ellen). The beautiful blonde little girl looked like a fairy-tale child. Eric would say "Hi!" and then sit and watch her for a long while, utterly fascinated, probably wondering what contribution he had made to this gossamer being and pondering how he could have been so lucky as to have fathered her.

On the baby's first birthday he made a page-long Gesell-and-Ilg type of analysis of all the activities she was engaging in, from shaking her head to indicate no, to smiling in the mirror, to greeting her papa with pleasure when he came home at night. But "he didn't know how to play with a kid," and, besides, "he never wanted to take her on his lap, although he was so crazy about her." However, he did write charming letters, either to or about Nellie, when he was away from her (which was more often than he would have liked).

Among Eric's personal papers are notes of the trip from Connecticut to Spokane. Eric said they left home June 5, 1943, and spent the first night at Easton, Pennsylvania, all four sleeping in the same room. The next day they landed at Carlisle, and stopped off to see Moe Margolick, who was soon to be finished with his training.

The second night they spent in Pittsburgh, the third night in Fort Wayne, Indiana, the fourth in "Chi" (Chicago), where they stopped to see Ian McRae and Betty and spend the day. Ian looked thin; he had had an operation. The next night Eric thinks they made La Crosse, Wisconsin.

South Dakota was beginning to remind Eric of the Near East. Conditions were bad: the countryside was arid, and the particular tourist cabins and washrooms they happened to strike were grimy and unappealing. Milk for Nellie was in short supply as well. (She was now drinking cow's milk out of a thermos.)

In Sheridan, Wyoming, they had a nice clean cabin and things seemed to be looking up. But conditions were terrible in Spokane.

Wartime housing in Spokane was as hard to find as in any other area with a burgeoning military population, in other words, virtually impossible. But Eric cleverly managed to work out an arrangement with an elderly Frenchman. They would share the kitchen with their landlord, who would keep his own bedroom in the large, dark, quasi-Victorian structure. The house sat on a hill overlooking the city, which stretched along the Spokane River below; it was surrounded by gardens "like an arboretum," with a network of underground sprinklers and "every kind of berry, vine and fruit tree."

The arrangement seemed ideal. Monsieur Dumont felt instant empathy with baby Ellen and her mother. Ellen was allowed to crawl happily about the garden with him, alternately admiring and massacring the flowers, as he tolerantly shunted her toward less sensitive spots. And Dumont found a kindred spirit in Elinor, with her twin passions for gardening and music. He soon took to sitting by the piano in his rocking chair while Elinor practiced, asking questions like: " 'Do you know the Brahms Intermezzo opus 117 no. 3, or the Chopin Nocturne in E-Flat, opus 9 no. 2?' He knew things like that specifically, which were beyond Eric." Elinor thought him cultivated and gallant, but Eric complained that he was taking up all Elinor's time and energy, hanging over the piano like that.

Jealousy! How was it possible to be so jealous of an old man, jealous even of the fact that when Elinor wasn't playing for him she was scrubbing every inch of his enormous, ugly old house? It was possible. Elinor was indeed wrong when she felt that Eric couldn't experience deep emotions over her and Ellen. He sometimes appeared cold, raucous and unfeeling on the surface, but the cruel, competitive world of Montreal had taught him to be wary; so he continued to be wary, not only of others, but of his own feelings.

This mover and shaker of psychiatry and psychology did not spring fully-armed from the head of the Olympian Zeus, nor was he a Rousseauistic child of nature, born perfect but destined to be corrupted. He made errors and he learned from them. Almost always running counter to the usual currents, he trapped himself into whirlpools of judgment errors and misplaced emotions, which he carefully and scientifically noted, while still whirling; and eventually he groped his way toward a theory of human conduct that made his suffering and mistakes worthwhile. With it he was able to help not only himself but others. But at this point he was still far from evolving his theory.

So he was wary and suspicious of the old man. He would

come home from Baxter Hospital after dealing with neurotic and psychotic soldiers all day, only to find the old man hovering near the piano, steeped in sonatas. He felt excluded and jealous. He had learned that in her childhood Elinor had teamed up with her brother Bill to play the game of the "clever and musically talented ones," while their sister Maxine had been "the excluded and stupid one." He wondered if his own feeling of exclusion was the result of some maneuver carried over from Elinor's childhood.

In an effort to get privacy, Eric would take his wife and baby for a ride in the convertible, but that didn't solve the problems at home. He began to build up a case against the Frenchman in his own mind. His letters to his mother and sister became full of complaints: Dumont was getting on Helen's nerves; he talked too much about his glorious ancestors; he trooped up and down the stairs to the bathroom incessantly; the phone was always ringing for him, and Nellie and Helen couldn't get calmed down for a nap.

"If I liked anybody at all, especially if it were another man, even in a barely friendly way, Eric got terribly jealous," Elinor said, "so I just couldn't like anybody."

Old Monsieur Dumont was extremely pious. He had a son who was a priest and a daughter who was a nun. Eric "became rude to the man" and took to saying "Creepin' Jesus!" religiously whenever he was around him. If the nun came home to visit and timidly apologized for using the kitchen to cut a slice of bread, Eric frowned and made her feel unwelcome.

"Goddamnit," he would say to Elinor afterwards, "we're paying the rent!"

Dumont soon whispered to Elinor that he didn't believe in divorce, but he didn't see how one could live with a man like that!

Elinor's mother came out to visit for a few days, so Elinor decided to go back with her for a brief spell. She took along her baby, of course, and her dog, of course. Eric's letters to his mother said that she was worn out from cleaning the big house and needed a rest.

In a letter dated in September 1943, Eric mentions he is moving into the bachelor officers' quarters, and that they are a dull group—mostly married men, and that everything about Spokane is dull. He is happy, though, that he is now in charge of the psychoneurotic ward, which is what he wanted. He reports that he is looking for new housing for his family in his spare time, but as fall wears on and turns into winter, he is still alone. "Helen," it seems, has migrated to Connecticut and plans to stay until the cold weather is over—the average January temperature in Spokane being 27.5 degrees and that of Norwalk, Connecticut, 27.8 degrees.

At Christmas time Eric thumbtacks blue metallic Christmas paper to the walls of his cramped quarters and gets a few articles of furniture out of storage, to cheer up the place. Although he shows interest in the prospective arrival of a new shipment of psychotics, he is still alone. And although Helen is lonely and is having to stoke the coal furnace all by herself she will continue where she is. Nellie is fine.

Sara was not fooled by a .3 degree difference in the average January temperature of the two locales. She said to Elinor, indignantly, "I know he's hard to live with. I know it isn't easy to be around him and put up with him, but you should be honored to *serve* such a man. Eric's not an ordinary run-of-the-mill person!"

But Elinor stayed on in their old shingled cottage surrounded by winter-bedraggled rosebushes, dogwood and bittersweet vines, where she had lived first with Ian and then with Eric. It was a picturesque place dating from 1738, one of the oldest and tiniest houses in that part of Connecticut. A trout stream ran behind it in a meadow where she used to pick watercress for their salads. Elinor tried her hand at "spot drawings," getting coaching from her Aunt Alice Harvey (Bransom, who was not just anybody's Aunt Alice but a cartoonist for the old *Life* and the *New Yorker*.) This didn't work out, and Elinor decided if she had to make it alone, it would be as a music teacher.

Eric had also had a few minor adventures since Elinor had left him. He had taken a trip in a flying fortress to Salt Lake City with three psychotic patients (wondering whether one or the other of them might attack the pilot). He had gone on a nature hike with an "eye man," Major Muir, through a weird

Washington landscape featuring lava beds and unusual plants. He had seen Glacier Park, and visited California and a bit of Mexico. The army had sent him through a training exercise where he had had to inch along the ground, his nose full of dust, while real machine-gun bullets zinged overhead.

Eric had been put in charge of the closed wards, and his peers were increasingly falling into the habit of saving up the hard cases for Lieutenant Berne. After hours, he now had time to resume his writing. He went back to typing short stories and trying to place his article on shock therapy.

One of these unfinished stories, "A Bleak House," was found among his papers dating from this period. It is a tale (in several versions) of an army medical corps couple with a baby sometimes called Nellie, a dog sometimes called Janie, and a wife sometimes called Elinor.

Strangely enough, Janie plays the role of an exemplary beast who dies from poisoning at the hands of an elderly French landlord, who has two daughters in a nunnery and two sons in a state hospital for the insane. The landlord is a religious fanatic who also poisons the baby. The locale in one version is in the South, while in another it is Spokane. The husband, although like Berne a doctor in the army medical corps, is described as short, which Berne wasn't.

Perhaps the husband's shortness of stature related to the fact that the wife in the story was definitely on a pedestal. Throughout the story the doctor is continually unable to appease her wrath because he made the error which resulted in the conception of their baby and the shotgun wedding which followed. Elinor's blue eyes are apt to blaze and she is apt to make acrimonious remarks or inform him abruptly that she hates him.

The husband thinks to himself how statuesque she is, how beautiful, and how unrelenting.

He is unable to look into her icy azure eyes. He tries, but her accusing look has made him lower his eyes ever since his error that led to the pregnancy.

In this story and in his letters home to his mother, Eric put forth the theory that it was the landlord who had driven Elinor away from him and the Frenchman's hilltop retreat. He now let things simmer until about the end of March, at which time he came East to wage a campaign worthy of Hannibal.

In his short story he had made the observation that love and hate are just polarities of the same emotion. Now he was apparently convinced that Elinor went by contraries, and soon after he arrived at their Connecticut village, Eric called on Aunt Alice, a few other friends, and a Miss Sembler, a photographer who had been fond of them both.

"And what do you think of Ellie now?" Miss Sembler asked Eric.

The officer answered, measuredly, "Well, the love is all gone, but I still think she has the most potential of anyone in the world."

Within minutes, the news got back to Elinor. Her first reaction was one of shock. "Really?" she asked herself. "How could he have gotten over it so quickly?"

And the ploy (if it was a ploy) worked, for shortly thereafter, the newly promoted Captain Berne, his wife with the icy azure eyes, the baby, and Janie set off for Spokane again.

Eric was probably confident that, this time, he had found the key to keeping his heart's desire at his side.

5

The Happy Days Lie Ahead

Some say that one-sided love is better than none, but like half a loaf of bread it is likely to grow hard and moldy sooner.

Eric Berne, *Sex in Human Loving*

"You can always trust a man who smokes a pipe," Flossie whispered to Shardlu.

Eric Berne, *The Happy Valley*

Eric wanted to show Elinor the Carlisle barracks, the Pennsylvania factory that had turned him out as an army officer. It was there, then, on April 4, 1944, that Eric bumped into Dr. Moses Margolick, an old "med school" acquaintance from McGill. Dr. Margolick was able to date the incident precisely, because eleven years earlier he and Lennard, as Eric was then called, were sitting in the classroom being bored to death by a "particularly dull lecture by our Teutonic professor, Dr. Horst Oertel."

Moses and Lennard had been slipping notes to each other, and one of them had remarked, "Today is 3/3/33—I wonder where we'll be on 4/4/44?" And sure enough, they had their chance encounter at Carlisle barracks on 4/4/44. They spent a pleasant evening together and agreed to look each other up, or at least write, on 5/5/55, 6/6/66, and so on, which they more or less did, but the string of magical chance encounters played out in '44.

The next day the Berne family was waved off by Dr.

Margolick and continued on its trip. Eric was not at ease with machinery. He ran over curbs, jerked to stops, and hunched over the wheel, peering forward as if he could hardly see. He had not fine-tuned the antennae of his intuition to pick up the secret messages from used-car salesmen at this point, so his impressive-looking convertibles tended to break down from time to time, but nevertheless the family crossed the continent without losing a diaper.

About half way on this trip to Spokane Eric's watch stopped. He searched out a jeweler who found a dog hair in the works. Eric returned to the car, fuming: "That goddamned dahg. We gotta get rid of that goddamned dahg!" But Janie hung in there. If any heads were to roll, it wouldn't be hers.

In Spokane, they moved into new digs and celebrated Nellie's second birthday. Also Elinor discovered she was pregnant, and soon thereafter they left for Fort Ord, California, Eric's next assignment. On the trip Elinor suffered a miscarriage.

"As soon as I had the miscarriage," Elinor said, "I thought: no matter what any doctor says, I'm going to get pregnant again right away. . . . I think I had a vision of eventually ending up alone and not wanting to bring up a little daughter as an only child. I wanted another child, frankly, by whom didn't matter. Obviously I wouldn't have got involved with anybody else at this point, and I already had Ellen by Eric, and it was convenient, but it wasn't that I particularly wanted a child by him. I just wanted a child."

Eric spent long hours puzzling over the reasons for the miscarriage. He finally blamed it on a cold he had had one night in Spokane when they had made love.

Once at Fort Ord, Eric and Elinor discovered nearby a town called Carmel-by-the-Sea, an ex-artists' colony not yet ruined by the commercial exploitation that is the conqueror worm of ex-artists' colonies. They may not have been at ease with each other, but they both loved Carmel. It was at that time equally as charming as their Connecticut village and about the same size.

If curbs or gutters had been installed throughout Carmel many oaks and pines that dotted the village would have had to be cut down. So the nature-loving citizens kept the trees, and curbless, gutterless streets meandered as best they might around the trees.

Robinson Jeffers lived on a rocky point near the bay (for Carmel-by-the-Sea is actually by-the-bay). Lincoln Steffens and Ella Winter spent many years in Carmel. Jack London (in his day) and Sinclair Lewis had been part-time Carmel habitués. "Sometimes the mysterious Garbo went into retreat at a little inn in the Carmel Highlands. Sometimes Jean Harlow was at the Del Monte Hotel, or Lady Diana Manners at Pebble Beach Lodge. Krishnamurti came for lectures."

John Steinbeck often came over the hill from Pacific Grove to drop in on his Carmel friends. Painters of seascapes and still lifes abounded. Edward Weston had his darkroom in his cabin at nearby Wildcat Creek. Lesser luminaries strolled the streets on their daily trips to cull rejection slips from their post office boxes, and those who weren't luminous at all gloried in the atmosphere and considered themselves artistic by adherence. There was not much prejudice here, except a slight intolerance for Babbitts, or those with Babbitt's habits.

Eric put an advertisement in the *Pine Cone*, Carmel's arty weekly: "McGill graduate and his wife want house." They soon found one, a rustic cottage with a "cathedral" ceiling, and settled down to as nearly normal a life as they had ever had. Elinor reveled in the woodsyness of Carmel, the fresh smell of the ocean and the pines in the air, the ice plant that grew around the house and the carpet of pine needles in the areas that the ice plant disdained (a mowed lawn in Carmel would have been a sign of sickness of the soul).

They began having a few fellow psychiatrists from Fort Ord out to dinner. Elinor busied herself with baking bread and keeping house; she rented a battered upright piano to practice on. And then she found out that she was pregnant again.

She wanted the child, but she wasn't totally happy—probably because, as she told us, "There never was a time I was with Eric that I didn't feel a sort of resentment against him. From the first minute he walked in the door and I was introduced to him, something in me reacted against him and I felt hostility and resistance. Even in the moments when we were superficially getting along all right, doing something we both enjoyed, such as driving through beautiful scenery, I still felt an underlying dislike for all he stood for."

It was his "crass physicality" that upset Elinor. "Now physicality is OK if there's something else there," Elinor said, but she had the feeling that "that was all there was to Eric. It was all he ever exhibited—what my mother called 'body-mindedness.' He was so 'body-minded!' "

A case in point was the way he approached love-making. When he was romantically inclined he would come toward Elinor with "this red, shiny tongue hanging out. . . . I think he thought it was sexually exciting. . . . Whenever he thought . . . [I] was open to a sexual advance he would start using his tongue, showing his tongue." This turned off Elinor completely. She thought: "He must have read somewhere that the tongue was an exciting phallic symbol, especially if freshly licked and shiny."

Elinor was dreadfully nauseated during this pregnancy. Already thin, she lost an alarming fifty pounds and seemed "unable to function at all." Eric hovered over her with a big needle, telling her he would have to feed her intravenously if she wouldn't eat, and he called in a practical nurse to look after things.

To Elinor it appeared that he agonized needlessly over the cost of the nurse. He seemed to count out her wages in nickels and dimes. But he never took Elinor into his confidence about money matters. In a letter to his sister Grace, earlier that year, he had explained his financial situation. He said he had $500 in stocks but $1200 in debts and no money in the savings bank. He had drawn out his last savings to pay Elinor's fare East. He was also sending his mother $60 a month. (Sara had had a heart attack and wasn't able to work, except for making costume jewelry to add a small supplement to her funds.) Elinor had had only two dresses since he had come into the army and neither he nor she had been able to afford new stockings or shoes. Eric ended by asking Grace not to tell his mother of their precarious financial state.

Soon after she arrived the nurse had sized up the situation and felt there was something very wrong with the relationship. She, like Elinor's mother and father, was a Christian Scientist.

One day she sat down with Elinor and said: "My dear, do you have any kind of faith?"

Elinor countered, "Faith?"

"Yes, religious faith."

Elinor answered, "Not too much."

"That's too bad, because I think it would help you now. You really need something to cling to, in order to get better. What about your family?"

"They're near Chicago."

"Why don't you go home to them?"

It hadn't occurred to Elinor that she could, at that point. The trouble was, she felt too sick to leave.

In their arguments Eric had more than once said that he would "rather see her dead than lose her." She had begun to wonder if he would really let her leave. By a coincidence her mother called that evening. When she understood the situation, her mother urged her to come home immediately; if she had any problems, she was to get the nice nurse to help her. So the two women set things in motion for the hegira.

Elinor was surprised that Eric, although he put up resistance, didn't forbid the move. He even packed her clothes for her but appeared to be in a towering rage. He dropped objects on the floor and broke them, slammed doors, paced back and forth, and slung things into suitcases.

It was, of course, supposed to be only a temporary arrangement. Even though he had to pay for another trip East, Eric was glad that Elinor's mother would be able to do any nursing necessary until the baby was born. But Elinor feels he had more than a premonition she wouldn't come back. She had been with her husband only six and a half months this time, but she never returned.

Onto the train again went Elinor, Ellen, the invincible Janie, and Ellen's maple potty chair, with a begonia in full bloom stuck into it. Eric, with a long, sad face, watched the train slowly slide out of the Salinas depot and disappear out of sight behind the lettuce-icing sheds.

After she got to Chicago, Elinor went to see various lawyers about a divorce. None of them wanted to take the case, especially after reading Dr. Berne's letters. Finally, a Mr. Van Winans, a Christian Scientist and family friend, arranged to represent her in Chicago. Ex-Judge Joseph Sam Perry would do any necessary trial work in Dupage County, Illinois. But she couldn't get a default divorce against a soldier, and a contested divorce while the war was on was almost equally out of the question. Eric was still convinced that this was primarily a battle between Christian Science and medical science. If he could just get Elinor away from that practitioner, everything would be all right.

Elinor tried to conceal the baby's arrival date. She was afraid Eric was so upset he would come to the hospital and make some kind of scene. He was still sending letters full of threats and razored-out deletions. Elinor began developing high blood pressure and skin rashes—she told her "cranky" obstetrician she was sure they were due to Eric's correspondence. When she showed the doctor some of Eric's letters, he assured her that they portrayed the "normal reactions of a concerned husband." Elinor's place was back in Carmel, and he urged her emphatically to go back there. "Can't you see he's just worried sick about you?" the doctor snorted indignantly.

Hoping that the baby would come early so as to confuse the issue, Elinor actually did manage to have him a little bit early. However, Eric found out. He was ecstatic and wanted to forget the ugly past. "He sent me a beautiful telegram: 'Thank God the hard days are over. The happy days lie ahead.' "

Captain Berne flew to Chicago, eager to see his newborn son, ignoring the divorce threat, and hoping that things could be smoothed over. He visited the baby at the home of Elinor's family in Wheaton. Bending over the crib he said, "Hello, little boy!" He was very, very moved.

"He was a good baby, placid and contented, and he was a boy," Elinor said. "Eric wished that I could have named the girl baby Sara after his mother, and he now insisted that I name the boy David after his father. He was opposed to the name I wanted which he said had nothing to do with anything, but I chose the name in both cases.

"When Eric came to see the baby it was really very touching—but then he hung around and hung around. My father told him he thought he ought to go; he'd seen the baby; he'd seen

Ellen; and there was nothing left to hang around for." (At least in the eyes of Elinor's parents.) But to Eric there was plenty. He was certain that with his brilliance he could get his family away from the clutches of his in-laws. So Eric wouldn't go.

"Finally, even my father got kind of upset; he shut the front door on him, and Eric walked up and down in front of the house, stopping anybody who came along and shouting: '"You know what those terrible people are doing? They won't let me see my own child, and I'm a serviceman too!'"

It was a quiet residential neighborhood, a suburban community, and people were out watering their gardens and walking their dogs. The neighbors sitting on their front porches pretended not to notice what was going on. Eric kept dashing up to the house, ringing the bell and demanding to see his children. About the tenth time around, Elinor's brother Bill answered the door and said it wasn't possible; Elinor and the children were napping.

Eric retorted: "But I'm the father!"

Bill answered wearily, "Well, after all, Elinor is the mother, and she's taking care of the children."

To which Eric shouted, "Well, she couldn't have done it without my semen!" The neighbors stared fixedly at their roses and irises, counting aphids with the utmost precision.

One afternoon shortly after that, Eric was given permission to take his beloved daughter out for a walk around the streets of Wheaton and nearby Glen Ellyn. But the "short, dumpy, little grandmother" trusted Eric no more than she would trust any member of the medical profession, and so she followed him with measured tread at a distance of 100 feet. And brother Bill, as ready reserve, followed behind her at 200 feet. As the parade made its deliberate way along the tree-lined streets, it passed a police station. Eric suddenly ducked into it with Ellen, shouting:

"Officer, arrest that woman!"

Policeman: "Why?"

Eric: "Because she is following me."

Policeman: "There's no law against following anybody that I know about."

The parade continued, but now the grandmother was indeed

suspicious that a kidnapping was contemplated. She closed in on the psychiatrist, and when he took Ellen up in his arms, her fears were aroused and she swung at Eric with her handbag, knocking the pipe out of his mouth. Eric was stunned by the attack. He put up his arm to protect his glasses and cried: "Don't assault me! Don't assault me!" He then put Ellen down momentarily to search in the gutter for his pipe. The grandmother, her worst suspicions unconfirmed but her free-floating anger given a focus by the clear evidence that this able-bodied man was still a slave to the tobacco habit, snatched up Ellen, shouting sarcastically: "That darned old pipe! You care less about Ellen than that darned old pipe!"

Elinor feels that if Eric had harbored any scheme for spiriting Ellen away, its only purpose would have been to get his wife to follow him. That way he could pry her away from her parents long enough to persuade her to return to Carmel.

Shortly thereafter, according to Bill Harvey's version, Eric showed up at the door with a fat bailiff dressed in plainclothes who insisted that Eric be allowed to see his children, and a "shouting match developed" in which Eric "mentioned his semen." At this time the grandmother angrily stated that the babies were the result not of semen but "of the intervention of God Almighty." Brother Bill Harvey, who joined the hullabaloo, twitted the bailiff with: "How do I know you're an officer? Where's your star?" The bailiff produced a badge, but nobody got past the front door.

"The whole thing was awful. But, you know, it was kind of sad," Elinor said. "Finally he had to go back to California. He came to the door and my father opened it. Eric was standing there with tears in his eyes and he said: 'Well, I have to go now. I'm glad you let me see my little boy. At least you were nice to me, Mr. Harvey.'"

As for the grandmother, she had found out long since that the things that Eric had written about Elinor in the early days weren't true, and she wasn't able to forgive and forget. It gave her another axe to grind against "men," and she had never liked men much to begin with. The fact that Eric was Jewish didn't help either. She also especially disliked psychiatrists, not to mention nonbelievers—so far as she was concerned Eric was a "heathen"—and his "awful physicality" totally repelled her. "Mother thought Eric was the devil incarnate," said Elinor.

"I remember V-J day. I was sitting at the table nursing my son when the news came. Oh, God! I thought, now I can be free of Eric. I never thought about the cessation of hostilities or the bloodshed."

As the date for the divorce hearing approached, Elinor and her lawyer were concerned as to whether Eric really would produce old left-wing newspapers with Elinor's address label on them in an attempt to demonstrate that she was a radical and, *ipso facto,* an unfit mother. Also, in one of his violent, if unrazored, communications he had threatened to have her lawyer disbarred—Mr. Van Winans had not used his own stationery in his latest letter about the divorce, but had written it on state bar stationery that showed him to be President of the Illinois State Bar.

Elinor doesn't mind now admitting to having been a "card-carrying Trotskyist" but, at that time, with the custody of the children at issue, she was totally distraught. However, Van Winans tried to reassure her that the letters which Eric had written her would provide her trial lawyer with good and sufficient weapons with which to retaliate.

During the pretrial negotiations Elinor felt that Eric's attitude was: "You think you're going to get me, but you're not! I'll get you! I've got more weapons than you have—I've got money!" She said, "No matter how your heart beat for him, no matter how much you knew that it all must have come from his old childhood suffering, still you just stiffened against him."

Eric showed up at the hearing wearing his new major's insignia on his uniform. He had hired one of the best known divorce lawyers in Chicago. At the conclusion of the two presentations, the judge asked if there were any possibility of a reconciliation. Elinor arose from her seat as if in a trance, reeled off her reasons for mistrusting Eric, and ended by answering the judge's query as to the possibility of reconciliation with a ringing "never, never, never!"

The major sat through the proceedings staring at Elinor with a fixed, hypnotic stare. She fearfully avoided his gaze. But he said nothing. Elinor was afraid that if he got custody of the children or shared substantially in their custody he would "try to mold their minds" and she "didn't intend to" (do so herself). Eric demanded custody of the children six months of the year. However, the lawyers worked out an agreement whereby Elinor retained full custody, but with reduced support payments.

It would now be up to her to make the major part of the family income from her piano lessons. Her child support payments to begin with were $30 per month for each child and a lump sum of $1300. This meant no luxuries, but she managed.

The basic median pay for army officers in 1945 was $2442 yearly, and an officer was expected to pay for his own food, housing, and uniforms. Basic pay plus allowances could run $3777 yearly, but after Eric had taken $60 out for his mother and $60 out for his children, plus something to pay off his debts, he probably didn't have a lot of spending money.

Later, after Eric had married his second wife Dorothy and was more solvent, he began sending more—$100 and, later, $120 per month. Dorothy, who was a gracious influence on Eric, persuaded him to do so, Elinor always thought.

With the lump sum payment, Elinor bought a lump of a car (cars being hard to come by immediately after World War II), a faded maroon De Soto with ripped and shredded upholstery but sturdy in the basics. It got the four of them, including Janie, safely back to their small New England town.

After the divorce, the importance of the razor-slashed letters waned as far as Elinor was concerned, but the fact that he had been so imprudent as to send such letters troubled Eric continually. Periodically he wrote to her and demanded they be returned "forthwith," but Elinor always said no.

After the two children were of high school age, and Eric had children by his second wife, he came to Connecticut for a visit, and he and Elinor found they had both mellowed. They went to dinner at The Crab Bucket—all four of them— looking like any happy family group. Eric and Elinor had both been through another tempestuous marriage and divorce. At home, later that evening, they expressed regrets about the fears and misunderstandings that had driven them apart. In this tender mood, and when they were by themselves, Elinor was suddenly moved to say she wouldn't mind relinquishing all 200 of the letters.

So she burned them, one by one, in the fireplace, as they both watched.

"I felt better for having done it. Besides, she added dryly, "I didn't want him hanging around for them forever."

6

Forever May Last As Long As Seven Years

Love is a sweet trap from which no one departs without tears.
                                    Eric Berne, *Sex in Human Loving*

It should be said again that being beautiful (like being successful) is not a matter of anatomy, but of parental permission. Anatomy can make one pretty or photogenic, but only a father's smile can make beauty shine from a woman's eyes.
        Eric Berne, *What Do You Say After You Say Hello?*

Back in Connecticut (after a year with her family in Wheaton), Elinor started putting the shreds and pieces of her life together, "trying to discover who I was." She took back Ian's last name, as she had given music lessons under that name before. Now she managed to teach her lessons even though she had a one-year-old and a four-year-old to care for, and no money for babysitters. "It wasn't easy, but I'd put the baby in his crib, say, at 2 o'clock and tell him 'Now it's time for your nap,' and that blessed little critter would lie there, or sleep, until I was through teaching at 6 o'clock and could go upstairs and get him!

"Later when Ellen went to school, she would come home afterwards and take care of him. She would go over everything she had learned with her brother. He was always two grades ahead of himself—in fact, when he started school, he was about ready for the fifth grade! He was so bored. Ellen was like a little mother to him.

"Before I left Eric I didn't have that kind of strength. I had to learn everything step by step. I did things in a funny order, but it worked out all right."

Meanwhile, the cool, hypnotic façade that Eric had exhibited throughout the trial cracked occasionally. On his way back from a New England visit to the children, perhaps a year after the divorce, he stopped off in Chicago and called on an old McGill Medical School acquaintance, Dr. Rachmiel Levine (now medical director of the City of Hope Hospital near Los Angeles). Dr. Levine was surprised to see Eric; he hadn't felt particularly close to him, and Mrs. Levine, a psychiatric social worker, was meeting him for the first time. The Levines never could figure out exactly what the visit was all about. There was a great outpouring of despair and remorse—it had something to do with the divorce. He kept asking them how to get his family back again, but since he didn't reveal all the facts, they felt powerless to advise him.

Eric was wracked by paroxysms of grief and guilt. The Levines were embarrassed to have a psychiatrist on their hands who seemed so close to cracking up—"it was pathetic, unbelievable"—but they did their best to get him to regain control. And years later Eric praised his old acquaintance highly. He told Torre, his third wife, that Rachmiel Levine was "the only man he had ever known who was smarter than he was."

Elinor could see only the coldness, the razored letters, the Machiavellian plotting when she looked at her ex-husband. But he hid from her the other side of the passions that swayed him.

Elinor told us: "Before he married Dorothy, Eric would write once a year and say he was coming to New York and would like to see the children. His letter would be very cold. I was always absolutely terrified that he was hatching some plot to get them away from me. But he didn't come very often (he was too far away) and he couldn't stay long. I was also afraid he'd get them alone and try to undermine me with them as he had done with my mother—tell them what a whore I was, for instance! But, then, there was nothing I could do. I couldn't say no. He had a right to visit them."

One time Eric brought along a "skinny, energetic, with-it" young woman "with melting brown eyes," named Rosabel Brown. Rosabel, a child psychologist, told us that she and Eric were in love at this time, even talking about marriage. Before they went up to Connecticut, Eric warned Rosabel that the visit was likely to be unpleasant.

It was. According to Rosabel, Elinor picked up the phone and threatened to call the police. She became "very upset" about Eric's visit and his desire to see his sleeping children. Finally, with the utmost use of her counseling skills, Rosabel convinced Elinor that she should wake the children, bring them downstairs, and let Eric see them in the forty-five minutes they had between trains.

Elinor thought Rosabel seemed trustworthy, sweet, gentle, and persuasive, but Eric was a different matter. As a mother, she was concerned about her vulnerability, because of what Eric might do to her through the children. She dared not relax her guard.

When Eric visited Elinor, however, the cold and calculating tone which he maintained in his letters disappeared. "As soon as he saw me, the minute he saw me, Eric would begin to be very tender. It would be as if nothing had ever happened between us." He gazed at this ethereal, blonde mother of his children, and it was "as if we understood each other perfectly, and he loved me dearly, and I was his devoted and dutiful wife. Before he left, he would come to me and say, 'I know I wasn't really a marriageable person in those days, but I think I've learned something. I think I should be able to be a good husband for you now. Would you take a chance?' And I would say no." (Elinor said this to us very quietly.)

On one of Eric's annual visits he swore to Elinor that she was the only woman he had ever really loved. If she had stayed with him, he would have been true to her forever. Unfortunately, after a brief pause, he couldn't resist a "take-away" line: "Or at least for seven years, which is as long as a man could be expected to be contented with one woman."

Elinor exploded: "You mean you would have left me, divorced me, after seven years?"

"Oh no," Eric replied, "never divorced, but I would certainly have been ready for something new. A man shouldn't be counted on to be completely faithful to just one woman."

Among Elinor's treasured memories is Eric's observation that their children demonstrated the best qualities of both parents, and Elinor agrees that this is true. "That's the one thing that made the whole thing worthwhile—all the misery and heartache."

Elinor told us that Ellen, a loving and understanding girl, became attached to her father as she grew older. Eric took her on two trips. The first was to the Canary Islands, where her brother subsequently joined them.

Over the years, Eric's feelings toward the children had changed. When Ellen was a little girl, he had paid most of his attention to her, but later he began to admire his son's assertiveness, independence, and his extraordinary intelligence. The boy was a musical genius, and even in his teens he spoke, read, and wrote five languages flawlessly. At the schools he attended he won all the prizes, and upon graduation he was offered a scholarship to Yale.

Ellen said: "My father was very taken with my brother. They did respect each other. He looked at my brother and he saw he was a winner, and I, at that time, wasn't.

"Eric said, 'Your brother's a prince! Why aren't you [a princess]?'

"I felt just terrible—utterly crushed. And I was thinking, I'm the one who cares about my father. The child who tries the hardest."

Eric, according to Ellen, "said I should have gone to Vassar. His daughter should have gone to Vassar and not N.Y.U. He said he was ashamed to tell people that his daughter was going to N.Y.U. He was ashamed that I hadn't lived up to something great—I was never quite sure what he wanted."

Ellen became a social worker and used TA in her practice for seven years. "I began reading the *TA Bulletin* and calling my father up and discussing cases with him, and we both got excited about it." (She has since become a librarian.)

Eric would be "out of his mind with happiness" to know that his oldest son, after pursuing a highly successful career as opera conductor until the age of thirty-six, has decided to become a doctor. He is tired of the arts and feels a strong desire for unselfish effort—something to help humanity, perhaps something along the lines of Albert Schweitzer's contributions.

About five years ago Elinor woke up in the night and thought: Gee! I'm a success! She believes that each person's life is a search for what her special talent is, her unique contribution. Hers, although she has many talents, is her ability to communicate her love for music to her pupils on a one-to-one basis. "It has nothing to do with fame, notoriety, or money. It's just that I have found my place."

Elinor identifies Berne somewhat with her hero, Richard Wagner. Wagner was a "monster of conceit," she pointed out, reading from a Deems Taylor biography. He was incapable of supporting himself, "borrowed money from everybody," was a breaker of women's hearts, was faithless both to his friends and his wife, wrote people begging letters, and felt that the world owed him a living—

"The women whose hearts he broke are long since dead," she read. But Wagner's music lives on. Elinor feels that, like Wagner but to a much lesser degree, Eric was a one-sided genius. She thinks it is "kind of interesting" in retrospect that she was part of the Eric Berne saga.

He was always in terrible conflict with himself. His intensive game-playing was in conflict with that part of him that developed the theory of games. He switched over from the Child position as gamesplayer to the Adult position as categorizer of games. " Very constructive! Which was fine!"

She believes that "never in his life did Eric feel real joy." For this reason he is to her "pitiable." She deplores "all that energy and ability" spent in what Einstein described as "perfecting means to achieve confused goals . . . a sickness in America." When she looks back on the years they spent together, she feels they were "bad, all bad." She feels no rancor toward him now, "but this is history, and it ought to come out."

She likes living by herself. Her marriage to the temperamental George, her Hungarian third husband, whom she describes as "sensational, irresistible, a dream lover," was "another astonishing story. I wouldn't get mixed up with a man again for anything on earth," she says—and she laughs uproariously. She enjoys being on her own, now that she is in her seventies.

She is still working in her garden, still conveying her passion for music to others, and she tells us: "I am an anthropomorphist, a disciple of Pythagoras, Rudolf Steiner, and Albert Schweitzer, who believes music to be the noblest, highest expression of spiritual order and balance—that the study of musical principles opens the mind to a more universal view of life and to an individual's indispensable role in relating to all life expression within the whole."

Eric continued to importune Elinor to go back to him for a long while after their divorce. In 1949, the week before he married his second wife, he asked Elinor to remarry him even though his marriage to Dorothy had been in the works for months.

Elinor says: "I knew there was a Dorothy; he told me about her. He put it to me that she was very interested in marriage. But he came to me a week before they were to be married and asked me if I wouldn't try once more. I had a feeling that if I said no, this time he wouldn't ask me again. And ten days later I got a note saying he and Dorothy were married. And I was so relieved! I had nothing more to fear from him."

Ω

Counterpoint 3

JUPITER'S SIDE OF IT

A woman connected with TA has suggested that we were giving a unilateral account—Berne's viewpoint wasn't being represented. Since Eric often wove his actual experiences into his writings, sometimes transmuted into myths, fairy tales, or fictitious case histories, she suggested that we print the following in rebuttal. It is the story of "Europa and the Bull" as Berne tells it in What Do You Say After You Say Hello?:

"One day [Europa] was in a seaside meadow gathering flowers when a beautiful bull appeared and knelt at her feet. His eyes invited her to get on his back. She was so taken with his melodious voice and friendly manner that she thought it would be fun to ride around the dell. But the moment she mounted, he took off over the sea, for he was really Jupiter in disguise, and Jupiter would stop at nothing when he saw a girl he liked. Europa did not fare too badly, however, because [later] she gave birth to three kings and had a continent named after her.

". . . in spite of Europa's wild lamentations and protests, she never expressly says 'Stop' or 'Take me back at once! . . . In other words, while she makes loud token protests, she is careful not to abort the drama, but instead resigns herself to it and becomes curious about its outcome. Thus her lamentations have the ambiguous quality, which in Martian is called 'gamy' or 'scripty.' In fact she is playing the game of 'Rapo,' which fits into her destined script of becoming the mother of kings, providing it happens 'against her will.' Taking a personal interest in her abductor is not the firmest way to discourage him; but her protests disclaim her own responsibility for having flirted with him in the first place."

7

Prince Lennie

> *Therefore a parent who wants to do the best for his children should find out what his own script is and then decide whether he wants to pass it on to them. If he decides not to, then he should find out how to change it, to grow princes where there were frogs before. This is not easy to do. It is even harder than trying to give oneself a haircut.*
>
> Eric Berne, *Sex in Human Loving*

During his childhood, Lennie Bernstein could well have felt that he was a prince. His father was a doctor and doctors were "the ideal . . . no different from . . . in America" of the Montreal Jewish community. The boy lived in a three-story brick castle, plain of façade (but with ten rooms and a fenced-in back yard) on quiet Sainte Famille Street. With its barred windows the basement playroom could easily have seemed like the dungeon of some king. The gold-leaf lettering on the thick glass in the transom of the front door which read "73 Ste. Famille Street" also seemed of regal elegance. Berne's sister Grace (who died a short time ago) told us: "I met somebody from Montreal only three years ago who happened to live on Sainte Famille Street, and I asked him if the house with the lettering on the transom was still there. He said, 'Oh! You mean the doctor's house?'"

The janitor, who lived in part of the basement and "took care of the house," also added a special touch. Grace elaborated on this: "We had a maid, a nursemaid, a sewing lady and a laundress. We had a beautiful home with lots of interesting people coming and going, whose culture rubbed off on us. My memories are of snowy linens and gourmet food on the table. We played tennis on real tennis courts and we paid tuition to go to one of the best schools in the city. . . . Our father, although he became ill, kept at his work and his writing [for medical journals] until the end, like Roosevelt. And come to think of it, our house was always busy, much like the Roosevelts. And we lived just as nicely, although more frugally after [our father] died. We had a maid, in uniform, all of our lives."

The father was ill with tuberculosis. And when he died, the little family, like characters in a fairy-tale, fell under a spell and henceforth had to struggle hard for a living. Lennie and Grace became a prince and princess in disguise. The mother, however, did not remarry and provide them with a wicked stepfather but toiled on alone, barely able to keep the fairy-tale illusion of royal status alive.

Another factor that may have made the children feel a bit regal in their younger days was that they didn't mingle with other children very much. They were forbidden to go to the neighborhood where their father's clinic was. After his death their mother was busy and too tired to get them together with the other relatives, especially during the long winter months when Montreal lay blanketed in snow. "Traveling about the city was by streetcar, and that was pretty rugged," said Grace. And they also weren't allowed to play with the children on Sainte Famille Street, where their house was. The reason for this may have been their parents' desire to protect their children from ethnic hostilities in the mixed neighborhood.

In a thinly disguised story of his childhood, Berne wrote about an incident in which a little boy was hiding behind the curtains playing peek-a-boo of a sort. His father (who was a physician) said to the mother that there seemed to be some kind of boogeyman behind the curtains, and if there was a boogeyman, they'd have to hug him to make him tame. After a certain amount of pouncing and grabbing, the boogeyman miraculously avoided capture even though delighted gurglings were issuing from behind the curtain. The doctor then observed that it might be a pirate and, if so, they'd have a lot of trouble catching him. Pirates were extremely clever and just about impossible to capture successfully. However, the mother did find him and said he certainly was a pirate.

This was, apparently, one of the few times that this smart pirate was ever caught. Whether the gurgler was Eric or whether the story was entirely fictional we cannot tell, but Berne seemed to be programmed to a life of swashbuckling and wearing pirate costumes to masquerade parties.

Another part of the unpublished story tells of how this blond heir apparent played in his father's waiting room. Dr. Bernstein had his office in his Montreal house, and the waiting room doubled as their family parlor. It had high-backed leather chairs, a fireplace, and a red carpet. Little Lennie would perhaps have shown his father's patients the treasures he kept in an old orange crate, just as the child in the story did: a crimson fire-engine with black, iron horses, some lead soldiers, marbles, etc. The waiting room captives never seemed to tire of admiring the little boy's possessions or of giving him their full attention.

But there's no story about his playing with children his own age. One fragment told of his sitting in the car while his father was making a house call. There were some dirty kids playing in the street. Sometimes they would gather around the Ford and stare at the boy, and he would be embarrassed. If he had an apple, he would eat it, concentrating his attention on the place where he had just had taken a bite. If he hadn't, he would take out a notebook and a little pencil his mother had given him and pretend to make notes. After a while the kids would drift away.

Born in Montreal, Quebec, on May 10, 1910, Lennie was the sole child in the household until he was four years old. Then Anna, his maternal grandmother, died very young. According to Grace, the grandmother died of overwork: too much fancy baking, starching of pinafores, and perhaps too many children over too long a span of time. (Her youngest child was younger than her grandson Lennie. This child, Jeanne, came to live, off and on, with the Bernsteins after her mother's death.) Another version of the story is that Anna was always an invalid, had five children, and died young of kidney trouble. Her daughters did all the housework.

One year after the grandmother's death, Grace was born, and Berne wove a similar event into another of his unpublished stories. He still describes himself as being very much on his own. He went downstairs to his father's waiting room, but no one was there to admire his toys; the patients had been sent away, and the room was empty. Mama had not come to breakfast, and the little boy asked where she was. The young servant was busy boiling cauldrons of water and said nothing. The father told his son to go out in the backyard to play; meanwhile a strange man arrived and went upstairs with Daddy.

Finally, the boy crept upstairs to look for his mama but saw that her yellow door with the brass handle was closed, and, as he had been forbidden to open closed doors, he stood there struggling with his conflicting emotions.

Eventually the baby was born, and the next morning the boy was allowed to eat breakfast on a tray in his mama's bedroom. She told him to look in the cradle and see the nice surprise which was waiting for him, but he looked at the baby and said his mama was fooling him because there was nothing there.

Later the boy found in the basement storeroom a collection of paraphernalia which he hadn't noticed before. A large yellowish rubber sheet reminded him of the color of his mother's bedroom door, and he impulsively cut the sheet into shreds with a pair of scissors. Then, after throwing up and dissolving in tears, he confessed to his father that he had been a *bad boy*. The doctor held his hand, listened with concern, and with perfect evenness of disposition and a gentle demeanor, reached for his razor strop. The boy began to moan, for he sensed what was in the offing, but the father was inexorable.

He told his small son coolly that it was important to learn not to destroy the property of others. Children could not allow themselves to get so angry that they took it out on other people's possessions.

He belted the boy twenty times with the razor strop and sent him bawling out into the backyard. Ten minutes later, the child, whose bottom was still smarting, spied a beetle out in the yard and got considerable satisfaction out of slamming it violently with the back of his shovel and flattening it against the earth until it was dead. The beetle, at least, didn't belong to anyone.

According to Pamela Blum, ITAA secretary from September 1965 through May 1968, Berne had a habit, when things went awry, of muttering "bad boy, bad boy" to himself sotto voce. She remembers hearing this innumerable times.

Dr. John Dusay, one of the TA leaders, once asked Berne if he thought that he (Dusay) should be psychoanalyzed. Berne said, "Well, if you want to find out who Buster is, as in 'Buzz off, Buster,' you can do that. I found out I was Buster at age five." Berne also told Dusay that his own script was that of Kronos, father of Zeus, who lead an uneventful life except for the fact that he castrated his father, married his sister and swallowed his children.

Dr. Bernstein, although a benevolent father and "a most gentle, benign and kind individual," was, according to one of Berne's wives, a stern disciplinarian. In an introduction to another unpublished manuscript called "Ramsbottom Horsely," which was mostly composed of cullings from his *McGill Daily* column, Berne dedicated the book to his parents. His father, he explained, had punished him when he had needed it and was the type of doctor who devoted himself unselfishly to the well-being of his patients. He died early of tuberculosis. His mother, he continued, had brought up her children to be fair, perceptive, and able to look at all sides of a question. She had the ability to enjoy life, even when there was little to enjoy. He also thanked his sister for turning the radio off when he wanted to study.

The doctor took Lennie around with him on house calls in his Model T Ford in summer and let him go on these rounds (bundled up in fur robes) in a horse-drawn "sleigh-taxi" in the winter.

"Kiss and hug my little curly-haired blond baby boy for me," the doctor had written his young wife, Sara, on a postcard once, and Berne later recounted this incident to his first wife, Elinor, as proof of his father's love. But even loving fathers can get disturbed when babyhood merges into childhood and living "by the rules" doesn't come automatically.

Dr. Lawrence Levitin, a close friend of Berne's in the last three decades of his life, said that he and Berne "used to talk about how it wasn't easy to be the sons of fathers who were rather tough and forceful in their own quiet way. Everybody else thought they were great, and we weren't so sure that they were that great." He and Berne agreed that "fathers were difficult, particularly if they had strong opinions."

From what Berne told Levitin, Dr. Bernstein was a "distant,

successful, idealistic, harsh, firm man, a controversial man himself."

Dr. Bernstein was a Zionist in the early days of that movement when Zionism meant radicalism. He set up a clinic for the poor and recently arrived Jewish immigrants, naming it after Theodor Herzl, the father of modern Zionism.

In 1918, when Lennard was eight, his father caught the World War I influenza. The doctor was overworked and he never recovered—the flu turned into tuberculosis. Too many people were now dependent on him, and he valiantly kept on with his practice. A screen porch was built on the roof so that he could sleep outside in the summertime. Often he stayed at the sanitarium, where he was the doctor, and his daughter Grace remembered visiting him there.

To the late Dr. Gerald Goodstone, who as a child came over to play with Lennie occasionally, Dr. Bernstein "was a shadowy figure; he was ill, had tuberculosis, and had his own little apartment—room—in the house. He stayed pretty much to himself. He lived a different life.

"I went to his room once when we were boys. I picked up this cup and opened it up. I didn't know what it was. I've remembered it ever since. It turned out to be a sputum cup full of sputum . . . a very disgusting sight. I didn't know people had to cough. I didn't know about such things."

Eventually, the father "just faded away. On the night before he died he had a message for each of us," his daughter Grace said. " 'Be a good girl,' he told me, and to Eric he said, 'Take care of your mother and sister.' "

Grace felt that for that community the thirty-eight-year-old physician's death was much like the assassination of President Kennedy. People crowded into their house; the place was filled to the rafters. "Many, many years afterwards I'd meet people who would say, 'Oh, I knew your father—he was such a wonderful man,' " said Grace.

But Lennard at ten going on eleven, couldn't do much then about taking care of his mother and sister. And his mother was busy trying to figure out how, at age thirty-two, with two children to support and care for and only a normal school education to fall back on, she was going to maintain a living standard appropriate to the survivors of a distinguished doctor. (Before she was married, she had helped put her husband through medical school by working as a teacher, but after the marriage she had not worked outside the home.)

Luckily, as Grace said, "she was smart." She divided the house into three flats and rented out two. She took up her teaching as before, using her middle name, Gordon, as her surname, until the day she received a letter from her employer, the Protestant School Board. The letter indicated that the board had discovered that Sara Gordon was really Sara Bernstein, no Protestant, and therefore her services would no longer be required.

Sara coolly told her progeny: "I'll have to do something else." Somehow she landed a job with *Canadian Jewish Chronicle* and later on switched over to the *Montreal Daily Herald,* working as a reporter or editorial assistant. In winter she often had to wait thirty to forty-five minutes for a streetcar to take her to work, and the street would be eight feet deep in snow.

Born with the "ten extra ounces of energy" that Eric also inherited, Sara managed it so that the children got into Montreal High, the school she had herself attended, and where she had been named "the Dux," the brightest in her graduating class.

She also saw to it that her children had good (if few) clothes. Grace said, "We were born with a silver spoon in our mouths. Fate took it away, but that changed nothing." She added, "I always had very good ski clothes, tennis clothes . . . , etc. The point is, we were born with those things and my mother was not about to let it slide. . . . Lennard's suit, too [he had only one], was the best."

Grace told us, "I used to say [to mother] that my brother's tuition was due and I was almost in tears, because I knew how hard it was for her to get the money."

The silver spoon must have been fashioned out of newly mined metal. Their grandfather (their father's father) had emigrated from Poland, where during the pogroms he and his brothers had been hidden from the Cossacks, who made a practice of shanghaiing little boys into the Russian army. In Montreal he was known as the "glasses man," a "traveling optometrist" who "went around with eyeglasses and tried them on until somebody found a pair that was good."

There was little money to spare in the family. His son David worked in a cigar store in the daytime and attended McGill Medical School at night—"no easy cinch."

Sara had been born in Pinsk, Russia, and had been brought to Quebec by her mother, Anna. Her father, Joseph Astrovsky, A.W.O.L. from the czar's army (probably he had been shanghaied into it, according to Eric's Uncle Isadore), served at least two years before he fled. Somehow he joined his wife and firstborn in Canada. On arrival in Montreal he started in the new world as a gravedigger, eventually setting up a second hand furniture-antique store.

Although he was an intellectual and had always wanted to become a rabbi, he stuck with his store and saw to it that his two eldest girls went to the normal school connected with McGill University and became teachers. (In those days only a year's training beyond high school was necessary for the teacher's certificate.)

Berne was always very proud that his father had been a doctor. He mentioned it frequently in his writings and, according to his sister Grace, decided when he was about two years old to become a doctor himself.

A year after his father's death Lennie had an opportunity to carry out one of his father's death-bed injunctions, namely, to take care of his sister. Grace and her brother had been tussling and she accidentally put her hand through the glass of a French door, cutting a blood vessel. Grace told us, "He just couldn't do enough for me—got linen out of the linen closet and bound it up. He was probably about twelve and I was seven. We were alone at the time. . . . He walked me over, not too fast, but not dawdling—to a doctor friend of my father's. . . . But it was remarkable—one minute we were two kids fooling around, and the next we were adults. It wasn't only that our father had died and left us alone; it was in our character. . . . We didn't emphasize self-reliance; we lived it."

At some point Lennie decided not to become a "real doctor" but rather a psychiatrist. He later told his secretary he could never have been other than a psychiatrist because he couldn't stand the sight of blood.

In another instance, Lennie again had a chance to show his mettle when Grace was found sleepwalking several times. Lennie asked his mother to leave this problem to him; he was going to be the doctor. He maneuvered Grace back into her room, sat down in her big overstuffed chair, and got her to tell him what was bothering her. Grace said, "My mother couldn't handle it nearly so well. He teased me—he was a pest—he was really terrible—maybe I sleepwalked on purpose because he was nicer to me at those times."

Lennie would often "go down to the docks and spend long hours there watching alcoholics. Any kind of strange behavior interested him," according to Grace." He was always a psychiatrist."

Their mother, according to Grace, was "very intuitive and perceptive." Lennard's Aunt Edith was also known to be intuitive, even psychic. Sara was always suggesting to her children that they write. "Go ahead and write," she would say, "you can do it! It's easy." Grace said: "She wanted me to use my brains, write and sell stories, not just piddle around and be artistic." Berne told one of his secretaries that he had written every day of his life, if only half a page, since he was fourteen. He had helped his mother with some of her newspaper articles, including making up the horoscopes.

The mother's Pennsylvania Dutch cream pitcher faced the children at breakfast with this motto: Do something good if you can, but do something.

But Sara Bernstein didn't push the children to be achievers, according to Grace. And this opinion is seconded by Dr. Albert Lapin, distinguished cardiologist, and Montreal High, McGill University and McGill Medical School classmate of Lennard, who said: "I knew the mother, Sara, and she appeared to be very easy going with Lennard. She wasn't critical of either of her children. She appeared extremely permissive. She was out working and they had the run of the house. She knew Lennard was brilliant, but she didn't push him. She admired him, but put no pressure on him or Grace. They made their own meals and came and went as they pleased."

Grace also said, "We never considered that just being 'family' was enough. Being interesting or superior in accomplishment *plus* being family would make relatives acceptable in the family circle. . . . For instance, we had one relative who thought she was pretty great because she had two children and brought them up well, put them to bed on time and fed them oatmeal in the morning. . . . Well, if that's all people want to do, just to live and do nothing else, then, like [my brother] said, they're just waiting for death or Santa Claus."

She continued, "My father left money in his will for a young cousin to go to McGill, but a young woman promptly got ahold of him and married him and that was the end of that. He took me aside later and said it was the worst mistake he ever made. Oh, his wife was all right; there was nothing wrong with her, but it put an end to his education. My mother was not 'ambitious,' but she hated to see brains wasted."

One of Berne's contentions is that every child is born a prince, but that oftentimes families, by mishandling, witch messages, and systematic put-downs, manage to convince the child that he is a frog. Once children are convinced of this, frogs they remain, according to Berne, unless "an excellent therapist, a severe trauma, or a religious conversion" breaks the spell. His mother and sister were not bent on turning Lennie into a frog, however, for they continued to see him as something so special that an acquaintance from that time said they believed Lennie could "walk on water." It seemed to be "the Bernsteins against the world."

At Montreal High, Lennie was "a skinny kid . . . who looked like Caspar Milquetoast" and who played the bugle every morning at the raising of the flag. At this institution (and many another in Canada) the girls and boys were kept strictly separate. They were placed on different time schedules so that they wouldn't meet going to and from school. If Lennard had attempted to talk to a girl at school, "he would have been killed," said Grace. The lone male in a household of admiring females, he was thrust into an all-male world during school hours.

Lennie studied hard. He would go to his room at night with a glass of water, pore over his lessons until three, and get up at seven. But he was beaten out in his senior year for the "Dux Board" honor by Albert Lapin and Michael Aronovitch, two future fellow classmates in McGill Medical School.

As an undergraduate at McGill, Lennie grew into a "tall, handsome figure." His college photos show him as positively photogenic. With a slouch hat and a pipe, he reminds one of an early vintage Leslie Howard or a blond, curly-headed Danny Kaye. Even so, his peers doubted that he dated very much, and he may have been describing his own situation when he wrote the following:

> After childhood the next period of strain is during adolescence. When the boy gets socially interested in girls his troubles begin anew. If he doesn't have the personality or the physical requirements to attract run-of-the-mill girls, they will desert him for other fellows who do. . . . But if his parents kept him feeling happy and emotionally secure . . . he has a good foundation. The feeling his mother loved him will give him more confidence . . . and he may try to develop himself in some way which will overshadow his drawbacks, particularly with girls of more than average good sense.

In later years, girls of more than average good sense seemed to lose their wits on the subject of Eric Berne. In the meantime, however, he had the stressful times of adolescence and young adulthood to go through. According to some classmates, the "Prince Lennie" phase didn't last through high school and college. The relentless leveling pressure of one's peers in adolescence makes it difficult to remain an individual, but this was not Lennie's problem. With Lennie, who followed no standard pattern, the problem seemed to be that his eccentric tadpoling antics were not to be repressed. They continued to make ripples in many an otherwise serene puddle for the rest of his life.

8

"Crazy" Lennie

> ... *When we wonder whether or not being gifted is worth the . . . excruciating sensitivity, inability to relate and/or tendency to over-analyze, all of us vote "yes."*
> Students of the National Symposium on the
> Education of the Gifted and Talented,
> *On Being Gifted*

> *I was too far out all my life and not waving, but drowning.*
> Stevie Smith, in
> *The Gifted Child and the Community*

At a certain point Prince Lennie went underground.

When Gerald Goodstone got home from school one day, his grandmother told him that "Crazy Lennie" had phoned. Although Gerry had never heard Lennard called that before, he knew exactly whom she was talking about, and that was the mental picture Gerry carried of Lennie for many years after that.

Son of his mother's best friend, Lennie was Gerry's best friend by mandate and a permanent embarrassment and torment to the conformist Gerald.

Gerald had known Lennie in his earlier "royal" phase. In those days Lennie had worn thick glasses, was "quite small" for his age, and unobtrusive. "He was shy," said Goodstone, "he was uncomfortable. . . . He hugged the walls everywhere he went." Early photographs show young Lennie to be a wistful and sensitive-looking little figure. He was encouraged to play in his own house and backyard, not to mingle with the neighborhood kids, thus he seemed programed to be vulnerable and a loner.

Even his contacts with Goodstone were attenuated. Gerald told us of a time when he was out of school for a while with a wrenched knee. One day his front door opened and in tumbled a large number of magazines for Gerald to read. Lennie had thrown them in, quickly shut the door again without saying a word, and headed back across town to his home, about fifteen miles away.

Also, Gerald remembered how he'd be awakened at two or three in the morning by a rapping on his window, and there this shy night owl would be, asking him if he wanted to play chess. ("Sometimes I'd play, and sometimes I wouldn't," Goodstone acknowledged.)

Lennie, it seemed, learned early that it was a "hostile world out there" and that there were few allies whom he could really trust. It was one thing being a prince in his own family and another being recognized as a fellow human being by his peer group.

On his way to Strathearn Grammar School on Jeanne Mance Street, a few blocks from his home, Lennie had to run the gauntlet of feisty French-Canadian street urchins who "harassed him and spat on him" and "called him a dirty Jew." The anti-Semitism around Montreal in the early decades of this century was not subtle. There were signs in some hotels, "No dogs or Jews allowed," and signs on public beaches: "Gentiles Only." Also, according to Berne's second wife Dorothy, Lennie's sister Grace once entered a public swimming pool and all the British-Canadians and French-Canadians ostentatiously got out.

Other forms of anti-Semitism were less crude, but even more intrusive. With their mother working, Lennie and his sister Grace were often left alone (when not in school) with a French-Canadian maid, some devoutly Catholic farm girl from the Gaspé Peninsula, usually about fifteen or sixteen years old. No longer were there the adoring patients of the doctor to exclaim over the virtues of the children. One day, one of these maids, shortly after arriving on the scene, asked the children: "Where is the picture?"

They replied, "What picture?"

She said, "The picture of Jesus that you spit on every day."

When the Prince Lennie phase faded, Lennie moved into a new category of loner. As his friend Gerry observed, there are loners who are alone because they are shy, and there are loners who are alone because people avoid them. When Lennie entered his adolescent reaction phase, he was no longer a loner merely by choice. "Most of the fellows avoided him . . . he antagonized most of them . . . so he kept by himself, more or less. He didn't seem to have any friends or be part of any group." And yet somewhere inside himself Lennard must have been screaming: "I am not to be ignored."

Dr. Gabriel Yelin reported that in college Lennie would "on occasion climb down from the grandstands at a football game and attempt to perform handsprings, somersaults, or other bizarre and exhibitionistic activity in front of the fans for no perceptible reason."

Another classmate, now a noted Montreal cardiologist, who knew Lennie from the third or fourth year of high school through medical school, also said that although he and Lennie enjoyed each other's company and were together a great deal, Lennie embarrassed him: "Here we were all conformists and we didn't want to be conspicuous, and here you are sitting with someone who is shouting and turning handstands in the middle of the game to draw attention . . ."

"To himself?" we asked.

"Well, to himself, but if you're part of the group—"

"Did those handstands happen once, on a bet, or all the time?" we wanted to know.

"Oh, all the time," our interviewee answered. "He was a funny combination. He had this great need to draw attention to himself, and yet he had the ability to do it for real."

In at least one instance, however, Lennie was put up to his unsolicited yell-leading role. Moses Margolick bet Lennie $1 that he couldn't walk on his hands the 200 yards back and forth before the bleachers at the Toronto-McGill football game. He did so, and "won the buck."

One year the *McGill Annual* appeared with Lennie's face beaming out of every men's group on the campus, because he'd stuck his head in all the pictures whether he was a member of the group or not.

On another occasion he borrowed a student's oil painting and rode back and forth on a Montreal streetcar for six hours one afternoon, holding it up significantly so that the riders could see there was an artist in their midst. On still another occasion he smoked a cigarette, cigar, and pipe all at once.

Such capers might be considered part of the high spirits of youth in many an American college, but they had all the aerodynamic charm of a lead balloon north of the St. Lawrence. Colonials are sometimes known to pride themselves in out-Britishing the British in the punctilios. (Even to this day in Australia there are headmasters who instruct their charges that it is "bad form" to cheer at soccer games.)

However, the self-protective chameleonism of Lennie's student associates had more to it than just ordinary colonial conformism. He was identified with the group of bright Jewish boys who had managed to get into McGill University and who would have to achieve even higher grades to survive the (unacknowledged but universally known) 10 percent Jewish quota system governing admission to the McGill Medical School. These boys above all wanted to blend harmlessly into the gray, bland Anglo-Saxon landscape in order to escape the oppressive anti-Semitism of old French-Canada.

So when Lennie did things like playfully "shadowing" his friends Ernest Crown and Gerald Goodstone when they went out on a double date, Goodstone was more horrified than amused.

Ernest and Gerald had taken the girls to the theater. After the play was over, they had all gone back to somebody's apartment, where they played records and danced and, after half an hour or so turned the lights down low. Suddenly there was a knock at the door. They called out, "Who's there?" A voice mumbled, "The telephone repairman." When the door was opened, there stood Lennie Bernstein. They asked him what he was doing and he answered, "I saw the lights go out, so I thought there was something wrong." They replied, "There's nothing wrong!" and slammed the door.

Goodstone also told us about the time in his senior year he

had planned to attend the "Red and White Revue," one of the big events of the year. It was a musical, full of the usual collegiate buffoonery, called *Off Key I Sing* (it was 1932 and the revue was a parody of the Depression smash-hit in America, *Of Thee I Sing*).

Gerald had told Lennie he was thinking of taking a girl to see it. Lennie immediately said he was going to go, too. Gerald countered that he really didn't know whether he was going or not, and explained to us, "To go out on a date with Lennard was a disaster, no matter what happened. . . . I sneaked out and bought two tickets and he apparently asked the guy at the ticket office to tip him off as to what tickets I was buying, because when I got to the theater with my date, he was sitting next to us. When the play was on, at certain points there'd be no laughter, but he would laugh and applaud. He'd stop the play and tell the actors they weren't reading their lines properly. He was attracting a lot of attention to himself, standing up and laughing loudly. . . . [Such behavior] was one of the reasons I didn't want him to sit near us. . . . He was pathetic. . . . Girls wouldn't date him. He had no social graces—was not socially adept at all."

Lennie not only attended *Off Key I Sing* but claimed he had written it. Several of his classmates felt he wasn't given enough credit for this feat. However, this was apparently another one of his pranks, as research by Faith Wallis of the McGill Archives Department revealed that all the records showed others had written it.

"One day I came home with Lennie," said Goodstone. "We came into the Bernstein living room, when all of a sudden he let out a sort of half-scream and fell apparently into a dead faint. And he just lies there. And his mother comes out; she pays no attention to him, and she says to me: 'Would you like some milk?' Apparently she was used to this type of behavior, because she didn't bat an eyelash. Eventually he got up and said he'd like some milk, too, and his mother made no comment. They played a game together, Lennard and his mother."

In later life Berne remarked to his TA associate Margaret Northcott that she and he were "stroke-hungry," having both suffered from a lack of parental touching and recognition when young.

Other anecdotes indicate that some of Lennie's classmates looked upon him variously as bizarre, arrogant, or self-centered, and they didn't understand him. His mother did not escape criticism either. She impressed some of the Montrealers and Americans who knew her as too aggressive, not at all attractive, inhospitable, suspicious, and so forth.

But these attributes did not show themselves in Mrs. Bernstein's attitude toward Lennie. One of Berne's ex-wives told us that from the moment the father died, Sara made Lennard the center of her existence, and she supported him in all his endeavors. It could have been, however, that her attention was conditional upon superior achievement, which was not easy for Lennard to come by in the group of well-adjusted super achievers surrounding him at Montreal High and at McGill.

Dr. Albert Lapin, who knew the family well and treated the mother in later life for her heart condition, did not find her cold and unsympathetic but warm and friendly, although somewhat cynical.

When the eight years of college and medical school rolled around, Lennie continued to live a financially pinched life with his mother and younger sister in their "flat." Therefore he had little campus social life and very few dates with girls. Goodstone told us he would be surprised to learn that Lennie had done any serious dating. The one time he and Lennard went on a double date together, Lennard brought his young aunt Esther, who was ten years older than Lennie (about twenty-eight or twenty-nine) and extremely pretty. Later in the evening Gerald was shocked to notice them necking in the back seat.

While at McGill, Lennard majored in English rather than pre-med, yet he managed to get through the course in eight years rather than the nine usually required of students who didn't take pre-med as undergraduates. He helped pay his way by caddying and bookkeeping at the Royal Montreal Golf Club and by selling shoes. He received scholarships in mathematics and psychology, and dabbled in athletics (running, particularly) and dramatics, sometimes earning his dinner at a local restaurant by putting on a nightclub act. He wrote for the campus literary magazine. He also wrote a humor column for the *McGill Daily*, peppered with Perlmanesque puns. The column appeared off and on for four years. Despite all this, Dr. Joseph Saltzer, one of his classmates, wrote us: "As far back as I can remember, Lennard impressed me as being a dreamer and impractical. When we all got into med school we thought Lennard was lucky to be admitted, as he barely scraped enough grades together under our quota system. . . . At times, I felt sorry for him because he seemed to be a square peg in a round hole in medical school. . . . He always had some comment on everything but it was never germane to our studies."

Berne's later success astonished Saltzer, because by the time they had finished medical school he was convinced that Lennard was "the one least likely to succeed in medical practice." Yet he "surpassed any of the medical scholars in achievement. . . . As far as I know," he said, "he is the only successful medical author in the entire class of 106 who graduated in 1935."

Dr. Moses Margolick wrote us: "From the beginning, it was evident that [Lennard] was unusual—a little different from the others. We were a fiercely competitive group, interested in excelling academically and making good grades, and while Lennard always made good grades, he seemed to have many outside interests, often exotic and even bizarre. He would tend to these interests until near the end of the session, when he would put in a very intensive period of studying and emerge among the highest students in the marking. Later on, in medical school, it was the same way. He was always able to master the anatomy and physiology, biochemistry and clinical medicine, but he seemed only mildly and peripherally interested. . . . He [was] much more interested in people and their emotional and psychological problems and very early on, somehow, I had the impression that he would be a psychiatrist."

Dr. Rachmiel Levine, now medical director of the City of Hope Hospital (near Los Angeles, California), worked with Lennie on the *Daily* and on the *McGilliad*; but, like most of the other classmates, he was surprised, when he read *Games People Play*, that his old schoolfellow had done such serious thinking. Lennard had always given the impression of being flippant and uninvolved when Dr. Levine had known him in school. Levine said, "It was the depression period—1929-1935. The prevailing attitude . . . among intellectuals was that you were in med school but didn't care. You were a man about town, sophisticated, blasé. This was, however, mainly a pretense."

With most of the students one could see through the pretense, but not with Lennie. Said Levine, "He was sarcastic, humorous, and terribly moody. Up and bouncy at times and then terribly down. He was not too much interested in political issues. He sneered at both sides.

"He just had to shock. . . . Many times I remember sessions of the bunch at the *McGill Daily* or over endless cups of coffee at Murray's restaurant. [Lennard] would have to say something to shock somebody, and we accepted it, without batting an eyelash."

Although there was much talk of sex among the students, Levine said, "The literary and intellectual group that we belonged to talked a lot about it in an esoteric way—James Branch Cabell, Michael Arlen's *The Green Hat,* James Joyce, Havelock Ellis—but didn't actually do much of anything. It was all verbal. We were kind of puritanical, actually."

According to Levine, Lennie was much taken with *Jurgen* and Cabell's other books, particularly the phallic symbolism. "He [Lennie] was somewhat pathetic. In a sense he wasn't taken seriously in our [*McGilliad*] group, which included David Lewis, who was later to become a member of Parliament at Ottawa, and Kenneth Cameron [the Shelley expert], who became a distinguished professor of English literature at N.Y.U. There was a lot of horseplay, but the rest got serious at times. [Lennard] never let down the mask of humor and cynicism.

"He was an outsider looking in and he wanted to be inside and at the same time he had to be outside the establishment. The yen to be on the outside and criticize the inner circle is probably the fear that if you don't stay on the outside, you won't be accepted."

Dr. Benjamin Bradford Whitcomb remembered Lennie as a "character," sometimes called "Bunny" because of his prominent ears. "Frequently," Dr. Whitcomb reported, "we would climb the hill [to medical school or hospital] together in the early morning . . . usually with the temperature 10 to 15 degrees below zero and Len never wore a hat. . . . We would watch each others' ears in order to recognize frostbite . . . so we could put our hands over the affected parts until the white changed to red.

"However, hatless Bernstein's ears always seemed to stay pink. One cold and windy day, though, he wore a hat and . . . his ears suddenly blanched with frostbite. . . . Len said: 'I'll never wear my hat again, because it obviously cuts down the circulation to the tops of my ears.'"

Dr. Whitcomb continued, "Our first class in the morning was a lecture by one of the clinical professors in obstetrics, who was a cocky, aggressive little fellow, who walked into the room and picked up a leather baby mannequin and the class settled down to listen to the lecture.

"However, Len Bernstein was still very engrossed in the morning *McGill News* which he was holding in front of his face. This apparently irritated the little professor, who immediately threw the leather doll with considerable force.

"It whizzed by my ear and knocked the newspaper out of Bernstein's hands, striking him in his face, to his great alarm, and the little professor said: 'When I walk into the room, I want attention.' You can just imagine how Bernstein's perceptive and critical mind sized up the lecturer."

Dr. Frances Cottington, a psychoanalyst who knew Berne off and on for nearly thirty years and who late in her career became enthusiastic about TA, read parts of our manuscript and was not surprised that Berne was out of sync with his classmates. Herself precocious (attending high school at eleven and college at fifteen), she has made extensive studies of "gifted and talented" children. She says: "Such uninvolved behavior is typical of the super-gifted; these students are easily bored, hate dull routine and often spend their time pursuing their own interests, cramming at the last minute."

She surmised that Berne's medical school associates probably were in the 120–130 IQ group, which means that they were bright but not so highly charged that they couldn't involve themselves completely in the demanding schedule they were required to keep and also in the unglamorous aspects of scholarship and research. Berne, she felt, was "super-gifted" and could well have had an IQ "perilously close to 200," as he once boasted. She would not have been surprised if his mother were also gifted, with a significantly higher IQ than her doctor husband, who might have fitted comfortably into the medical scene with an IQ in the 120–130 range. She told us: "Gifted people are very inner-motivated and amused by people who are anxious to conform to the expectations of others."

One out of a hundred people have an IQ of 130 or over, but few of those people end up doing something "great." It seems clear that genius requires another element besides mere IQ. Whatever that element is, Lennie had it. It worked in him, damped down and smoldering, most of his life, giving out bursts of smoke and soot at embarrassing moments, until, in the last dozen years or so, it blazed forth with a pure and brilliant flame.

To the many thousands in the mental health field who have been touched by the beauty and aptness of the TA and the "I'm OK—You're OK" philosophy, Eric Berne has taken on a godlike stature, and his inability to integrate with his peer groups in his youth may come as a suprise. Warren Cheney said in the memorial issue of the *Transactional Analysis Bulletin* after Eric's death:

> It would be difficult to cite another example of a trail blazer and pioneer in the fields of psychiatry and psychotherapy who was more widely regarded with love and affection by those who knew him personally than Eric Berne.

Even we, who didn't know him personally cannot help but feel a warm regard for him since we are using almost daily the concepts set forth in his works or those of his disciples.

Is it necessary in studying his life to dwell on so much negative material? How did he turn himself around to become well integrated to his TA and other peer groups? How, out of a strange and outrageous early life style, did he come out with these invaluable concepts? Evidently early peer group evaluations are poor indicia of future power and greatness. To us there is a fascination in the discrepancy itself.

In discussing the question of "greatness" as it applied to Freud, Ernest Jones mentioned these attributes: a strong personality, and accomplishment of emotional or intellectual feats which we recognize to be far beyond our own capacity, feats having some moral quality, "so that when we admire them we also recognize that what has been accomplished has raised the level of general culture."

Freud himself struggled with the problem of writing a biography of a great man (Goethe). Freud says that even at best the biographer's research will not be able to show us where the genius's talent comes from, but biography helps us get closer to the man as a human being. However, in getting closer we find that there is an element of "degradation" involved—as we "learn more about a great man's life we shall also hear of occasions in which he has in fact done no better than we . . . as a human being."

Nevertheless, Freud declared the efforts of the biographer to be legitimate. Since our reverence for our fathers and teachers is mixed with hostility, it is impossible to avoid this ambivalence "without forcible suppression of truth and [this] is bound to extend to our relations with great men whose life histories we wish to investigate."

Thomas Mann, in speaking through his novelist hero Aschenbach, describes genius as a lack, saying that "almost everything conspicuously great is great in despite: has come into being in defiance of affliction and pain, poverty, destitution, bodily weakness, vice, passion, and a thousand other obstructions." Mann feels that if we could meet the artist in person we would recognize that "This repulsive worm is the reality of the glorious butterfly in whom all those deluded onlookers thought to see realized all their own secret dreams of beauty, grace and perfection! He is just like one of those disgusting little creatures which have the power of being phosphorescent in the evening. . . . For when you come to think about it, which is the 'real' shape of the glowworm: the insignificant little creature crawling about on the flat of your hand, or the poetic spark that swims through the summer night?"

It is evident that many, if not all, of Lennard's McGill classmates saw him as an unidentified crawling object rather than a poetic spark flying through the summer night. Yet, being put down by his early peer groups didn't break his spirit. It was in these years that the groundwork was laid for Berne's fireworks later to come.

9

There's Only Room For One

> There's only room for one
> There's only room for one
> At the resident's gate
> At half past eight
> There's only room for one.
>
> Folk song

Lennie and his sister Grace sang this song together as children. Grace didn't know what it meant or why they sang it, but it stuck in her mind. And when her brother graduated from McGill Medical School, he found that there was only room for two—only two Jewish graduates could become interns in the Montreal hospitals. (These were Albert Lapin and Michael Aronovitch, the top men in their class.) Other Canadian hospitals followed the same system, so it was off to the United States for young Bernstein and many of his classmates.

This was in 1935, when everyone was pretending that "recovery" was on its way. Berne's classmate Joseph Saltzer wrote us about those days, saying that internships were hard to get because "we were in the *Real Depression* and none of the intern residents wanted to leave the protection of the hospitals to go into medical practice, as no one had any money to pay their doctors."

The result was that there were even fewer openings than usual. "I remember that year in 1935 or 1936, I took eight or ten different examinations in different boroughs of New York for an appointment. At Mt. Sinai in New York I was one of 250 applicants for twelve to fifteen jobs.

"At times I felt sorry for Lennard. . . The last time I did see him, he had just obtained an internship at a Newark hospital." Although he had to wait 12 months before the job started, Lennard seemed extremely grateful to get it, the only reason he got it being that Dr. Saltzer had turned it down to take a better one. Saltzer continues: "I don't know what happened to him then. I assume that during this wait for his internship he found his natural bent for psychiatry, and whether he ever pursued the internship at the Newark hospital, I don't know."

In fact Eric (he now called himself Eric) didn't have to wait a year. He found a position at the Englewood Hospital on Engle Street in Englewood, New Jersey. It was a three-story brick building surrounded by many outbuildings, with an ample grassy lawn. Nearby were the Palisades where he could get a view of New York City and the three-or-four-year-old George Washington Bridge.

Nurses outnumbered the interns considerably. Leo Kohn, a fellow intern at Englewood, tells us all this. He says the quarters were filled when Eric arrived, so he was given a room on the corridor. "He always left his door open so he could say Hi! to all who came by."

Englewood personnel were somewhat awed by the young medic from Canada. "We were quite impressed by the fact that he played chess with Dr. Heller, a young 'attending.' We would often go by his door and see him squatting on the bed playing the game and to us who had never learned chess, that seemed like the ultimate intellectual achievement."

This was a new experience for Eric. No longer did he have to strive for status. To the other interns he was "a brain," and his sometime puzzling behavior was laid to his being a Canadian. To the nurses he was a doctor.

But there were occasions when there seemed to be no explanation for the puzzling behavior. "In his time off, Eric would come over to the interns' quarters for companionship and find all the doors closed and locked to the individual rooms." Young interns and nurses had all disappeared. "He would bang on the doors and yell, 'I know what you're doing in there! Come on out! I know what's going on!' But silence reigned."

What was going on in the rooms was never made clear, but soon Berne got in the swing of things and "would sometimes be seen with a smug look on his face, escorting a pretty nurse from maternity and what was going on with Eric was apparent, but unspoken.

"I recall one pleasant afternoon walking through the cemetery with Eric in the company of two pretty young nurses . . . the sky was blue; the grass was green; we were young; the girls were young. After a while we came back to the quarters, and Eric and the other girl were together for a while in one of the rooms. Later he observed to me that she was a 'shark.' He didn't say why. I didn't ask why. I often now wonder why she was a shark to him. Was she sexually voracious, did she keep her mouth open, or what?"

Kohn never found out. "He expected me to ask him to explain . . . and I, equally difficult, refrained from asking."

Eric's sister Grace remembered how Eric relished breakfast in the Englewood common room where nobody made conversation and one could read his paper in peace. Eric seemed "an ebullient young man, undoubtedly talented and intelligent." He was "bouncy and energetic, with his hair in some disarray, usually, and his conversation was all of one piece [with his hair]; it bounced along also by erratic fits and starts."

But Englewood was no pleasure dome. Calls for interns came in at all hours of the day and night. The pay was only $20 per month, and from this one had to provide uniforms.

There was no lack of drama. The two ambulances were frequently called out, each with one intern aboard. Sometimes they picked up a psychiatric patient, and sometimes they sped to the scene of a gory accident on the George Washington Bridge.

First-year interns were assigned to medicine, pediatrics, obstetrics, nose and throat, laboratory and surgery on a rotating basis. The second year the interns became house surgeons with junior interns as assistants.

At some point in this year at Englewood Eric made a pivotal decision: no more general practice for him; he would not continue his internship there for the second year. His real interest lay in psychiatry, and the following fall he was enrolled in the Department of Psychiatry and Mental Hygiene at Yale.

There young Dr. Bernstein worked hard fourteen hours a day and was paid $50 per month. He lived in at the New Haven

Hospital, and in 1937, his second year, he became an assistant resident and also a minor member of the staff, doing laboratory work consisting of research into the pituitary glands of rats and frogs.

On August 14, 1937, an excited young Dr. Bernstein set sail for Istanbul. Eric had borrowed the money to go because he wanted to take a look at the Levant before World War II, then threatening, broke out. He also planned to write articles on psychiatry in these parts and thus further his career.

His arrival on Turkish shores was something of a let-down, however. He confessed that the achievement of any goal usually gave him the same feeling. As he pointed his movie camera toward a skyline filled with Byzantine domes, surrounded by their attendant minarets, the perverse thought occurred to him that the scene bore a distinct resemblance to the Bronx as viewed from Fort Lee, New Jersey.

The camera was to get Eric into trouble: he was thrown into a Turkish prison for taking pictures of military installations. His brief but frightening experience wasn't wasted, though; he used it as the basis for a novel in which the hero was locked up in a Turkish dungeon and was later executed as a spy.

This lengthy, much-worked-over romance was called *Maisie Atkins*, after the name of its heroine. It was never published. In it, however, are many exchanges of conversation between the young psychiatrist-hero and his mother, which could well have been straight reportage of conversations Eric had had with his own mother, who had now found a job and an apartment in New York.

In one scene the young psychiatrist tells his mother that he is once more going to Turkey in the summer. His mother objects that he has just come back from Turkey and that he has hardly finished paying for his last year's trip (Berne went to Turkey in the summers of 1937 and 1938). His mother then wants to know why he doesn't go to some swanky place in California or Florida and find himself a nice girl.

Her son replies that he doesn't want to get married. He wants to see Europe and the world before a war breaks out. He then details a trip he currently plans—through Poland to Russia, then to Teheran, Baghdad, back by way of Beirut and Turkey. He figures he can do it for a few hundred dollars now that he knows his way around. His mother thinks this is a lot of money to spend, but the psychiatrist points out that his credit is good since he paid off last year's debt (if she will endorse the note).

His travels, then as later, were not solely to glean material for novels; rarely did they fail to produce at least one serious article he could submit to some medical journal and which could be referred to later in a scholarly bibliography in a book. Thus his Levantine travels of 1937 and 1938 bore fruit in his first published article on psychiatry called "Psychiatry in Syria," which appeared in the *American Journal of Psychiatry* in 1939.

In 1937 Eric's sister Grace decided to get married, but Eric and his mother viewed the move with concern. The prospective groom, McGill graduate Arthur Rose, was taking his M.B.A. at Columbia. Grace and he had been dating for six weeks. It was not surprising that Sara opposed the marriage. She felt they hadn't known each other long enough, and, besides, Sara had opposed every family marriage on record, according to her younger sister, Edith Albert, who still lives in Montreal and was seventy-six at the time we interviewed her.

Mrs. Albert said: "My sister Sara was a snob. My late sister Esther never got married on account of her, because nobody was good enough for my sister Esther . . . Esther was very, very quiet; if you told her don't do this she [wouldn't do it]. I was a fighter and I still am a fighter. But with my sister Esther, I still remember, there were a couple of doctors. . . . Esther was a very, very pretty girl and she had men [admirers] and every time she wanted to get married, my sister Sara put a stop to it. They weren't good enough for her, so she never got married."

We asked Mrs. Albert whether Sara had taken over the role of mother to her younger sisters.

Mrs. Albert replied, "She was bossy, very, very bossy, but she couldn't get very far with me. . . . From what I remember, Grace was engaged to a very, very wealthy man in New York and my sister broke that up. No, she had her finger in every pie, Sara. The only one she couldn't handle was me. . . ."

A few days before Christmas, 1937, Arthur and Grace secretly filled out the forms for a marriage license in Teaneck, New Jersey. There was a three-day waiting period. Walking along the streets of New York with Eric and Sara after having seen a friend off on the steamship *Normandie*, they casually dropped the bomb. Sara was taken aback, especially since she was slated to go into a hospital almost immediately for an operation.

Arthur said, "The scene along Tenth Avenue was really something out of a movie. Eric would walk along with me trying to convince me to wait awhile and her mother was with Grace, and then they'd shift sides and try to convince both of us. We were insistent. So, finally they gave in [and] accompanied us. We got to the Teaneck police station where the license had been left, as the government buildings were closed the day after Christmas. The police had our license and we asked them if there was anybody available to marry us. So the cops were lined up with all the available telephones, calling the mayors, the justices of the peace, and so forth, and not getting any satisfactory answers. Then the shift changed and we had a whole new lineup of policemen. . . .

"Finally, we got the mayor of Bogota, New Jersey. We had the most charming set-up there. The mayor and his wife were the epitome of what they should be, just what you'd see in a movie, very distinguished looking, and they had the fireplace decorated with Christmas decorations and so on. Eric and his mother were our witnesses, willing or not, in spite of previous protestations."

They got back to New York and Arthur bought Grace a bouquet from a street hawker; but in his excitement he had forgotten to bring enough money with him and Grace had to pay for it. Then Eric and his mother and the newlyweds went to a small restaurant for dinner.

Arthur, a responsible executive for a huge company, taught business administration at a large midwestern college, and through wise investments he became a prosperous man. He felt that Sara was a strong-willed, independent, and capable woman. She became fond of Grace and Arthur's children, frequently babysat for them, and sometimes stayed with the family for extended periods. Eric and Arthur also developed a good relationship.

In the spring of 1938 Grace and Arthur sailed to Europe via Montreal. They had driven Arthur's car to Canada and left it with a friend, as Eric was coming up later and had promised to drive it back to New York. When Eric arrived in New York with the car, he was unable to find a suitable parking place, so he left it temporarily in front of a fire hydrant and promptly forgot it. Eric then sailed away on his second trip to the Near East. Their ships crossed in the Atlantic as the newlyweds were sailing back. They found their car safe and sound where he had left it. (Cars weren't towed away in those days.) It had been sitting for six weeks in front of the hydrant, and it didn't even have a ticket on it. "That was Eric," Arthur commented.

Upon coming back, young Dr. Bernstein received an appointment to the Ring sanitarium in Arlington Heights, Massachusetts (near Boston), as assistant physician in charge of instructing the nurses. We find him there in early 1939, working on his spy novel *Maisie Atkins*—an amalgam of New Haven, Ring, and Turkish experiences. It was more than 200 pages long at this point—not yet finished—and he apparently never did finish it.

He was also writing an article entitled "Who Was Condom?"—a Rabelaisian spoof on a purported scientific inquiry into the well-known if not well-loved prophylactic. The article was eventually published in *Human Fertility*.

His sister Grace had a different attitude toward marriage than their mother did. While Sara might have preferred that Eric marry for status, Grace felt that Eric would have been happier with the "good egg" psychiatric nurse he went around with at Yale. To illustrate this, she told us a story about the time that Eric came to visit her and Arthur, when their first child, David, was six months old. The year was 1939.

All the relatives and some friends were gathered for Sunday dinner. Grace told us: "We were all walking down the street. Eric brought up the rear, carrying his nephew David. He was totally unused to babies but thought he'd like to try carrying one. He was wearing a beret, looking very French, and carrying the baby very efficiently. And all of a sudden I heard this baby crying. I looked back, and away down the street there was this poor forlorn baby sitting in the middle of the road—fortunately, it was a quiet street—and Uncle Eric had joined the group, and was busy talking. And I said: 'You were carrying the baby; what happened to him?'

"And Eric said, 'Well, I got tired of carrying him. Let him walk.'"

Grace added that the nurse Eric went around with at Yale was the type of girl who would have run back and picked the baby out of the middle of the street without making a fuss about it. She would have taken care of Eric in all circumstances and stuck with him through thick and thin. But she wasn't glamorous enough for Eric, and Eric wasn't interested in marrying her.

Although Canada had entered the war in 1939, and Eric was still a Canadian citizen, he was left in peace for a time. He changed jobs and began work at a sanitarium in a small village in Connecticut, the village in which he met the McRaes. After he had been working hard there for about a year but before he encountered Elinor, he decided to treat himself to a stay at a dude ranch in Larkspur, Colorado (between Denver and Colorado Springs, but closer to the latter).

Mona Williams of Carmel, California, ran across Eric in the summer of 1941 in Colorado, little suspecting that he would turn up later in her own home town. Mona and her husband Henry, both writers, and Mona's sister and brother-in-law (who happened to be a real-life cowboy) had rented a large ranch near Larkspur for several months. It was a stylish ménage; they'd hired a resident cook and a handyman. The ranch was called Hasta la Vista.

One day they were looking down at the main road through a large plate-glass window and saw a man struggling with a horse. "This man obviously didn't know anything about horses," said Mrs. Williams. "He had gotten off his horse and the horse wanted to go in one direction and the rider wanted to go in another. The man was trying to push him and coax him and he was absolutely frustrated by the whole thing."

The cowboy brother-in-law began to laugh and said: "Ah think that pore fella needs a drink and ah'm gonna go down, take care of his horse, and bring him up here."

"We all began to laugh, as we were very horse-ified by then," said Mrs. Williams, "at this poor Easterner who obviously didn't know one end of the horse from another. And, as we were living in such a lonely place, we were very pleased, really, to have a little diversion."

After a few drinks, the inept rider, who was Berne, said in "a kind of sullen voice that the thing that was so frustrating was that he had been taught that the best way to cure an inferiority complex was to get a man on horseback. There he would be higher than the cars, and would look down on everything surrounding him."

During their Colorado stay the Williams group had Eric over for drinks several times. They lost sight of him after that until a few years later in Carmel. Marie Short, Eric's Carmel landlady, had invited the Williamses to a party at her house, but when they arrived she told them that her new roomer, Dr. Eric Berne, a psychiatrist, had refused to leave his room when he learned that Mona and Henry Williams were coming over. Intrigued, Mrs. Williams went to the roomer's quarters, tucked away in an isolated part of the house, and asked him why he was hiding from her.

According to Mrs. Williams Eric explained that "he didn't want to see me and Henry, that we had seen him in such a humiliating position that he just couldn't bear it, he just couldn't bear it. He was afraid we were going to tell everybody the story." Mrs. Williams got him to the party by promising not to tell the story, and has kept it a secret until now.

Underneath Eric's jauntiness and eccentricity was a vulnerable, sensitive human being.

10

The Martian Finds a Haven

. . . All my kidding is serious if you can read it right.
Eric Berne, *Sex in Human Loving*

Dr. Russell Williams, Berne's personal physician, once told us, "There are some people who never should marry and Eric Berne was probably one of them."

After Eric reconciled himself to the rupture with Elinor, he found out that Carmel was the ideal place in which to be unmarried. Although its artistic Bohemianism tilted toward the bourgeois, the atmosphere was highly congenial to people between marriages.

Eric's explanation to his acquaintances for Elinor's defection was that she couldn't stand the cobwebs in the cathedral ceiling, and that her mother's Christian Science indoctrination made it difficult for Elinor to be at one with an M.D. They accepted this without question.

He was fortunate to find a bachelor's nest in an apartment over a garage owned by a retired army officer recently back from the Far East, a Colonel George Stuart. The colonel's wife, Kippie, was a writer of children's stories and, although generously proportioned in every respect, she was extra-sensitive and perceptive and thus much loved by the villagers. These two "rotund, beaming people" made Eric feel "very welcome and comfortable" in their home, which was "the typical, blowsy, well-worn and sat-in" rustic Carmel cottage, according to Rosabel Brown, a child psychologist from southern California.

Meanwhile, over at Fort Ord, Berne was getting recognition

as a therapist. The original aim of the psychiatric program at the Fort Ord Regional Hospital had been to weed out soldiers with mental problems as undesirable, but a change of policy decreed that sick soldiers were to have "psychiatric reconditioning," and Berne was chosen to head the program.

So far as his private life was concerned, after his day's round of duties was over, Eric had the choice, he said, of going up to the officer's club at the fort for a round of drinks or coming home to his eyrie and working on a book. So *The Mind in Action,* his first full-length work, was started in his flat over the Stuart garage.

He also renewed an old acquaintance with Frank Lloyd, whom he had known in Montreal. Frank had gone through Montreal High and McGill with Eric and was unaware of the name change. They had a few awkward moments until Eric saw that Frank and his English-born and Montreal-bred wife Marjory were the embodiment of the unstuffy Carmel spirit. They accepted people for what they were and shunned labels.

Marjory remembers that on their first encounter Eric warily asked her if she had ever played golf at the Royal Montreal Golf Club. He was afraid, no doubt, of a possible resurgence of the old Montreal snobberies if she had recognized him as having been one of the lowly caddies on the course.

Professor Francis E. Lloyd, Frank's father, who had retired to Carmel, had been Eric's revered botany professor and the subject of one of his first short stories, entitled "The Old Man," printed in the Canadian *Adelphi* magazine in 1933. So it was not long before Eric became closely attached to the whole Lloyd family and came to appreciate from their example how free spirits could flourish in Carmel.

Frank had once been a pre-med student at McGill but had changed course to become a sports writer on Montreal papers, a shipyard worker in World War II, a commercial fisherman, an electrician, and finally for a time the editor of the *Carmel Pine Cone,* a weekly of as much charm and individuality as Carmel itself.

A handsome man with an aura of elegance and *je ne sais quoi*, Frank was also something of an attraction to the artistic ladies of Carmel. Frank and Eric discussed the beautiful Jewish girls they remembered from Montreal High days and went from that subject into long, philosophical colloquies about the lovely ladies of Carmel—to whom they humorously assigned code numbers—the code being based upon the last four digits of the ladies' telephone numbers. Eric dropped into the Lloyd's house frequently. He kept Frank and Marjory on their toes by starting up conversations in Latin—McGill students were nothing if not well-grounded in the classics. The Lloyd's cosy cottage was a place where Eric felt free to go when he felt low, and their warm, undemanding but lively personalities never failed to cheer him up.

The time was ripe for a resurgence of Jurgenism. Eric also fell back on his *McGilliad* formula for maximizing his energy by keeping repression at a minimum so that he could be acknowledged as a genius (which his mother had convinced him was his due). At the same time, he reconsidered the flaws that Elinor had exposed in him. If he didn't like dogs or animals enough, he would by all means begin to like them. He would learn to appreciate music.

With a friend, Katie Martin (Schlepp), he began to listen to symphonies, concertos and chamber music. Katie, a multifaceted, talented writer for the *Pine Cone*, Little Theatre faithful, pen-and-ink quick-sketcher, and music lover, came to appreciate his brilliance. In the first hour she knew him she was quite put off by him and thought he seemed "dreadful." After that he was "dreadful and wonderful." When she had known him for a while, the wonderful impression grew, but the dreadful didn't entirely disappear.

Eric had a clarinet, and he and Katie would play duets and Christmas carols together. "He was not unmusical," Katie said. "He could have played many instruments. He loved to listen to music."

He did an about-face on animals. Katie remembers that on a trip back to Carmel from a psychiatric meeting in San Francisco he hit a mule which "came out of nowhere." It was foggy and late at night. Eric stopped a few hundred feet down the road and said to Katie: "We've got to go back and see if that animal is hurt and get it off the highway—otherwise other cars might hit it." They went back and searched for about twenty minutes, but no trace of a wounded mule could be found. "Eric was very responsible," said Katie.

Another friend said he loved dogs and has a snapshot of him patting a dog lovingly on the head at Fort Ord.

Many people in Carmel remember him for his kindnesses or whimsical, thoughtful gestures toward others. On Christmas day in 1944, he left a Santa Claus sack of toys on his landlord's doorstep, full of "little, odd, humorous and playful things, which he had collected during his travels abroad."

Rosabel Brown, with whom he spent that Christmas, remembers coming back to find the Stuarts ("very loving people") surrounded by their goodies. He hid similar presents for Rosabel in obscure places all over his apartment and turned her Christmas into a combination Christmas–Easter-egg hunt.

"He was grateful for genuine people and any small acts of friendship," said Katie. "I think he must have had a rotten childhood. Because, you know, he just couldn't believe in people for a long time. I always had a feeling he'd been terribly hurt by something or somebody."

After her husband died, Kippie became very sensitive about being left out of parties. Katie and Eric found that a local hostess had forgotten to include Kippie in one Carmel gathering and dispatched themselves to herd her into the fold. The slippery path to the street was too muddy for Kippie's long dress, so Eric slung the heavy woman in a fireman's carry and ferried her downhill to the car. They rousted her out a second time that winter to a party. Nevertheless, what had seemed to be a solid tie did not last. Soon Eric was evicted from his flat, and no one knows for what. The Lloyds happened to have a friend looking for a roomer for her spare bedroom, so they brought the two together.

Katie used her fifteen years of *Pine Cone* newspaper expertise in helping Eric edit and rearrange some of the chapters of *The Mind in Action*. "At that point he was definitely pure Freud," said Katie. He "admitted Krafft-Ebing, however," and she remembers that his favorite limerick at this time was:

There was a young man from East Anglia
Who was into the sexual new-fanglia.

> His mind was a webbing
> Of Freud and Krafft-Ebing,
> But his loins were a mass of old ganglia.

"I certainly enjoyed Eric," said Katie. "Everybody did. I liked his . . . wicked sense of humor, his conscience."

"Everybody did" is a new one for Eric. For the first time in his life, Eric was able to move in a society that tolerated the offbeat side of his personality, that enjoyed his zany sense of humor and his refusal to kowtow to the establishment.

But even Carmel had an establishment of sorts. "Everybody" in Katie's book didn't include the lumpen bourgeoisie who ran the gift shoppes and lingerie emporiums, and the prosperous retirees drawn to the growingly slick quaintness of the town—the people who made up Carmel's counterculture. These did not appreciate the poker-faced psychiatrist, who seemed obviously intent on observing others. They feared his continual challenge to their herd instincts and his scientific scrutiny at parties. "How can you have that man around? How can you stand to have him in the house?" one lofty individual asked Marjory Lloyd.

His social worker assistant during this period, Virginia Mitchell, wrote us: "Having generally disliked gossip, at times I was literally horrified at the maliciousness of the remarks . . . made about my boss, mentor, and colleague, Eric Berne. There were a few times that I took umbrage and rather righteously told people off. . . . A psychiatrist who shuttled back and forth from San Francisco, had been divorced, and refused to talk shop at parties, was a prime target."

Dr. Talcott Bates, a Monterey pediatrician who was acquainted with Eric in the late forties and later on became a devoted follower and a great admirer of his TA theory, remarked: "I knew him pretty well during this period, but I don't think anyone was close to him. You could have a great feeling of mutual affection, but . . . not carry on any conversation. Berne would go to a group or a cocktail party but he wouldn't say anything, he just listened. ("Usually with an inscrutable smile," Katie added.)

"He loved parties," Bates continued, "but sometimes stood

in the middle of them watching with his baleful and myopic eyes to the discomfort of other and perceptive guests. He would disappear periodically. I asked him, 'What do you do?' And he said he would just stand on a street corner and watch. Most people couldn't do that; they have to be with other people and talk."

At other times, perceptive guests noticed that these mysterious vanishings coincided with the disappearance of some blonde—usually tall and buxom. There would be an elaborate ritual of going out for more soda water, whose procurement from the corner liquor store would take about two hours, or otherwise the pair might merely disappear to the bottom of a host's garden.

A woman we interviewed who knew Eric well during this period, but who doesn't wish to be identified, said she had an affair with him of about three to six months' duration. She said Eric had some serious talks with her about himself. He felt he had psychological problems and she recommended more analysis. It had to do with the peculiar and defensive way he related to people in social situations. Eric exhibited more hangups than anyone else she had ever known, and she found it remarkable that a psychiatrist would have that many hangups.

Berne's clown-like capers and piercing stares made some people uncomfortable and kept them at a distance from him. Perhaps this wasn't an accident. Berne gives an example of the use of weirdo behavior as a weapon in the social ramble in *The Happy Valley*:

> Abe asks: "Do you know why you have to face the front in an elevator?"
> "No," says Dulcy.
> "Neither do I," responds Abe, "So I always face the rear. It makes everyone as nervous as a cat!"

Whether or not their conversation had anything to do with it, not long after this Eric again took up his didactic analysis, this time in San Francisco with the well-known and highly respected Erik Erikson, who had moved to the West Coast.

On the other hand, Rosabel Brown, the Los Angeles child

psychologist who for two years was also very close to Berne, has written us that she and Eric both went into long-term analysis at this time because they were in love and were trying to find out "if it was right."

Eric had been with Rosabel in Los Angeles on November 17, 1947, the night that his mother had had her third and final heart attack. He had been planning to present a paper on *The Nature of Intuition* the next morning before a "Los Angeles Psychoanalytic" meeting; on receiving the news of her death he made a decision: that Sara would have wanted him to go ahead with his speech.

Immediately after the speech was finished he and Rosabel took a plane for New York. From there Eric flew to Canada for the funeral. Rosabel said that Eric presented his mother to her as a heroic figure, a feminist who had struggled successfully against tremendous odds. "I wished I had known her—learned how she made her many transitions," said Rosabel.

Although Eric may have been suffering from "hangups" and was somewhat hampered by them, he kept on functioning on a high level as a nonstop psychiatrist and theorist in his daily life. He was impatient with those who used their underlying conflicts as an excuse. "Underlying conflicts don't have to keep people from functioning," he said, later on. "The therapist is likely to have as many underlying conflicts as the patients."

His acute pronouncements on the perversity of human nature, which got their widest audience in *Games People Play*, came from perpetual observation. He is remembered in Carmel more for his stance as one who stared at others than as a garden satyr or fetcher of soda water. "He was a spectator at life's feast, but he wanted so much to belong—be a part of things. It took him years to learn how to get along with people," said Katie Martin (Schlepp).

However, he soon found a circle where he could both "belong" and be an observer without going to the bother of learning how to get along with ordinary people. The leader of this circle, which contained most of the artistic element in Carmel, was no blonde innocent of the type glorified in "The Mythology of Dark and Fair." Rather, the conservative Carmelites looked upon her as a raven-haired witch, suitable for framing. She was more like the Queen Anaïtis Berne had read about in *Jurgen:*

> . . . who was a delicious tall dark woman, thinnish and lovely, and very restless. . . . And . . . her more affectionate moments . . . positively frightened [Jurgen]: for transports such as these could not but rouse discomfortable reminiscences of the female spider, who ends such recreations by devouring her partner.

The center of this circle, or rather the vortex, was Marie Short, his new landlady. A landlady like no other, raving witch and/or raving beauty, she had a coterie of admirers, friends, and near-enemies who took delight in characters who stood backwards in elevators. In this circle Eric found he could both "belong" and be an observer without having to explain his sudden role switches to the Philistines.

Marie Short is still remembered by remnants of the old Carmel artistic circle as the only person in the village who ever had anything approaching a true salon. She had been a San Francisco–Woodside–Pebble Beach debutante, and socialite, who had married well, divorced well, and lived well. "I don't know where she got all the celebrities for her salon," Carol Steinbeck Brown, John Steinbeck's ex-wife, wondered. "Maybe she flagged down incoming buses."

Marie didn't have the financial wherewithal to be the complete Mabel Dodge Luhan of the far west, but she had the same ability to spot the comers in the artistic-literary-intellectual firmament. And, like so many intellectuals of the era, she was associated with numerous left-wing causes. With Ella Winter (Lincoln Steffens's wife) and her friend Langston Hughes, Marie Short had once organized an auction in San Francisco for the Scottsboro Boys, with James Cagney as auctioneer.

Marie had her own form of being a patron of the arts. She would rent out the one extra bedroom in her beautiful Spanish house to people she felt were worthwhile, for a small amount. At this point her antennae picked up Eric Berne as a suitable roomer, and Eric moved into her house and thus became even more integrated into the Carmel scene.

Marie's interests and tastes were far-ranging. She was equally devoted to Ella Winter, the left-winger, and to Una Jeffers, the Irish and ultraconservative wife of Robinson Jeffers. She was still fond of her ex-husband Douglas, who during their married years had accepted (under protest) the two months' sabbatical she took in New York with a married male artist friend of theirs. She was even more devoted to her current lover, young enough to be her own son, and bound to write the Great American Novel when he got free of his writer's block. Van Wyck Brooks proposed to Marie but could not tempt her away from the younger man.

Marie was the female embodiment of the energy-releasing principle Eric expressed in his *McGilliad* article, and it no doubt did his heart good to see his principle in action in gorgeous, living color. She was lithe, she was tanned copper-colored, and her hair was of an "anthracite blackness." And she was a free spirit.

With a previous roomer Marie had leapt into bed early one morning, to see if he were a homosexual (he was), but sex was not an aspect of her relationship with Berne. The chemistry was not right for an affair with the new roomer, but they supported each other as fellow free spirits, and they both reveled in an enormous vitality.

Rosabel Brown tried to get Eric to move away from this offbeat, insular little village, where he was the only psychiatrist, and get to the center of things, for she too recognized him as a comer. But Eric never strayed far from Carmel or for long; he did, however, begin commuting to San Francisco for part of each week, just as he had done between Connecticut and New York. In San Francisco, a few years later, Eric created a little colony of "free TA spirits" who appreciated the brilliance of his eccentric genius, but it was probably Marie Short, as much as anyone, who shook Eric out of the doldrums he suffered as a result of the disaster of his first marriage, and got him back on the track of exploiting his full energy potential.

In the "Acknowledgements" in *The Mind in Action* and in the revised reissue of the book a decade later (*A Layman's Guide to Psychiatry and Psychoanalysis*), Berne mentioned his Carmel friends of this period:

To those who read the manuscript, or who listened while I read it at the Short home in order that they might make suggestions, I offer a toast of Carmel wine in memory of much help and many pleasant evenings. These include Marie Short, Jake Kenny, Mr. and Mrs. John Geisen, Muriel Rukeyser, Dr. and Mrs. Russell Williams, Mr. and Mrs. Frank Lloyd, Sam Colburn, Gretchen Gray, Katie Martin, and a score of other Carmelites.

Two novels were written about the legendary Marie Short, *Laughter on the Hill* by Margaret Parton (1945) and *No Marriage in Paradise* by Myron Brinig (1949). Both made her into more of a devil than she really was. The following passage from the first book gives an accurate description of Marie's house according to Kraig Weston, Marie's daughter, and Kraig's husband, Neil Weston, son of the photographer Edward Weston:

> The rambling house . . . was approached by a sandy path, which led in from the road through a thicket of live oaks to a flagged courtyard, circled with hanging baskets of purple and pink fuschias. . . .
> [Marie] stood up then and nonchalantly brushed the dust off her rear. A wiry woman with a lithe body, she wore blue jeans with a Mexican silver belt, scarlet sandals and a scarlet shirt. Electric [jet black] hair fell now over glittering dark eyes and her derisively curved lips were brilliant with lipstick. I remembered [the] phrase 'haggard beauty,' discarded the haggard and retained the beauty.
> . . . Books lined the walls of the living-room, and a chased silver urn filled with moss roses stood on the old spinet in the corner. An enormous Gauguin print hung above the fireplace, and [red-orange] window curtains picked up the oranges of its Tahitian sunset. Everywhere, on the long refectory table, the carved desk, the mantelpiece, rested great curled shells, their polished inner surfaces faintly pink, glowing in the filtered green light. Three Siamese cats curled in a warm triangle on the deep corduroy couch in front of the fireplace. . . .

[Marie] rushed over to them and scooped them up into her arms . . .

"Oooooo" . . . she crooned. 'You beautiful animals!"

The cats seemed beautiful to Marie in more ways than one—they embodied for her that independence and decisiveness she so much admired. Many a house guest who came in late electrified the household with a blood-curdling scream because one of the cats had decided to sharpen its claws in his back and hang on there.

A certain free-form nudism was also celebrated. Guests at Marie and Douglas Short's Big Sur hideaway would be encouraged to strip and sunbathe, and would suddenly discover to their surprise that the practice was flagrantly coeducational.

Short-sheeting and water fights were also the order of the day. The scientist and observer in Berne noted this all down, but provided no inner resource of tolerance when two of Marie's children opened the window to his bathroom and threw their bantam rooster in on the doctor as he was taking a bath.

Berne insisted, however, that the rooster (a "wee, tiny thing" which wandered around the house all day) be put in the cellar at night so that absolute silence could be preserved in the interest of his writing program.

Marie started right off (according to Gus Lannestock) by enlisting her new roomer's services as a psychoanalyst, but was taken aback when she received a bill for $25 for the first hour. She promptly raised Eric's room rent by $25 and the subject was dropped.

Kraig Short Weston also remarked on the soggy-cornflake syndrome. One night two of Kraig's high-spirited teen-aged cousins, Sheila and Brenda, were visiting. Eric called out to them: "I have fifteen minutes while my cornflakes are soaking, girls. Come on in the kitchen, Kraig, Shenda and Brilla, and sit on either side of me and talk."

The three girls went into gales of laughter, but then they would often giggle at just the sight of this hunched-over man, whose eyes, behind his high-powered glasses, seemed so inscrutable, as if he were gazing at them, wizard-wise, through the bottoms of Coke bottles. The right lens was measurably thicker than the left, giving him a dizzy, one-sided look. One eye appeared to be half an inch higher than the other, due to the refraction.

Kraig also remembers that the household was required to tone down its boisterousness when Eric was working on his book in his room. She remembers the many nights he would rap on the ceiling of his bedroom with a broomstick to calm her bursts of laughter over Thurber's *The Day the Dam Broke,* or similar tidbits. He'd shout: "Shut up! Shut up! Go to sleep! Go to sleep!" and she would have to settle down in a hurry.

Some of Marie's children despised her freewheeling life-style and longed to revert to earlier established, old-fashioned values. One evening Kraig came into the house after a date and ran upstairs crying. Eric followed after her to find out what was the matter. Kraig explained that Neil didn't ever want to get married: he saw his freedom going down the drain; he wanted to have adventures, sail his boat to the South Seas, etc.

Eric said: "Wal, there are only two things you can do: forget the whole thing, tell him you are through—or, you know, he's got to marry you."

So the next night, the beautiful, raven-haired Kraig said: "OK, this is it—we're through."

But that wasn't it at all, as far as Neil was concerned—and they did get married. Four years afterwards, Kraig and her three-months'-old daughter came down with polio. Kraig was in the hospital, feeling very depressed, and her mother decided that she really needed to talk to a psychiatrist.

She asked Eric to visit Kraig.

Kraig's doctor, who was pooh-poohing the idea of her needing a psychiatrist anyway, expected Berne and Kraig to talk within the hearing of the other patients on the ward. Finally he was persuaded to let them talk in a cramped little room the size of an overgrown closet. Kraig couldn't even sit up at this point; they wheeled her in. Eric sat down and said, "Now, tell me how you feel."

She replied, "Well, one thing, I *hate* my doctor."

Berne then said: "Good! It's good for you to hate someone. Go ahead and hate him! And don't forget, all doctors are jerks!"

"He said that (about doctors) all the time to my mother," Kraig reported. "It was one of his favorite expressions."

When the lions prowled the salons, Eric knew enough to melt into the background in his observer role. At that point he was just another army psychiatrist, who lacked the firepower of Dylan Thomas, Ramon Navarro, Henry Varnum Poor, John Steinbeck, Roland Hayes, Henry Miller, Langston Hughes, Frieda Lawrence, or Robinson Jeffers. When Marian Anderson showed up one night at somebody's soirée after a concert and did a switch by playing the piano, while an amateur basso of the neighborhood sang "Ol' Man River," Eric "put on his amused look."

But he didn't seem particularly impressed by these big-name guests. "He cared only for the essential human quality," said Carol Steinbeck Brown.

When only the "regulars" were in attendance, the "Crazy" Lennie of old might cut loose at any moment.

At the first of Marie's parties Eric attended, he would "take a couple of beers or something and it was like a real, royal drunk-out. He would just act weird." Realizing that alcohol was not for him he gave it up, but social occasions at Marie's so exhilarated him he needed no inhibition-releaser.

Carol said: "[Sometimes] he got quite manic. There was a strange streak in him. If he was accepted in a group he sort of blew his top. I've seen him stand on an upholstered chair and jump up and down and scream like a child. I think there was an inadequacy there . . . well, it was rather frightening and sort of pitiful—in a man who was supposed to have other people under his control."

Kraig said: "He was a very energetic person, always jumping around and dancing and rough-housing." At one gathering there was a mad scramble to remove Eric's shoes. All the others had taken theirs off. Eric resisted (probably, Neil Weston suggests, because his socks bore the inevitable badge of bachelorhood—vast open spaces with perhaps a big toe rampant.) In the melee Eric knocked over "a very tiny little woman" and cracked her ribs. He switched into his doctor role the next day, went to her house, and bound her up with tape from his medical kit.

Some say he broke the woman's ribs by jumping off the dining table. ("Could have been another set of ribs," suggested Neil.)

Sometimes at parties Eric would respond to the ringing of the doorbell with cries of "Dames! Dames!" and would slide across the floor to fling the door open with a flourish. The women guests thus heralded generally let out little bleatings of terror or distress, not knowing the correct social amenities to be observed after such an overture. Even more difficult to formulate was the appropriate response when Berne, in the middle of a frenzied tarantella, would clutch his partner and roar: "Off to the bushes!"

"You always had the feeling he might just pounce," said Katie.

One time the diffident daughter of a Fort Ord commanding general was greeted at the door. Grabbed by Eric, she was waltzed and whirled into a nearby coat closet. The door was slammed shut and a long interval of silence ensued, followed by a cacophony of rudimentary jungle noises. On emerging, the diffident one failed to find any appropriate remarks from the Army Field Manual of Phrases to Utter at All Social Occasions and left early.

At other times (on new sock night, perhaps?) Eric would voluntarily take off his shoes and walk around the room on his hands (firmly embedded in his shoes) for five minutes without saying a word. Sometimes he would stand in place and do a "sort of French-Canadian shuffle." Or he might dance on the dining room table. In one Carmel house he would swing by one arm from the beams in the living-room ceiling—the other arm curled up and his feet drawn up under him.

"Pretending to be a monkey?" we asked Katie.

"Pretending?" she replied. "He was a whacking great ape!"

If the room were crowded enough, and after he had bumped into several dancers, he might clasp his partner to him and shout: "At last we are alone together!" While he went through these pranks he would have a "funny, evil smile on his face—wicked and wonderful."

Parlor games were also played at these gatherings. In one case, while other guests were wracking their brains over how to work certain little-used letters of the alphabet into a proposed telegram to President Truman protesting the atomic bomb, Eric came up with three versions: one in prose, one in poetry, and one in Jewish dialect.

In Carmel, even Eric's posture was a plus factor. According to Katie, "He looked like an eagle or a vulture. He hunched, and he had a craggy profile, and a strange, heron, crane, stork sort of stalk. And he always kept that little semi-elliptical smile on his face; when he didn't smile he looked angry. Without that smile, his eyes were like x-rays—analyzing you. Whenever there was any tension between him and anybody, he looked grim, and dour, and mean."

In this period, Eric spent much time at the beach. The psychiatrist would often stride over the sand dunes and say, "Any dames?" with all the assurance of a well-built adolescent. To Marie's son John Short, who was the recipient of this and similar remarks, Eric "seemed kind of scrawny." Berne brought down all sorts of elaborate snorkeling equipment, masks and whatnot, stuck a mammoth thermometer in the water for five minutes and, after carefully noting the temperature (usually 51 degrees), would put on his inflatable life preserver and swim, no matter what the thermometer said. But even this apparently droll caper was linked to one of Berne's scientific experiments.

A woman whose house overlooked Stewart's Beach, near the Carmel River, used to see Eric down on the beach on Sunday afternoons doing startling exercises which looked like some strange primitive ritual, almost as if he were praying to a sun god. He would do them for about ten or fifteen minutes, seemingly oblivious of others. "I don't think he was trying to attract attention to himself," said this beach friend. She added that she and her daughter, who was a medical student, got to know him well and that "Eric should not be portrayed as some sort of freak—he was a really marvelous person."

The Carmel River, like most California streams, has manic-depressive tendencies. For most of the year it is dry, but if an extended rain soaks up the hills and fills the dams, it can be floodsville. The sandbar that closes its mouth during the dry periods is swept away, and branches, fence posts, sheds, logs, and other debris are propelled seawards. "If a dog should fall in, it would be curtains, the end," Virginia Mitchell told us.

"Eric was utterly fascinated. He used to go down there every Sunday at that time of year and gradually it spread to other times of the year. He would go to see the torrent raging and to meet his friends, his 'river buddies' as he called them, who also hung around the mouth of the river on Sundays. He really enjoyed being a part of something. It was bigger than he was, the river, and took him out of himself."

It was into the lagoon near the river mouth that Eric and another man plunged one day and pulled out a teen-aged boy struggling in the water. The beach, in fact, is one of the least safe beaches of the area, and northern California beaches are notoriously unsafe for the unwary. The scene gives an overall sense of peace and beauty that the tremendous slamming waves and the river at flood play counterpoint to.

The combination of great beauty and great hazard in women as well as in beaches fascinated Berne more than once during his life. He was a man who liked a challenge, and he had the supreme confidence that his cleverness would see him through. For the hazards of the surf and flying he had his inflatable life preserver. He took it on the plane in his briefcase every week on his commuter flight to San Francisco, in case the plane should undershoot the landing and end up in the bay. On some flights he also carried a flashlight, a life raft, and a police whistle, and, according to his daughter Ellen, "he would push people aside in his anxiety to get a seat near the exit."

He asked a private pilot friend of his, Howard Brunn, what he thought of the life preserver. Brunn didn't think much of the preserver's practicality. "Can you imagine getting that damned thing out of your briefcase when the plane hit the water?" he asked, but Berne continued to carry it nonetheless. For the hazards of the joust with the female sex he had similar remedies, as the self-assurance in *Sex In Human Loving* evidences.

Early in 1946 the army took Berne away from his beach and his haven and sent him on a circuit between Fort Lewis in rainy Tacoma, Washington, and Bushnell General Hospital in Brigham City, Utah. In the six months away from Carmel he did a certain amount of group therapy with soldier patients, and he also treated some civilian patients in Ogden, Utah. After Carmel, he found both Brigham City and Tacoma dull. In July 1946, he was sent again to Madigan General Hospital in Fort Lewis to be phased out of the army.

From there Eric wrote his old mentor, Dr. Paul Federn (no doubt with jubilation), that he was due to get out of the army on July 16, 1946. He was worried that the army might change its mind, though, as he was the only diplomate in psychiatry left in the army on the western shores of the United States.

At the same time he was waiting for his divorce to go through and wrote to his lawyer, Mr. Davis, that he was concerned that the matter might conclude without some specific provisions for his visitation rights with his children. He was also concerned that the complaint charged physical cruelty. He didn't know what the future might bring; he might want to go into politics some time.

Elinor told us, however, that at no time did Eric ever actually hit her—the most he ever did was hold her wrists in a viselike grip while they were arguing. The physical cruelty probably crept into the complaint out of an excess of zeal on her lawyer's part.

A letter from Eric to his mother stated that he was anxious to get back to the beach in Carmel. To Sam (Colburn) he wrote that Marie had been awfully nice—she was going to let him stay at her house again until he could get permanently settled. (Apparently this was to be temporary, as Marie had reassigned his room. Marjory Lloyd told us that eventually Eric was "evicted" by Marie, but she doesn't remember any of the details.)

The army didn't double-cross its remaining diplomate on the West Coast; Eric got out as scheduled and was made a major to boot. He sent Marie Short $10 and asked her to use it to buy "seltzer water" for a little celebration upon his return to Carmel. After a short stay at Marie's, Major Doctor Berne found his own house up in the Carmel Hills and began putting the finishing touches on his book, *The Mind in Action,* which he had decided was a bit too audacious and not steady and reliable enough. He had been receiving advice and criticism from Federn and Henry Simon of Simon and Schuster.

He also set up private practice in a second-floor walk-up in the old Goold Building in the Carmel business district.

Having his own house allowed Eric to launch a weekly party-giving program. Such parties had been a big thing at his mother's house in Montreal. His first attempt at a weekly salon in New York had died for want of a second, and the sporadic parties during his first marriage had only whetted his appetite.

Kraig said: "He had a lot of mad parties. I think the idea started at my mother's house. He loved those parties because he could go completely ape if he wanted to—so then he decided he wanted to have a lot more parties."

But ape-ward though Eric might go, his party-giving wasn't entirely purposeless. No doubt it was all part of his master plan for observing people at work and play. In *The International Journal of Group Psychotherapy* he wrote a surprisingly dull article about his "salon" experience, saying:

> For a period of about three years, the writer held 'open house' one evening a week in the same village. Specific invitations to individuals were relatively uncommon, but it was "generally known" that anyone who cared to was welcome to come and bring friends. The attendance at this series of social meetings approximated closely a series of appropriate random numbers. One week there would be two guests, the next 58, the next 23 and so on.

"Everyone would bring a bottle of wine or some cheese and crackers or other refreshments and drink and talk," John Short reported.

John told about the sensation he and other friends caused by showing up at one of these parties with a caricature of Wilhelm Reich's orgone box. "It had gauges on it and instructions and fake dials, one of which was called 'Peter Meter' . . . another, 'Whang Control.'" People climbed in and "were instantly psychoanalyzed or maybe their characters were read," according to Neil Weston. "It was wild. Everyone was having hysterics around that box."

"Eric was much amused," said John Short. "He loved things like that."

Carol Steinbeck Brown told us: "Eric wanted to give at homes or something after he moved into his new house and so we all put in command performances and turned up on Sunday nights—and there'd be a poker game going on in one room and a little wine drinking and chatting in another. It was pleasant."

At one party Howard Brunn remembers Eric lying on the floor "croaking and flapping his wings, being a seagull. And he sounded just like one, too—and he looked just like one."

Rosabel Brown said that Berne described his series of parties as follows: "Everyone will eventually come. I shouldn't be surprised if Freud himself walked in that door."

However, Eric *was* surprised when the "Dorothy la Desirée" of his wildest Jurgenesque dreams walked in that door. When Dorothy de Mass Way swept in, "in all her piquant gorgeousness, with her tip-tilted gold-green eyes and retroussé nose and 'dark blonde' hair and tall and gracious elegance", thoughts of Freud flew out the window.

He wasted no time. The next night he had to be in San Francisco, but he called her from there for a date for the weekend. Once again it was full speed ahead in pursuit of the goddess, a stunning divorcée-manquée with three sparkling, energetic children, in short, a goddess to end all goddesses—and besides, Dorothy had a "twinkle in her eye" and was thoroughly nice.

11

Jack in the Beanstalk Meets Cinderella

. . . First, he sees her for the first time, standing and moving, and he thinks, "Maybe this is it." That feeling already makes life worthwhile, and if he has too many doubts he should go no farther than glimpse her face, so that he can regret it sweetly for the rest of his life.

But if he dares the possible disappointment of talking to her, he may end up knowing, "This could be it."

After that, when he is alone, he starts to dream about seeing her again.

When he does see her again, he wants to be with her all the time.

He starts being with her all the time, and then he need no longer have dreams, for his life has become one.

Then come the first quarrels, the partings and reunions, for they cannot bear it long apart, and the only question is which will stop sulking first.

Then they move in with each other, married or unmarried, and between lovings they quarrel about money.

Twenty years later they are inseparable. Their love has been tamed into an affection that will unite them till the grave. . .

Eric Berne, Sex in Human Loving

She had been having dinner with a jolly group of friends at the old Sade's Restaurant in Carmel (now The Matador).

Someone had suggested that they all troup over en masse to Dr. Berne's "at home." Dorothy's escort said he didn't want to go. Dorothy, however, had heard about Berne and was intrigued. Berne's secretary, Millie, who lived next door to Dorothy, had told her about her peculiar and puzzling boss ("a strange man to work for"), and Dorothy had retorted, with a ringing, silvery laugh, "I'll meet him and I'll tell you what he's really like, ha! ha!"

Millie had talked to Dorothy about Berne's first book, *The Mind in Action*, which had been on the *New York Times* bestseller list for several weeks, and had told her about an article by Berne in the July issue of *Vogue*. Dorothy promptly spent some time at the library searching out the *Vogue* article. Major Doctor Berne, chief of the Psychiatric Reconditioning Unit at Fort Ord, author of a successful book and the only psychiatrist in the village of Carmel, was a highly eligible bachelor. Besides, Dorothy liked the doctor's sense of humor.

Dorothy had seen pictures of Eric and she had noted his tawny leonine looks. (She had always fancied lions.) The *Vogue* article did nothing to dissuade her from setting out to meet him; bidding adieu to her reluctant escort, she went with the group to Berne's at home.

So it was no accident that Dorothy la Desirée opened the door that evening and thoughts of "Maybe this is it" blanked out thoughts of Freud in the mind of Eric Berne.

Berne knew quality when he saw it and class when he saw it, and Dorothy had the manners and poise of a socialite. Her father's family background reeked of money and power; the family owned a company whose product was (and is) a household word. And shortly before she met Eric, her father had died and Dorothy had been made the recipient of three trust funds.

She was irresistibly self-assured, tall, curvaceous, full of savoir-faire, armed with intelligent questions about his work—and besides, she was nice.

The Carmel cure had worked to rid Berne of *le cafard* that gripped him since the divorce. The old confidence had come back. And a boy from the respectable but limited milieu of Sainte Famille Street could dare to pursue a fairy princess. His sister Grace thought that Eric's script was that of Jack who climbed the beanstalk and dared giants to bring back treasure. Well, here was indeed a treasure, and Eric dared mightily—he was always one to challenge himself. He once wrote that he was a little disappointed when he couldn't eat one more egg during his evening snack of cornflakes and six eggs. The czar of Russia used to eat six eggs every day, and he always felt that he could at least outdo the czar.

Dorothy had had a French-Canadian grandmother (the de Mass strain), and we asked Frank Lloyd if that was part of what had brought the two together.

"Oh, no," said Frank, "it was pure sex appeal. She had a lot of sex appeal. She still does."

But the pursuit was not entirely one-sided. Dorothy had her research to do for her neighbor Millie, and it was not seemly to leave an unstalked lion lying about.

Certainly Eric courted Dorothy indefatigably. Often he took her to the Pine Inn, an establishment caravansary where he now ate his dinners. And he would walk down from his office every morning at eleven o'clock when he got his break to see Dorothy for five minutes at her rented house on Camino Real.

And, quite often, right after work at 5 P.M., they would take off for San Francisco for the ballet, the opera, a concert, or a play, returning home at 2 or 3 A.M.

The beautiful heiress had traveled in her youth from Chicago to New York to Florida in the private railroad train of her father's family—"it had about three cars." She had gone to all sorts of marvelous parties in the days when parties were "super"—the days of "wonderful nonsense," she said, "it doesn't exist any more. It was just so marvelous! I just had such a ball!"

"I had been married before to a playboy. I was a playgirl, so naturally I married a playboy," Dorothy said.

Her first husband had shared her social background and was also, like Berne, a wizard—he invented computer devices and credit-card processing equipment. He was the type of person who elicited gasps of admiration from their friends. But the two of them had gotten out of phase, and they were separated.

Dorothy had been in Carmel for a few months before she met Eric and had been wined and dined by eligible male sharks and wolves. She had enjoyed the dating game again, but she "was always looking for a father." Her own father and mother had been divorced when she was a babe in arms, and her mother had remarried. She had never actually known her father—he had been the family wildcat and had moved from the East to Rancho Santa Fe in California, but she was well acquainted with her father's family. The inevitable yo-yo effect caused by the gap between ordinary life with her mother and the Great Gatsbyism of the paternal branch sometimes left Dorothy feeling that she didn't belong to either side. Some days it was back to the cinders, other days it was riding in the golden pumpkin coach. Maybe Eric could offer her the stability and authority she had been searching for in her lost father.

At first, she was mostly fascinated by Eric's mind. But gradually she began to fall in love with him. "The love kind of grew" until finally she was "crazy about him. . . . I never thought of another man while I was married to him. . . . I never felt for my first husband any of the feelings I felt for Eric. But I was horrified at the idea of a divorce."

At the beginning of their relationship Dorothy remained very independent. She had always been like that during courting days. Her mother used to say she'd be sorry for the way she treated her suitors.

She was dating a man in Palo Alto, and there was also a local runner-up. She would tell Eric all about these dates, shaking her dark blonde curls and laughing her silvery laugh, but she wouldn't tell him their names. She would tell him the local's initials were "J.S.," but nothing more. Eric was insanely jealous and would telephone her every hour on the hour from San Francisco or wherever, until she finally got home from these dates. J.S. gave her "pints of Chanel No. 5." The more capricious she was, the more both J.S. and Eric seemed attracted by her. If, during the courting period, Eric got in a gloomy mood and refused to talk or be interesting, she would just walk out.

Eric seemed "foreign" to Dorothy, "quite European. He pronounced some words differently, like 'garage' to rhyme with 'Madge.' The children and I never stopped cracking up over that!" He was completely unused to Christmas, for instance, and would watch the festivities with fascination, but would never join in, saying, "they just didn't celebrate Christmas that way at home." And he didn't seem to be at all accustomed to gracious living. "You had to make allowances for Eric. He wasn't like the other boys I had gone around with."

Eric told her his childhood was a bleak, bleak time. "They really lived in a ghetto because he said they did. He always had to feel guilty about his mother's having worked so hard. I saw some of the letters she had sent him, saying 'Don't worry about me. It's perfectly OK, because I'm your mother and I haven't minded getting a heart attack because I had to work so hard.' He became a compulsive worker, just consumed with ambition, to make up for her sacrifices."

Eric's Sunday night at-homes had begun to lose some of their allure for him now. At times only three people showed up. And, aflame with his new romance, Eric began to resent "his obligation," because it took him away from Dorothy. Dorothy had attended his parties a few times but had become bored and refused to participate further. So on Sunday afternoons, over at Dorothy's, he would often say, "It's almost time for my at home. I wish I didn't have to go." He evidently felt gripped by the iron tradition that "the salon must go on, come what may," but when he could get out of it, he and Dorothy joyously took off for a whole weekend in San Francisco.

Dorothy sometimes helped him buy the party refreshments—cold sliced meats, cheeses, lots of bread, and lots of salted peanuts. People never brought their own food, to her knowledge.

Dr. Russell Williams said: "Eric gave good parties for a period in his bachelor days. He had a lovely and vivacious lady (Dorothy) to host them . . . and there were always psychiatrists from San Francisco visiting. Good parties."

Williams called this Eric's halcyon period. "The nicest period in Eric's life. He was free, no children as yet, with none of the responsibilities of marriage.

"But he married the girl. Who's to say it was a mistake? But it turned out to be, as the divorce [later] testified. He should have lived with ladies, but not married them. He was too set in his own ways, his ideas, his work, his need to take off on far-flung trips, to be bent to domesticity. Too bad for him that fashion still dictated marriage."

In the summer of 1948, before they were married, Eric took

off on a "far-flung" trip around the world, on which he visited seventeen mental hospitals in the Philippines, Hong Kong, Singapore, Ceylon, India, and Turkey. Dorothy didn't go—she had her three children to take care of—but she decided to rent Eric's house and fix it up for a surprise. "It was a mess," she said. She and a cleaning lady scrubbed, painted, and slip-covered all summer and planted a garden.

The place looked wonderful when Eric returned, and he was awfully pleased. He had called her from India and England and had written her practically every day. When he got home, Dorothy, ever conscious of the proprieties, moved out again until they got married.

Eric had been gung-ho to make Dorothy his wife almost from the minute they'd met in 1947, but, as he was in didactic analysis with Erik Erikson, he was admonished to wait until he had completed the analysis. However, Erikson had told Berne during a therapy session that he was "already married to Dorothy in his mind." By the time the marriage actually took place, Dorothy said, Berne had dutifully completed two years of training. According to Dr. John Dusay, Berne decided to "divorce Erikson" before he had completed his training—and marry Dorothy.

Dorothy, however, "didn't have her divorce yet and kept putting it off and [putting it] off." Eric was disturbed by that and thought it showed she still cared for her first husband and was ambivalent. "I have a very hard time terminating relationships of any kind," Dorothy explained.

Once she had her interlocutory decree of divorce, she kept forgetting to pick up her final papers. ". . . It got to be a thing. I didn't go and I didn't go. Eric would keep asking and we'd set the date—and it was just terrible! I still hadn't picked up the papers!"

Eric, too, may have been ambivalent. In *Sex in Human Loving* he wrote: "The best age for a bachelor is 39. He is neither too old for the interesting young ones, nor too young for the interesting old ones. It may come as a surprise—an unwelcome or even a distasteful one—to people under thirty to learn that some of the sexiest women are fifty." Eric was thirty-nine when he married Dorothy, and he had asked Elinor to marry him again a week or so before the ceremony.

It is certain the wedding very nearly didn't come off.

Dorothy says: "I literally tried to get out of it the night before the wedding. I really had made a terrible, terrible mistake and I said, 'No, we've just got to call it off.'"

The evening before the wedding Eric had planned to take the family out to dinner. "He said: 'Now, I don't want you to be all tired—tomorrow's your wedding day.' But [Eric] wasn't crazy about going out with the children—he liked them up to a point—he always said one of the most attractive things about me was that I had three beautiful children—and that was fine and dandy as long as he could look at them, watch, and when it was over, zzzzt, that was it.

"So this particular night we were going to the wharf. . . . Each of the children had received a check from their father for Christmas, and my daughter said something about, 'My Daddy sent me a check,' and *jealousy*—Eric just flared up and made some very cutting remark to her. And I don't know what I did, but my heart turned over and I thought, oh boy, this is never going to work out! And I couldn't eat and I was all choked up.

"And I just couldn't see how he could have answered her that way—and not even seen how a little girl would have been so pleased to have heard from her father, when she hadn't heard for a long time. Eric saw how I felt. I was sitting there with tears falling down on my plate.

"We came home and I put the children to bed and I said, 'OK, I simply can't marry you tomorrow. And so we called up Marie Short, who was going to give the reception, and she said, 'You can't do this to me! The arrangements have all been made!' And Eric said, 'Dorothy simply won't listen.' And all night long he stayed and talked and we were in touch with Marie every hour on the hour, and finally he went home about four or five o'clock in the morning and we had pretty well settled that I would [go through with it].

"When I woke up it was all bright and clear (it was Christmas Eve)," she continued, "and I thought, OK, I guess I'll go through with it."

Long-time Montreal friend Gerald Goodstone, a Beverly

Hills psychiatrist, had been asked to be best man, but on such short notice that he couldn't manage it. He remembered, though, that Eric was marrying "a widow with three children," but that Eric told him he wasn't going to have to worry about the children as he was planning to install an iron door on his study.

The sun still shone that afternoon while Dorothy and Eric were married at the Church of the Wayfarer in Carmel. Meanwhile, back at Marie Short's, where the reception was to be held, Marie's three Siamese cats began the festivities early by devouring the turkey. Other refreshments were hastily substituted, and the affair went off smoothly. A guest who offered to psychoanalyze the culprits was convinced that the cats had been put up to it by a caterer hostile to Eric.

The happy pair honeymooned at the St. Francis Hotel in San Francisco. "We entertained a lot of our friends, and I remember we went to hear Artur Rubinstein. We did a lot of fun things." But then on a trip to Berkeley, Eric decided he had to dip into the University of California library to check on a point that was troubling him in an article he had been writing.

"He said, 'I won't be long,' and he left me sitting in the car for three solid hours! Waiting in a parked car! And I didn't have the gumption to get out of that car and leave. No, I had a problem—if I could just sit there and take something like that!"

Shortly after their return to Carmel, the Bernes bought one of the oldest houses in the village (on Carpenter Street) and remodeled it into a comfortable and rambling white house that could have come right out of a *House and Garden* article—as the perfect country cottage. They settled down with their ready-made family of three children and three years later produced a boy of their own, Eric, Jr., called Ricky.

The *Carmel Pine Cone* of March 28, 1952, announced Ricky's arrival, saying that Dr. Berne "reports that his son is already sporting a head of reddish-blonde hair that bears a marked resemblance to the color of his father's moustache." The whole household was looking forward to the coming home "next Sunday of Mrs. Berne and the latest genius in the family."

Three years later Ricky's blond brother Terence (called

Terry) appeared, as beautiful as an angel in Carmel's general opinion.

In these early years, Dorothy went around the village saying, "Happiness is being married to a Jewish psychiatrist," according to one informant.

Eric was also very happy in the early years of his marriage, judging by a chapter from an unpublished manuscript written in 1953 and found among his papers. It has for a hero a psychiatrist born in Canada who uses group therapy in his practice. When group meetings are held at his office at night, he thinks wistfully of what is going on at home, a wistfulness accentuated perhaps by the nights spent in San Francisco away from his home in Carmel. He imagines his wife settling down with her crocheting to The Nutcracker Suite. One daughter would be looking at movie magazines, another practicing pliés and entrechats to the ballet music (his stepdaughter Roxana). One son would be cutting out pictures of sports heroes, another playing the flute, while the littlest would be sudsing around in his pre-bedtime bath. (Dorothy confirms that this was indeed a good description of their family life at the time. It would have been Eric and Elinor's visiting son who was playing some musical instrument.)

The psychiatrist then admits that when he was on a trip to Alaska, he had come home earlier than he needed to, because, for the first time in his life, he was homesick.

The doctor wonders about all the places in America where he could possibly live and ends up with a love song to his small village, on the California coast, not too far from San Francisco, where the mountains plunge into the ocean and one is surrounded by growing things. In this small town were people whose skeins of life had become enmeshed with his.

So, in his early forties, Berne had his first taste of well-rounded family life with a loving wife and a sizeable complement of happy children. And Dorothy was glad, too, to be the center of a well-ordered household after the high and flighty living of her earlier years.

Dorothy had the household running like clockwork. The days clicked off as if automated for an assembly line. Dorothy got up at 7:30. Eric, like his father before him, got up slightly later, about 8:15. They had breakfast, and Eric left for his office, a few woodsy blocks away. Every day he telephoned her exactly at 11:00, even after they were divorced. He ate his lunch in town from 1:00 to 3:00, and very often Dorothy met him at the restaurant. Evenings he would come home, have a nap and then dinner. He would play with the children for forty-five minutes precisely, look at his watch, and disappear out to his study (a little rustic shack especially built for him in the backyard) where he wrote every night until 2:00 or 3:00 A.M.

A large roll of white paper, such as butchers use, hung on the wall and fed into his typewriter so that he didn't have to interrupt his thoughts to change papers. "On a good night," he would say, "I can write about four yards."

And every Sunday afternoon exactly at three o'clock he took the five kids to the beach where "he talked to them as if they were in college," according to an admiring acquaintance of his who lived near the beach.

"He did everything methodically, so he didn't have to use any of his energy or mental processes for unimportant details, you see, so there was not much of anything that was spontaneous," said Dorothy. "Even his clothes I arranged so he wouldn't have to think of anything. With his rigid schedule here and in San Francisco, if he was a minute off, it could throw his whole day out of kilter."

Dorothy had been a playgirl, and nothing in her life had prepared her for anything so regimented. With the help of her wonderful housekeeper she managed it all—even though she found that "having to take care of all those children and never have it interfere with him . . . and have everything done so that things were exactly the way he was used to having them when he came home—you can't believe the pressures!"

The assembly-line analogy was not at all dispelled when in his Acknowledgements in *Transactional Analysis in Psychotherapy* Berne wrote, "Finally, I have to thank . . . my wife for keeping my machinery running smoothly and for her patience during the many evenings I spent in my study."

When Eric was writing his books they had virtually no social life. "We never went anywhere or did anything." He didn't like movies "and he hated concerts." However, it was necessary to have some social contacts in order to be able to observe how people behaved in social situations.

"You see," said Dorothy, "he was really an anti-social person. It didn't seem like that because he went around a lot, but the only reason he went around was to study people. They were all grist for the mill. He really didn't like most of the people.

"He really didn't have any Child. He wasn't a bunch of fun. Some of the time he was—when he was rambunctious. He would decide to have fun. You could almost see the wheels go 'round. You could see him say, 'OK, I'll take three hours off and I'll have fun.' And you could see him turn it off—but don't wake up with a hangover the next day because the fun is over—well . . . I didn't like hangovers anyway."

Ellen Berne remembers one time when she was visiting in Carmel and they had a party. Eric was acting out his usual scientific scrutinizer role. "You really felt he was watching you," said Ellen. One of the guests arrived holding a glass of iced tea. Eric took her coat and asked her if he could get her a drink. She demurred, pointing out she had brought her own tea. "But pretty soon she changed it for a scotch, and then she got [totally rip-roaring] drunk. I said, 'Look, she's drunk!' And Eric responded, 'That's what always happens when they bring their own iced tea.' "

Once Dorothy gave a formal dinner party. Ellen said, "Dorothy is kind of a social person and she likes to do things nicely." The dinner was proceeding sedately, when Eric found things too stiff (or the center of attention shifted unduly, or the need for scientific observation became acute). He left the room suddenly and then "sprinted through it in his undershorts."

Ellen noticed, too, when she visited, that Eric kept an unabridged dictionary in the bathroom and read it each time he used the facilities. He urged her to ask him, at random, the meaning of any word, claiming that he knew by heart every page in Webster's. Ellen doubted this, but after numerous quizzings found that Eric never slipped up. He particularly asked her to search out the most obscure proper names and not to go lightly but to ask for the hardest, longest, most impossible words.

When Eric "went off on those marvelous trips," Dorothy was longing to accompany him, but she was too conscientious to leave five children, some of them small, in the hands of overworked hired help. "Eric went to the Caribbean every year, sometimes twice in one year. He was in Havana when Castro walked into his hotel with machine guns."

Dorothy particularly wanted to go because "we were always so happy when we were alone." When she and Eric went away together, it was perfect. "He wanted me to be like a mistress."

When Eric was traveling by himself, Marie Short would say to Dorothy, cattily: "'Don't think for one minute he's being faithful to you in Tahiti . . .' Marie loved 'Uproar' and played it all the time."

Dorothy, in her heart-to-heart talks with Marie, used to tell her (according to Marie's daughter, Kraig Short Weston) that "she and Eric fought like mad and that she loved Eric but he was impossible to live with." Dorothy said: "Marie would come storming over to the house and confront Eric with: 'How can you go to the Fiji Islands (or wherever) for a month and leave Dorothy to cope with all this?' And Eric was not used to having anyone stand up to him like that and was flabbergasted at her assault."

Hassles over money seemed endless. There was always a difficulty in getting agreement as to what part of the bills should be paid solely or jointly, and Dorothy ended up turning over to Eric most of the income from her father's trust funds. "If I could have continued to be independent financially, it would have been better for our marriage," she said. Eric also believed in making major decisions without consulting her. When their first-born was still a baby, Eric phoned one night from San Francisco and said, cheerily: "You are now the proud owner of a twenty-seven-room house in San Francisco." He said he expected the family to move up there very soon.

Dorothy went up to look at the place. It was an enormous mansion of three floors on Pacific Avenue with front stairs and back stairs and fireplaces in every room. It had a back pantry and a front pantry—"simply enormous! I asked my marvelous housekeeper, who had been with me since our older boy was born, if she would come up with me, but she said she couldn't." The idea was that the family would all move to San Francisco for weekdays and keep the Carmel house for weekends.

"Well, I had lived up there with my first husband," Dorothy continued, "and I'm not a big city girl any more—I'd gotten away from that—and I didn't want to move to San Francisco. That is, I didn't know I didn't want to move—I just broke out in huge hives. Finally, Eric said: 'I know what's the matter with you, you don't want to move!' I was also having hay fever attacks which I hadn't had for years and so—well, anyhow, we kept the house for a while and he used it to practice in. We finished the upstairs, the bedrooms, just enough so we could go there on weekends. We all had beds and a couple of chests of drawers—there were linens and things—but we didn't even eat there (except for breakfast). The kids were of the age to go to the Ice Follies and the zoo so it worked out pretty well."

Afterwards when it was sold, they kept a San Francisco apartment which they used on weekends.

"In a way," Dorothy reflected, "we had a happy marriage." [They were together fourteen years.] If Eric had been a little less relentlessly ambitious" and had given more time to the family— "and if I'd been a little more mature [she had been in analysis for a time even before she met Eric], we . . . could have made it."

"Twenty years later they are inseparable.
Their love has been tamed into an affection that will unite them till the grave."

When Eric wrote these words in *Sex in Human Loving* in the year before he died, he was contemplating remarrying Dorothy after twenty years of off-and-on-again togetherness since their first ceremony. He had been through another marriage and divorce and had proposed to Dorothy again, and she was considering it.

"I started to say, 'Well, no,' you know, when he asked me," Dorothy told us, "but he said, 'Don't give me an immediate answer. Let's go on a trip. We've always gotten along so well on trips.' It might have worked out; . . . the pressures were gone. The children were mostly grown. The conflicts over the children had always caused difficulty."

She couldn't help thinking "how peaceful it had been without Eric." But, on the whole, she believes she might have accepted his offer.

Remembering the ins and outs of what they had been through and especially the unpleasant or dreadful years of 1952–56 must have given her pause. Those years were to be like the trials of Job. Perhaps if it hadn't been for those years, with their tragedies and traumas and law suits and Eric's being rejected by the psychoanalytic establishment, the pair might have managed to stay together.

12

Poker

Where there is a hare and a tortoise it is better to be a winning hare.

Eric Berne, *Sex in Human Loving*

Poker was more than a pastime with Berne; it was a prime game for exposing the true nature of winners and losers. In *Sex in Human Loving* he said that it is easy to distinguish winners from losers in poker; you just count "what they have in their pockets when they get outside the door."

A *New York Times* ad promoting *Games People Play* said that Berne was a master poker player and that he had financed visits to mental institutions in thirty countries with his poker winnings. In our assiduous pursuit of the story of the Conquistador of the Poker Chips we came up with some interesting results.

We asked Dr. Rachmiel Levine about Berne's poker playing at McGill. Dr. Levine said Lennard wasn't very good at it. "He didn't have the face for it. He played but he never won."

Eric played some poker at Marie Short's when he roomed with her in Carmel, but these were penny ante games, and Berne would withdraw to a corner and read a book when he exceeded his $2 limit, despite chaffing from others about his being a cheapskate.

Eric's serious poker playing started with a Carmel group originally organized by lawyer Bill Stewart. A core of dedicated players (all male) developed out of this first group, and although some newcomers would show up from time to time (because the old hands "needed new fuel all the time, otherwise they just fed off each other"), the solid core stayed constant.

After a series of losses, the tyros would drop out and new blood would be recruited. Among the steadies, Berne was considered one of the better players, and by some the "second best." There was no consensus as to who was the best. The regulars all won from time to time, "otherwise they wouldn't have hung in there," said Stewart.

In *Sex in Human Loving*, Berne wrote:

> . . . a loser . . . thinks poker is a game of luck. So if he gets bad cards he gets mad and says: "My luck's not with me tonight." Maybe he even slams his cards on the table. Second, he If Only's and I Shoulda's . . . Thirdly, after the hand is finished, he wants to do it over, and says: "Let me see the next card that I woulda got if only I'd got the next card insteada this card." The winners may say the same thing to be good fellows, or to con the other players, but they don't really mean it. They know that if they lost the hand, they played it wrong or got bad cards, that's all there is to it, and cursing won't help. They can wait for the next hand to do better.
>
> A winner is a person who sets out to do something he decides to do and gets it done if possible; if he doesn't get it right the first time, he gets it right the next time. He knows that everybody makes mistakes—except winners. He doesn't let his Child or his Parent impair his judgment.
>
> . . . Of course a loser wins occasionally, but he makes sure not to keep it, and a winner loses occasionally, but he makes sure he gets it back.

According to Dr. Bob Goulding, who was one of Berne's chief teachers of TA and is now a TA star, author and trainer of therapists, "Eric was a GREAT poker player, really unbeatable. He made a lot of money playing poker. . . . He was marvelous."

But Goulding wasn't one of the regular poker group. He played in a group of his own, which sometimes traded players or provided fill-ins for Eric's regular group. In the regular group Berne savored the excitement and cut-throat competition, and was able to carry on his research in social psychiatry without hindrance from his tolerant companions. Howard Brunn, successful merchant and Carmel city councilman, said, "Eric wasn't what you'd call a social animal. He'd make some pretty strange remarks, but we'd just ignore them and accept him for what he was. We weren't trying to analyze the guy."

Brunn remembers that Francis Palmer, who held a Ph.D. in psychology and who considered himself their best poker player, grated on Eric's nerves. When Palmer would win, he would bellyache loudly: "There isn't enough in this pot to make it worthwhile. There ought to be more."

"He did it on purpose to make everyone rattled so they would play badly," said Brunn.

"Did Eric get rattled too?" we asked. Brunn replied that he did, "but when he did, he just got calmer."

One time Palmer got Eric so annoyed that he said Francis was "the Nixon of Psychology." This was before Watergate, but Nixon was already considered an awesome mess in many Carmel purlieus, and Palmer seemed "totally stunned by this."

The players took turns hosting the games at each of their houses, and some served elaborate late-night suppers, competing with each other to provide the best.

All Eric ever ate, though, was heavily salted, butterless bread. When he was a bachelor and it was his turn to have the group, he opted out of the Julia Child sweepstakes. The other players would kid him about the meagerness of his offerings. ("He would put some bread out there, I mean, literally, and some water . . . and a little orange juice . . . and a little bit of booze.") To these scoffers he would reply rather gruffly: "We're here to play."

We had been told that Brunn was probably Berne's best friend in Carmel, but he declined the nomination, saying: "Eric wasn't a warm, outgoing person. I always felt a little bit on edge around him. I just never had a close rapport with him. I don't know if he liked me. I don't think he did. . . . Well, we were very polite to each other, but we weren't close. I doubt if he was close to anyone."

If Berne won enough at poker to finance trips to mental institutions in thirty countries, it wasn't in his regular Carmel group.

Bill Stewart said: "He couldn't have won enough to pay [for those trips] even if he'd won every time, which he didn't. He lost as much as he won—we all did." Francis Palmer agreed that $400 was the top sum for a game and (although a person could lose $200 to $300 in an evening) he, Palmer, who was the best player and took the most home, only made about $1000 a year. Bill Stewart suggested Eric might have won a lot in Australia in some games he got into over there.

Bill Fassett, owner of Nepenthe, a far-out, far-above-the-ocean restaurant at Big Sur, reported that Eric couldn't have won much in these poker games, because he was transparent—so cautious that everyone knew that when he stayed in he must have a *great* hand, so everyone immediately dropped out.

Brunn mentioned one particularly memorable trip which the poker group took. "We called ourselves 'The Highlanders' so we would get a group rate. We went to Las Vegas and took our wives—rented an extra room and played poker for three days. All the wives wanted to go to shows and do other things. It turned out to be a complete disaster. Some of the people got divorced after that trip . . . I was one of them. . . ."

But it was not a disaster for Berne. Dorothy told us she and Eric were never happier—had a marvelous time. "Eric was feeling no pain because he was winning at poker, and it was like a second honeymoon for us."

For twenty years, when he was in Carmel, Berne could be found at the poker table on Friday nights. The testimony of his partners indicates that he was not a carefree macho Marlboro man staking empires, loves, or old homesteads on the turn of a card. He played as he drove his Maserati, cautiously, methodically, and systematically—no wild plunging or derring-do. He stayed out of the hand if he didn't like his cards.

Fanita English told us that Eric played poker with her son Brian on one occasion and that she had talked to Berne about poker more than once: "I can't tell you that I saw the books, but Eric claimed he kept separate books on poker from all his other accounts and all his other sources of income, and thereby he could prove to himself that he was a winner. Because on the total year's poker budget, he always ended up with a plus. There was no year that he ended up with a minus.

"In another way, it was pathetic. He claimed that he was using poker as a method of observing others, but to me it was a sad way of reassuring himself."

He did not play for camaraderie. None of the regulars in the Carmel group felt close to him even after twenty years of playing together. They did have a "memorial poker game" in his honor right after he died, but that was all the personal involvement that the members indulged in. It is as if poker acted for Berne in the same way psychiatry did—it afforded him an opportunity to observe people under stress without becoming personally involved, and it certainly fed his mystique about winning.

13

"The Dorothy Who Did Not Understand"

> Knowing that Santa Claus is just Father is the beginning of wisdom. Knowing that your husband is just Santa Claus, so that you don't expect him to be real or there every night, is the end.
>
> Eric Berne, *Sex in Human Loving*
>
> . . . the Duke of Logreus and the Lady of the Green Castle parted later on the most friendly terms.
>
> James Branch Cabell *Jurgen*

At mid-century it appeared that the young psychiatrist from Sainte Famille Street in Montreal had fulfilled the family recipe:

He had graduated from one of the world's foremost medical schools, McGill.

He lived in one of the most "in" towns on the West Coast: Carmel, California.

He was married to a beautiful heiress.

He had published a best-seller, the popularized Freudian handbook *The Mind in Action*, for which A.A. Brill, the *fons et origo* of Freudian orthodoxy in America, had written the introduction.

He was in didactic analysis with Erik Erikson and expected to be accepted soon as a member by the San Francisco Psychoanalytic Institute.

He had a comfortable psychiatric practice in Carmel and claimed to be the only psychiatrist in America practicing in a village of less than 5000 population.

His book *The Mind in Action* gave no hint of defection from strict Freudian principles. His two mentors, Federn and Erikson, both had their problems adhering to the Freudian line but had stayed within the fold. Berne expected to do the same.

But there are some things that the human spirit can't hide. His inability to cloak himself with the mantle of orthodoxy was apparent to the San Francisco Freudians. He and his childhood acquaintance, psychiatrist Gerald Goodstone, were both taking their didactic analysis at the same time. Berne asked Goodstone how he was coming along with his training. Goodstone replied, "Fine, how are you coming along?"

Eric then said, "Well, I don't think I'll ever be a member."

The problem seemed to be that in his analysis he would tell his three training analysts that he was dealing with a lot of his material using extrasensory perception, according to Goodstone.

Eric said: "They'll either throw me out or make you a member long before they make me a member."

Goodstone was aghast. He thought this was one of Eric's typical self-destructive maneuvers, so reminiscent of Lennie's adolescent behavioral oddities (see Chapter 8, "Crazy" Lennie.) He asked Berne, "Why do you do it?"

Berne replied, "Well, that's the way I feel about it and that's the way I have to handle it."

Dr. Donald Shaskan, a friend of Berne's who was later a chief of the Veterans Administration Psychiatric Clinic in San Francisco and for a time Berne's boss, was a candidate at the Psychoanalytic Institute in the early fifties. He remembered Eric's being in certain classes that he attended and said that he didn't think Berne deliberately insulted anybody. "I didn't see him do that, but he made it very clear to his mentors and everybody else at the Institute that when Hans Selye came to town he would far rather have heard Hans Selye speak than to attend Institute functions. He didn't realize how important it was to be tactful."

Berne's close friend Dr. Lawrence Levitin was taking his didactic analysis at the San Francisco Institute at the same time as Berne, and his relationship with the Institute was terminated at about the same time, but for different reasons.

At any rate, according to Levitin, Berne was advised by the

San Francisco Institute that he was not eligible for membership. The exact date of this occurrence is not known. According to Dorothy, he was told that perhaps after three years of supervised analysis of another patient and additional training he might apply again.

This was a terrible blow to Berne. He had not only subjected himself to the weekly visits to the San Francisco Bay area, and paid the cost of his didactic analysis—"over 300 hours of training,"—but also he had taken away time from his own patients in order to go into this training.

Mel Boyce, one of the early TA adherents, says that Berne's script was the same as Freud's. Berne, in *What Do You Say After You Say Hello?*, described Freud's script as that of a hard worker who decided to be a great man but who, when he tried to get into the Establishment, was refused admittance. "So he decided to look into Hell instead. There was no Establishment there, and no one was paying any attention to it. So he became an authority on Hell, which in that instance was the Unconscious. He was so successful that after a while he became the Establishment."

With the loss of the orthodox psychoanalytic connection, Berne threw himself into developing his own system. Dorothy said: "I think he was very happy the first years we were married—until things started to change. He began dreaming up this TA—this was really a huge thing to start to prove. Everything changed and he threw himself into that and it meant that he had to work every night until about two in the morning. His home life just went by the board. He got home from the city on a Thursday and saw a couple of patients—got home from that about seven and was out in his workshop by eight and worked out there from four to five hours. And then he would wake me up and read me what he had written, and I wasn't the best audience that ever was, at that hour of the morning."

When Dorothy found that one book followed another and more and more time was being taken up by the burgeoning TA movement, she felt the whole arrangement was grossly unfair. She told us "it wasn't in the contract" for him to devote himself to TA and have no time for the family. When they married, he had been simply a practicing psychiatrist, and she felt his involvement in this new venture was at the expense of normal family life. She said:

"For years afterwards he said he had given in to my 'whim' for a divorce—there was no reason for wanting it. He just simply felt that I should have been completely self-effacing! And I wasn't about to do it. You see, I don't revere Eric for the work he did in the same way that an awful lot of people do, and none of my children do, and for this I'm really glad. However we feel about him is about his personality, his personal charm, but certainly not for the work he did. It took a lot out of me and it took a lot out of the kids.

"You see," Dorothy continued, "Eric doing all that writing didn't endear himself to us. You know, we really didn't give a damn about the books. We felt that if he wanted to be a psychiatrist, he ought to be satisfied to be a good psychiatrist and write his reports for the journals and if what he wanted to be was going to take up his entire life, that he could pay for a housekeeper.

"I was no help to him whatsoever. I was no inspiration. I didn't set out to be. I felt very gypped because he didn't keep his contract to me that he made before we got married. . . . It was really a sterile existence. . . . As time went by I got more griped about it all the time."

TA people got to know another side of Eric from the side that she and the children knew, Dorothy felt. "They sort of deify him. It's kind of hard for his family. We had a more down-to-earth attitude toward Eric."

In some respects Dorothy had been very supportive of Berne's commitment to psychiatry. When Berne's first analyst Paul Federn was old and ill, he telephoned Berne from New York. His beloved wife of many years had died, he was facing a third cancer operation, and he sounded extremely depressed. Berne, with the encouragement of Dorothy, proposed that Federn come out and live with them in Carmel. Federn turned down the offer, "although he had no one left," and subsequently committed suicide. Dorothy still has the letter Federn wrote thanking them for the offer of a refuge, which he appreciated but felt he couldn't accept.

From the early fifties on, Berne's contact with his family was slight. Not only was he out of town from Tuesday to Thursday (Monday to Thursday in his psychoanalytic days), but his Friday night poker game with his Carmel male friends was also a weekly ritual. His vacations were usually spent solo, in faraway places. An article in some scientific journal was very often a by-product of these trips. However, one of his sons told us that Eric used to spend a great deal of time catering to his interests, such as skin-diving, fishing, rebuilding old radio cabinets, and going to the airport to watch the planes.

Dorothy had reported to a friend that she and Eric had a very good physical relationship. "She made no bones about it," said Carol Steinbeck Brown. "She is the soul of candor." But the pair was separated by Eric's work habits and Dorothy's care of the children. Mrs. Betty Burney, their housekeeper, told us, "The divorce could have been both their faults. It could have been—she was too wrapped up in her children to go with him, you know, when he was traveling. . . . She seemed to me a pretty perfect mother."

Dorothy expressed disgust at some of the Carmel parties "where married men could be found in the bushes, kissing other men's wives. People even brought their kids to these affairs. I would never have brought mine."

But there were other stresses in the marriage. Dorothy's daughter, Roxana—the one who practiced pliés to The Nutcracker Suite—was killed in an automobile accident when she was just fifteen years old. Eric wouldn't allow Dorothy "any period of mourning. . . . He didn't want it to intrude into his life, his schedule," said Dorothy (even though Eric, too, was very upset). He was "so impatient with the whole thing—so anxious to get on with his own work."

Frank Lloyd thought the marriage was never the same after the blow it received that night. Virginia Mitchell, who was Berne's first office assistant and associate therapist, said that Eric was "absolutely devastated" by the wreck and its aftermath. He was crying and very bitter about the teenager who drove the car. TA's Dr. John Dusay told us that later on in a lecture Berne said that "the death of a child is something from which the parents never recover."

In *Transactional Analysis in Psychotherapy* Berne described the personality of Dr. Quint, a social scientist, who like himself was an observer: ". . .in time of need he could neither father his wife nor offer his students paternal inspiration." This type of personality Berne characterized as that of an "excluding Adult" in that it functioned almost solely as a data processor. Berne often said that a person who has lost a parent early in life, as he did, is unable to function fully in his parental capacities.

At about this time, too, Berne's careful observation of how people had fun at social gatherings got a little jumbled in his data processor—what his computer may not have picked up was that there is a difference between hormone-happy adolescents and a middle-aged psychiatrist at a dude ranch. Among the memorabilia left in Berne's office at his death was a cartoon of two teen-aged glamorettes sitting beside a swimming pool. The one with harlequin glasses says to her blonde friend: "Herb hasn't pushed me off the side of the swimming pool all week. I wonder if there's someone else?"

The cartoon dates from the 1960 edition of a San Francisco paper, but it undoubtedly was clipped by Berne because it brought back memories of an incident mentioned in the *Monterey Peninsula Herald* on August 16, 1956. The article reported that Eric Berne, a Carmel psychiatrist, was being sued for $36,173 by a Mrs. Hildretha Chase, operator of the Chase School for Boys at Thousand Palms, California. The complaint alleged that on September 2, 1955, the psychiatrist had "beat her and kicked her, inflicting on her contusions and lacerations, hemorrhaging of the leg and nervous shock."

According to Dr. Goodstone, Eric called him up when he came through Los Angeles sometime after this incident. Goodstone asked how things were going.

Eric answered: "Things are going beautifully. I threw a woman in a pool and she's suing me for a quarter of a million dollars."

"I asked him, 'Why did you do that?' and Eric claimed she did something or said something he didn't like, so he just pushed her in the swimming pool."

Some of Berne's Carmel friends said they understood the story was that Eric was tussling with a woman at the side of the pool. Berne threw her in the pool, and it was that woman who had landed on the injured party.

As the lawsuit dragged on, the financial aspects of the prank began to bother Berne. Members of his Carmel poker-playing coterie remember Berne's mentioning it worriedly over a number of years. The eventual outcome is unknown, but five years later Berne mentioned in a letter to his sister Grace that a judge had awarded $3300 to a woman who had been suing him.

The next incident wasn't amusing either. Berne was called upon by the government to prove that he wasn't a security risk. Berne's contract as consultant to the Veterans Administration came up for renewal at the height of the McCarthy malaise. The government decided to call for a hearing to determine whether it could still continue to employ this successful and sought-after northern California consultant.

Berne had to write to various old friends, mentors, and colleagues for testimonials. He was able to line up a couple of hospital chiefs, a retired colonel, and a corporation lawyer. He also asked Dr. Albert Lapin, well-known Montreal cardiologist and old-boy McGill compatriot, to provide a notarized affidavit.

Eric, it is true, had associated—strictly as an onlooker—with Trotskyists in his youth in New Haven and had been a roomer of Marie Short, who was "left-wing, to say the least." However (Berne wrote Lapin), it was probably the fact that he was a member of the American Civil Liberties Union, had talked to certain suspicious colleagues at medical meetings, and had refused to sign a loyalty oath, that had put the witch hunters on his trail.

During his San Francisco Psychoanalytic Institute period, Berne had formed a warm friendship with an interesting couple, Dr. Lawrence Levitin and his wife, Evelyn. Lawrence and Eric usually had dinner at Maye's Oyster House after their sessions at the Institute were over. (Berne always ordered boiled—not broiled—salmon.) Eric soon became an habitué of the Levitin house, a big, gracious place in the lovely Forest Hill section of San Francisco. Sometimes he called up and invited himself to dinner—he was always welcome.

Mrs. Levitin was a radiologist, practicing as Dr. Evelyn Siris. She had taught at Stanford and had often talked with Berne about his ambition to develop a workable system for making x-rays in color.

The Levitins were among the first to get acquainted with Dorothy. The four double-dated at a medical-meeting dance in Los Angeles, during which Dorothy and Eric decided they would get married. Eric broke the news to the Levitins this way: "I want you to meet my wife." Actually it was a year and a half before the nuptials took place.

Lawrence and Evelyn both said, "Eric loved us, and we loved him." The feeling among some TA people that Eric was incapable of real intimacy surprised Levitin.

Subsequently, Lawrence said both he and Eric refused to sign a loyalty oath. He added: "The Eric I knew wasn't at all skittish about taking a stand."

At the time of the VA hearing Eric wrote a letter to Dr. Albert Lapin, dated 4 April, 1955, in which he said that his contracts with the army and the Veterans Administration came due for reexecution when McCarthyism was at its peak and now, much later, his hearing was coming up to prove he wasn't a danger to the government.

He said he was asking people who had known him since high school days to reassure the government that he wouldn't reveal to Communist spies the fact that one of his VA patients was suffering from night sweats and grinding his teeth and that no glamorous blonde spy would be able to wrest the secret from him even under threats of performing on him several infamous crimes against nature specifically mentioned.

He signed it "Hubsch." Lapin told us that "Hubsch" was a standard signature that both of them used in their letters, a leftover habit from college days. Somewhere along the line it had amused them to find that an awkward German word stood for "handsome," and it amused them even more to adopt it and apply it to themselves.

Lapin did write a supporting letter, and Shaskan, Eric's boss at the Veterans Administration, believes that Berne was probably cleared. Eric's insistence that the burgeoning TA movement should not become involved in political struggles may have come partly from this experience.

Among the critics of this apoliticalism was Robert Coles,

whose blistering attack on *Games People Play* in *The New York Times* bore down heavily on TA's "shallow . . . self-centered . . . insulting" philosophy, "the cult of self," and Berne's obliviousness to the general misery of the masses.

But Berne had his own way of doing things. Not only did he resolutely take a stand on the loyalty oath, but he continued his open support of the American Civil Liberties Union and subscribed to its magazine for years after this hearing took place. He and Dorothy and the Levitins remained good friends throughout the years. Eric called Evelyn and also talked to Lawrence from the hospital the week before he died.

Rarely does an outsider know what really causes a marriage to be troubled, and even the principals themselves often are baffled.

"Quite a few times," Dorothy said, "I literally fled. When [our younger boy] was two years old [1957], Eric came home and we were all gone. . . . I had moved out of the house completely, crib and all, moved two blocks away, without telling him. The [older boy] was five; he was in kindergarten. I had it all planned. The minute Eric left in the morning, I had this man who used to work in the garden—he rented a U-Haul and took us up to this little furnished house I had rented.

"Marie [Short] arrived at 9. [Marie delighted in matchmaking, but she also highly enjoyed matchbreaking, according to Virginia Mitchell.] We just went en masse with all the things we thought we needed, like the skillet and the toaster. Eric came home, no note, nothing. I did quite a lot of this running away over the years. . . . I felt I was being slowly destroyed."

We asked Dorothy what happened after she moved out of the house.

"Well, I stayed a couple of days, and then I called him to let him know where we were, you know. He had no idea. And he would come over and get [the older boy] and take him to the Carmel Woods School for kindergarten. And I hated the rented house so much that as soon as Eric left for work I came over here [to the house on Carpenter Street] and brought [our younger boy] and spent the day here, making Eric's bed, naturally, and washing the breakfast dishes. We ate over here and then about four o'clock I'd go home. . . .

"And then Eric got sick; he had to have an operation [gall bladder] and then there was going to be a dance of a psychiatric society at the Naval Postgraduate School and a lot of our friends were coming down and Eric said, 'Please, won't you go, because they'll all be asking about you,' and I did, and then he said, 'Please won't you come home again, and—' "

She did move back, and Berne made an effort to change. "And it would be all great for just a few days and then he would get back to the same old thing. There was no way he would change . . . and he made me so dependent on him, financially and otherwise, that I had to ask for everything."

At Berne's suggestion, Dorothy began going to San Francisco to see a strict Freudian analyst, "sweating it out for four hours a week."

It was not so simple as Berne implies in *Sex in Human Loving,* written some years later. There, he complained:

> Women and their mysterious ways. Griping and nagging and then knitting you a sweater and cooking your favorite chicken. Saying they will not stay with you another day, and then, if you say, "My, you look beautiful this morning!" they will stay with you forever. But once you are truly bound together by children, all this is less important, and then what?

The results of the psychoanalytic treatment were unexpected. Berne had urged Dorothy to go but was indignant when the upshot was that she decided to get a divorce. "I couldn't believe I would do it, but my analyst made me believe I could. . . . Eric wrote him a letter about it. The analyst said: "You can tell your dear husband for me that if he thinks I'm going to change you so you can live with him and put up with this, he's mistaken. I'm just going to strengthen what you already know, which is that you should be divorced from him and lead your own life."

Later Eric remarked in *Sex in Human Loving,* "No man is a hero to his wife's psychiatrist."

The divorce came in 1963. By this time there were transactional analysts proficient in marital therapy. But the fountainhead of TA was hardly in a position to submit his problems to one of his disciples. Later, however, he said that psychoanalyis is inadequate for marriage counseling—it lacks the proper tools for the purpose; to get results it is necessary to use transactional analysis instead.

When Dorothy went to court to get her divorce in 1963, California divorce law still required a finding of fault on the part of one of the spouses. She had a difficult time making a case. Judge Anthony Brazil said to her: "'I don't see how I can give you a divorce, Mrs. Berne, unless you tell me more than you are telling me.'

"My lawyer was champing at the bit, and I was saying, 'I will not say anything nasty! I will not have that kind of thing.' So anyway, Judge Brazil was kind of sweet about it and he said, 'Well, I can see I'm not going to get anything out of you, and I'm just going to have to read between the lines—I'm sure you wouldn't have come in here without a good reason.'"

That night Eric moved across the street, where he had rented a little blue house, "as it wasn't legal any more. But he didn't have any furniture; so I helped him, got a bed out of the attic, and my children and their friends moved my chest of drawers out of my room, gave him dishes and made up his bed with my linen. I'll never forget my clothes in neat stacks on the floor. But I felt sorry for him. I couldn't help myself. . . . Oh, it was terrible, too. . . . We really were devoted to each other, but I literally had to do it. I had no identity whatsoever. . . .

"I can't tell you how many years it took me to unwind from that kind of life. . . . He always told the kids—he'd sit right here at the table and say: 'I'd still be here if your mother hadn't kicked me out.'

"Anyway I was never sorry I divorced him. I was never unhappy after I divorced him. We remained fantastically good friends, you know. He lived across the street for three years.

"He came over every morning [he was in town] and kissed me goodbye. He called me up every morning at eleven and every night he'd come up the driveway at seven o'clock and sit down and eat dinner—for three solid years, until I was beginning to have dates. Suddenly I said, 'I just can't stand this any more!

We're not married; we're not married, really—and we're not divorced. It can't go on!'

"It was great for the kids, of course; they didn't notice any difference. They thought it was pretty funny. If they wanted to go see him, I just said, 'Watch out crossing the street.' Eric was in the back garden using his study and in the refrigerator getting 7-Up. He ate up all my cookies—life was still going on. He never rang my doorbell—he just walked in."

Sometimes, Berne would get a crab at the wharf and make dinner for Dorothy and the boys, and afterwards Dorothy "would be over at his house cleaning up."

After two years of this, Dorothy decided to take the children and move to Coronado Island, near San Diego. Her departure was delayed for six weeks because Berne got appendicitis followed by an embolism. When he got out of the hospital, Dorothy took care of him. He flew down to spend Thanksgiving and Christmas with her and the family. Dorothy told Eric she was already homesick and longed to return to Carmel, but not with him living across the street. Eric agreed to move and found a house on Hatton Road, not far away. They wanted one nearby so the children wouldn't have too far to go on their bicycles nor would they have to be chauffeured.

"It was terrible for Eric—the divorce, and all that happened afterwards resulted from that."

Eric's comments on divorce in *Sex in Human Loving* were bitter indeed:

> Middle-class husbands are like appliances. They come with a manual of instructions which you are supposed to read before you install them. They are guaranteed by the Church and Good Housekeeping, but the guarantee is void if you don't follow the instructions. There are maintenance manuals on every newstand telling you how to keep them oiled properly. And when you have worn one out, madam, you can turn him in for a good price at the courthouse, after which you can stop worrying and send your clothes to the laundry. Then you will have plenty of free time on your hands, which you can use to sit around the house and bite your nails.

Middle-class wives are also like appliances. . . . The difference is that instead of your wearing her out, sir, she wears you out, and instead of your turning her in and getting part of your money back, she turns you in and you have to keep up the payments. What kind of washing machine is that? No wonder some men prefer the laundromat.

The payments Eric had to keep up after his second divorce were more impressive than those from his first—$1200 monthly. Even so, Dorothy divorced him just before *Games* came out, so her share of the community property was considerably less than what she would have been entitled to if she'd waited a while. Dorothy pointed this out to Carol Steinbeck Brown one day in the aisles of the local Safeway—"which passes in these parts for the Groves of Academe," said Carol.

Dorothy hated *Games* anyway ("it took eight years out of my life"). Eric had been "very resentful" of her attitude about that; he had said, "I don't want you ever to benefit one cent from that book." She added: "I wasn't about to fight with him about the money."

"At that point," Carol said, "Dorothy had separated from Eric half a dozen times—it was off again, on again."

It was on again, too, during the interlocutory period of the divorce. In an effort at reconciliation, Berne persuaded Dorothy to leave the children with her capable housekeeper and fly away with him to Europe. They had a marvelous time there, all by themselves. Dorothy enjoyed playing the mistress role, free from household cares. On the plane from England to San Francisco, Berne said wistfully—and his eyes were moist—"I know we're going back to what we were. It'll never be the same."

The day after they got home, they went to the beach with the children. Lying in the sand, Eric turned toward Dorothy with tears running down his cheeks. "It's not the same," he said, anguished. "It'll never be the same!" He said if he called his lawyer and told him they had been living together the divorce would be void, but Dorothy begged him not to do it. "There was no way we could handle marriage with the children in the house," she said. "Even with the kids, he would come home and countermand everything I had told them."

Several years after they had been divorced, Dorothy woke up in the middle of the night. Eric was standing at the foot of her bed in the moonlight, gazing intently at her. He must have let himself in with his old latchkey. She didn't know how long he had been there and she was too sleepy to wake up properly and ask him what he wanted.

Besides, the next time she opened her eyes, the apparition had vanished, leaving behind not so much as a wisp of smoke.

Eric's second wife Dorothy (c. 1955).

Eric exercising on beach in Guadeloupe.

Eric on lawn of his Carmel house, Torre period.

Eric and Torre (c. 1967). Photo by Kurt Hartman.

Eric and Torre arriving for the Young Presidents' Organization Conference, Hawaii, 1969.

Group picture of TA members at a summer conference (c. 1966). Back row, l. to r.: Ray Poindexter, Mel Boyce, unidentified member, Jack Dusay, Tom Harris, Jacqui Schiff, Ellen Berne, Ken Everts, Viola Callaghan, Bill Collins, Joe Concannon. Front row, l. to r.: Fanita English, Mary Goulding, Gordon Haiberg, Frank Ernst, Hedges Capers, Zelig Selinger, Steve Karpman, Martin Groder, unidentified member. Foreground right: Dave Kupfer, Claude Steiner. Photo by Eric W. Cheney.

Eric Berne and Fritz Perls.

At the Vienna Conference, l. to r.: Jack Dusay, Pam Blum, Eric Berne, Claude Steiner.

14

The Unsinkable Dr. Berne

> *I was born with a something lacking that is requisite for anyone who aspires to be as thoroughly misled as most people and you will have to love me in spite of it.*
> James Branch Cabell, *Jurgen*
>
> I don't think Eric would have made it in an establishment situation. He couldn't have stood it to work patiently from within.
> Rachmiel Levine

About the time he left the Psychoanalytic Institute, Eric seems to have dreamed a dream that was so disturbing that he broke one of the cardinal rules group therapists followed at that time: "Don't get too familiar with your group."

In a manuscript evidently intended for publication, Eric recounted the story of "Ben," a psychiatrist. On October 21, 1952, Ben revealed one of his own dreams to his patients, saying that a band of brigands was chasing him with guns and he holed up in an elevator where he found friendly people. The friendly people symbolized his therapy group while the brigands were the older established therapists who were critical of his methods. He admitted that it was not at all the usual thing for a psychiatrist to discuss his own dreams in his group. Although there was nothing harmful about such revelations, it was not standard practice.

After the meeting was over Ben talked about the incident with his co-therapist. Possibly without realizing it he had wanted sympathy and support from his group, he said, and that might make the members feel fearful. The last time he had been with his training analysts he had spoken out too strongly about his opinions, and then afterwards had told them he was sorry for having been so abrasive. His analyst said not to worry, he was used to that sort of thing and it didn't bother him. This remark apparently made Ben feel worse and was the main cause of his agitation.

The cocky façade that Berne assumed may have led others to think that he was indifferent to the crushing blows he received in the fifties, but he couldn't fool his nightmares.

Dr. "H," a prominent teaching member of the Psychoanalytic Institute, who asked us not to identify him, was very good about giving us an interview, although some people told us he would simply refuse to talk to us. We were attempting to find out as much as we could about Berne's departure from the Institute, the date of which that organization had been unable to clarify. A member had written for this information on our behalf, but the Institute had replied that it no longer kept such data. The Institute doesn't retain its records for more than five years. Eric's analyst, Erik Erikson, also had (understandably) declined to comment.

On the book jacket of *A Layman's Guide to Psychiatry and Psychonalysis* [1957] Berne had stated that he had continued his training with the San Francisco Institute until 1956. Both the Canadian and American *Who's Who* variously listed him as in training with the Institute until 1956 or 1957. But several people we interviewed had told us he had finished his training at an earlier date.

Dr. H warned us against the use of the word "finished." "Terminated" was the appropriate word, he indicated. Then he added, "God knows why Berne said that. I know he terminated long before that." He said the Institute would never challenge Berne, never write to the newspapers and say that he was misrepresenting himself. "But," said Dr. H, "I don't think he did it because no one would challenge him. I think he did it for the kudos he would get for having been with the Institute that long."

In late 1952 or early 1953, Dr. H became a member of the education committee which evaluated candidates at the Institute—he consulted his notebooks to be certain of the dates—and at that time Berne had already left the Institute. "He was no longer a factor and his case was not even being discussed. He was never even mentioned during the rest of the 1950s," said H.

Dr. H continued: "Somebody put out a story that Berne was kicked out of the Institute because of his unorthodox ideas. I don't know who could have put out such a story if it weren't Berne himself. But it wasn't true. I don't think Berne was kicked out because of nonadherence to dogma, unorthodoxy, or not sticking to the party-line. My feeling is that it was because of the severity of Berne's personal problems—the intensity of his personal problems."

In a later telephone conversation and also in a letter H amplified his remarks: "I recall the only meeting of the Education Committee where his name came up. It was in the early fifties when the then chairman said that in net effect Berne had withdrawn and we should not expect any letter of resignation from him. I am certain that he was not asked to resign or withdraw from training. I can date this because of where the meeting was held in the old Institute offices prior to the move to Sutter Street." He also said "My hunch is that Berne was told that he would never make a good analyst."

(While this may seem confusing there are evidently fine distinctions to be made. Apparently it wouldn't be appropriate to use the word "finished," because he didn't actually complete the training. But the institute didn't terminate Berne, according to this version; Berne terminated his studies there when confronted with the probability that he would never be accredited as a psychoanalyst by the institute.)

Dr. H added that Berne, so far as he knew, "never even got to the point where he analyzed a patient. I doubt that he ever did supervised work."

Berne had other mini-disasters and failed sagas in the fifties. In 1953 he lost his job at Fort Ord. Mt. Zion psychiatrist Haskel Bazell told us: "I arrived at Fort Ord in August of 1953 and Berne was still a consultant there then. That was very short-lived because there were allegations of some left-wing connections. It was around the fall of 1953 that this crystallized. It's my impression that it was only a couple of months that he was still a consultant for us at the Mental Health Consultation Service. Berne spoke to me in rather bitter terms about having been fired from the job."

The army apparently fired first and found out why later. The government hearing, which also jeopardized his position as a consultant for the Veterans Administration, was held two years later, and probably cleared him; however, he never worked for the army after 1954 nor for the Veterans Administation after 1956.

It was perhaps as a result of these investigations that Berne's group notes of June 25, 1953, indicated that upsets in his personal life were giving him insomnia.

Bazell said, "Eric was well-liked, in some quarters, anyway; he was bright and had elaborate language skills." And besides, "he had a good sense of humor." Bazell added: "Eric was among the brighter people I have known, and I have known quite a few bright ones."

This was the decade in which Eric had made a lot of "mistakes." He had made the "mistake" of being too independent and cocky around the Institute. He had made the "mistake" of being too overtly "liberal" in refusing to sign a loyalty oath. He had made the "mistake" of throwing a woman in a swimming pool, etc. However, he was able to be philosophical about mistakes when the subject came up in a group on June 29, 1953. Berne took the position that some mistakes were inevitable and not always preventable. Also he didn't propose to dwell on each parapraxis, Freudian style. He said that one had choices. One could retreat into a shell and be very cast down, or one could figure out how to do things differently the next time.

He noted that it is when a machine goes wrong that we find out how it runs. A talking parakeet, he said, can be drilled into repeating phrases faultlessly; it never makes a mistake, but also never learns anything further. And if a person takes lessons, she may learn what the teacher teaches but nothing more. It is only when people strike out for themselves that they make mistakes—and learn.

This was advice which Berne himself followed during this period. Six months later, on November 24, 1953, he made what he considered a grievous error, which he carefully analyzed in order to avoid repeating it.

He had tried to curry favor with a newcomer at the expense of his old group. The new patient attacked the way Berne's group operated. She contended that group members had to go back to their childhood traumas and find out how they felt toward their parents and siblings.

She accused the doctor of not being forceful enough. Instead of meeting her challenge head-on, the doctor was conciliatory, while the regular group members hotly resisted her ideas. His notes reflected his concern that he did not ward off the agitation this attack caused the group. He discussed it with his co-therapist, Mrs. Y.

As a parting sally, the new patient said she didn't know whether she would come back to the group or not. Berne felt the important question was whether the *other* group members would drop out or return. It would be more of a compliment to his co-therapist than to him if they came back.

But the group's warm feelings toward the doctor would probably win out. His final assessment was that the group grew closer together as a result of this outsider's attack on their unpsychoanalytic way of doing things. They were able to take it and defended him—but the fact that he seemed to side with her he considered inexcusable.

Berne's own approach at this point consisted of a blend of conventional group methods with strong emphasis on intuition and ESP. Dr. Benjamin Weininger, who was at one time a training analyst for the Psychoanalytic Society, told us: "Eric was having trouble getting accepted by the . . . Society. I gather that since he believed in extra-sensory perception that was one of the stumbling blocks to being accepted. He discussed extra-sensory perception with me—at that time Jules Eisenbud from Colorado was the only analyst sympathetic to and interested in this kind of work." Dr. Weininger was friendly with Berne over a number of years and Berne mentioned him in the Acknowledgements in *The Structure and Dynamics of Organizations and Groups*.

Berne also retained Freudian concepts but mixed them with budding TA insights. It was a period of germination and confusion. In September 1954 he started a rudimentary Transactional Analysis group composed of patients with borderline psychoses, patients who had recovered from a psychosis, or who were suffering from an out-and-psychosis.

Earlier in 1954 he had become very discouraged and complained that Transactional Analysis didn't work (group notes, January 25, 1954). It seemed to him to be more like transference analysis, at least with the women—all transactions taking place between the group leader (Berne) and the patients—instead of with each other. The men's group seemed to have some transactions taking place between the members. On March 12, 1954, the notes contained the plaintive remark that he had lost his touch. On March 16, he was disgusted with group therapy. But there must be some way of doing it, he felt, and so he plowed ahead.

Sometime before 1960, Berne's seminar for the training of residents at Mt. Zion was phased out. This was due to another "mistake." Berne had not been psychoanalytic enough in his approach to the group. He had had been running it with a young doctor assisting him since the early 1950s, but had steadfastly refused to occupy himself with the housekeeping and administrative chores, throwing all the burden of such things on his assistant.

It was the only seminar at Mt. Zion in which group therapy teaching methods were expounded, and both staff and outsiders eagerly attended, according to Maggie Northcott. She remembers the excitement and enthusiasm the seminar engendered, and yet there was a day, in perhaps late 1959 or early 1960, when Berne came in with the news that the following year, Mt. Zion would offer no more group therapy seminars for residents. His assistant asked Berne: "What reasons did they give you?" Berne paused significantly and then answered: "I forget."

A Dr. J, who is highly placed on the psychiatric staff at Mt. Zion but who does not wish to be identified, told us that Mt. Zion is the only open-staff hospital in the area and that Berne or any other doctor was perfectly welcome to do group therapy there if he wished, as Mt. Zion was very tolerant of unorthodox ideas. In fact Berne gave a lecture at Mt. Zion on his version of ego states in 1952 or 1953, according to Dr. J's recollection. About a year later Berne gave a second lecture at Mt. Zion—his first presentation to the public of the concept of Transactional

Analysis, according to Dr. J. Dr. Haskel Bazell said that it may have been true that Mt. Zion welcomed group therapy, but "there were others who felt otherwise."

Mary Goulding, who was taking her M.S.W. training at Mt. Zion, had still another point of reference. She said the hospital higher-ups "did not like anybody on their staff to go to Berne's meetings. I listened to his first lecture on Parent, Adult, and Child, and my supervisor said, 'I suggest you do not go any more, it will only confuse you.' Since I was already in hot water for doing dreams with patients and all kinds of things that social workers aren't supposed to do, I decided that would be the last straw. So I didn't attend and neither did anyone else from Mt. Zion whom I knew."

Bazell continued: "I remember Eric as having been a little perplexed about being squeezed out of the seminars. My recollection is that they were abruptly stopped and my impression was that they weren't sufficiently analytic to satisfy the people who were running the show at the time." He added: "I believe one reason Eric was kicked out from so many places was because he was cocky and people like to put cocky people down."

After the seminars for the residents and staff on how to do group therapy ended, Eric kept on with his own TA therapy group at Mt. Zion until 1962, when he transferred it to the McAuley Neuropsychiatric Clinic. Clinical social worker Jules Levaggi reported that Berne stated "that the psychiatric staff [at Mt. Zion] conveyed a displeasure in his techniques and the presentation of his theories. [Mt. Zion] was committed to an individual psycho-analytic approach and had very little time apportioned to group therapy. . . . Eric sought out Dr. [Michael T.] Khlentzos because he had heard of the work in group therapy that was going on at McAuley Institute."

Interspersed with the gloomy downs of the period were a few reassuring ups. Berne could take comfort in the fact that some of his clients swore by him. A whole group, which had become acquainted with his style as a therapist in Ogden, Utah, in 1946, when he was stationed at an army hospital nearby, pulled up stakes and moved 668 miles to California when he moved. He had led the group for only thirteen weeks, and was not the army doctor who had started the group, but seven persons crossed several deserts and sierras to be with him and stayed with him almost seven years. Berne wrote up some of the details of this group in a journal, but the excitement of the hegira and the implied compliment to Berne as a therapist are missing. One of the four group members we interviewed told us that this "Seven Year Group" "loved him dearly," and "he had a powerful effect on. . .our lives."

Way back in 1952, shortly before he "terminated" from the Institute, Eric was already using terms that were later to become key words in TA parlance. On July 1 and October 28, 1952, Berne's San Francisco group notes mentioned "transactions" and "games." He described "Let's You and Him Fight" as a needling transaction. On October 7, 1952, and a year later in September, 1953, he went rather deeply into "script" theory. He told the group that people act out scripts they adopt in childhood. They act the same drama over and over, changing the cast of characters to include new acquaintances. But the scenario is based on early attitudes toward one's parents or siblings. Ambivalent feelings toward the mother, for instance, could cause the mother role to be divided into several parts and played by more than one player. If there were only one woman in the person's life, he could sometimes hate her, sometimes love her. If there were two women he could hate one consistently and love the other. If there were more than two, he could subdivide his feelings even further. On June 30, 1953, Berne was exploring the Adult-Child relationship (the Parent wasn't in the picture at this point). He said that instead of six people in the group there were really twelve since each one of them had an Adult and a Child. On July 14, 1953, he wrote that he was in process of formulating a new theory of group psychology. On October 13, 1953, a few months later, he called his new approach "The Transactional System of Group Therapy."

Virginia Mitchell, one of the first social workers Berne supervised in private practice, reports that the Parent, Adult, and Child theory seemed to be germinating in 1951-1955 but wasn't actively discussed in the Carmel group which she audited. He had her keeping notes of the group sessions, but not until a day or so elapsed. He felt that tape recorders "interfered with the flow" at this point and suggested she "wait a few days and consolidate her memories before writing the notes down."

Virginia said: "I think Eric taught me more than any person I ever worked with, and not in any didactic way at all. He was trying to teach me not just to listen but to conceptualize what these people were like as children. He seemed to have an intuitive understanding of the person and would give them back what they needed. He had a positive genius for seeing where the person was at and what he or she was looking for.

"In spite of the fact that our supervisory hours were sparse, he shaped my practice in ways for which I am grateful. "First of all, he set out to free me from psychiatric jargon. . . . This distaste for 'lingo' has stayed with me, although in later settings I had to try to readapt . . . lest I be seen as a 'dummy' by my psychoanalytically oriented friends.

"Even more important than language, however, he suggested that I pay less attention to the content of the interview and more to facial expression . . . and body movement. I remember his saying 'try to imagine what the person was experiencing as a child, by observing eyes, mouth, hands, feet and voice tone. I found to my amazement that I began to see and hear people differently."

The Eric Berne of those days had "great timidities," and Virginia believed his TA theories were partly a means of working his way out of his own difficulties.

When she first started working with him, he got an invitation to speak to the local PTA "and he was just appalled at the idea of speaking in public." But Virginia encouraged him to go ahead and make speeches. He tried it a couple of times, and one day, maybe in 1952, he said elatedly: "I did get up and talk at the meeting of the Mental Health Association and now I feel I can do anything!"

"To listen to him speak, you'd never have known he had stage fright," said Virginia. "He was a marvelous speaker even then."

She told us: "When I first met Eric I thought he was a cold, forbidding person. But I was willing to go along with the situation because he was connected with and recommended by the Psychoanalytic Association."

Later, in TA days, Eric "was a different person, much more carefree and boyish . . . he changed greatly . . . for the better . . . emerging as a warm, loving human being instead of a reserved psychiatrist. The TA people had an entirely different impression of him."

There were other indications that Eric must have changed. Two psychotherapists, friends of TA's Mel Boyce, told Mel that in those days they had considered Eric "just an ordinary, third-rate psychiatrist," having completely missed the signals of future greatness.

Not everybody was busy battering Berne in the fifties. Joe Concannon picked him up on his antenna and remained a staunch friend for the rest of Berne's life. Concannon was a social worker for the Veterans Administration clinic in San Jose, California. Two VA patients claimed that Berne was overcharging them. So Joe made a study and found that Berne was carrying more patients than any of the other doctors in the four counties supervised by his clinic, and that he also sustained the patients longer. He went down to see Berne. Concannon said: "I told him I was a social worker from the Veterans Administration, and he replied, 'Oh, you *help* people!' He dug social workers, but that was a joke."

"Berne acknowledged that he charged more—he was charging about $1 a visit more, or $2, depending on whether they were working . . . and one fellow who . . . was doing really well was being charged $5 more a visit.

"That was his belief, unless you paid for it, etc.—it's a fond belief of psychiatrists that if you don't pay through the nose you don't get cured—but some patients were coming all the way from Berkeley to Carmel [about a three-hour ride in those days] because he had been their psychiatrist at Fort Ord. That's the highest compliment you can pay. I was rather impressed by Berne. I thought he was very honest. His patients did not want to change doctors. They could have changed to a psychiatrist in Berkeley at the going rate, but they didn't want to. They wanted to complain . . ."

Concannon was so impressed that soon he was driving down to Carmel from Oakland with two of his social worker friends to get training in therapy. When we said that more than one of the people we had interviewed (three to be exact) had suggested that, although Berne was a great theorist, he was not very effective as a therapist, Concannon replied: "Well, I disagree, and I was in a position to know. When people were in and out of the VA hospital and I hooked them up with Eric, not one of those people went back to the hospital over a period of two years and they all swore by him. He knew what the hell he was doing at all times! (He pounded the table angrily.) He was a damned good therapist!

"I had to get ahold of these patients and write up their cases in order for them to get their disability. So I knew all about these cases. I don't know who made that statement, but Eric Berne was a *good* therapist!"

No man may be a hero to his valet, but Berne was a hero not only to his landlord but also to his secretary. John Gamble, a Carmel architect who was a part-owner with Berne (and later landlord) of the office building Eric occupied in Carmel, told us: "I would say that as far as Eric Berne was concerned there wasn't a more honest man around . . . I don't know that he ever let anyone down. He was one of those guys that you knew you could rely on anything he said. I would have trusted him with anything in the world. Anything he said was OK."

The late Mrs. Allen Williams, who acted as Eric's secretary in his Carmel office from 1958 to 1970, a twelve-year period that covered the beginnings of TA in Carmel and San Francisco and its *Blütezeit* in the sixties, also sensed his drive toward excellence. She had no doubts about his effectiveness as a healer. She remembered vividly how seriously he took his obligations to groups and felt that he did his patients "100 percent of good—in two months what a difference! They would come in all hang-dog and in two months they would be standing straight and looking you in the eye. He was a dynamo himself, and it was quite a job to keep up with him."

Mrs. Williams said: "He would come bouncing in like a genie out of a bottle and stand right behind me and demand certain things. I would say, 'Please go out of here. I can't think with you standing there! . . . it was just that he was so revved up. He was keyed up, high strung.

"He was a very complex person, really complex. His integrity in dealing with his employees was 100 percent and in dealing with income tax forms and things like that. . . . He was full of integrity about everything he did—or with anyone he hired—he always paid me and gave me appropriate raises and did everything just right. And as soon as he saw I could function all right he left me alone."

Mrs. Williams said: ". . . He had fifty ideas in fifteen minutes. I don't believe his mind ever stopped racing. It was very tiring to be around him. . . . I really worked so hard at that office, phones ringing, everything interrupting, files wanted, manuscripts to figure out. He never had time for me to ask him any questions. He wanted me to do the best possible job and I had the interest in doing the best I could. That's what we had in common."

Mrs. Williams was an unusual secretary—a physician's wife (her husband had been ill for years and it was necessary that she support him), she had been educated until the age of twelve in England. "Eric hired me because he had a use for someone with a better-than-average knowledge of the English language—not so common as one would think, and somebody who could read his writing, which was [so hard to read] . . . and so quick. Everything he did was quick. He was one of the quickest if not the quickest person I ever met. . . .

"He had a phenomenal memory and had read more extensively than anyone I ever met—well, one person in England had, perhaps, read as much. . . . He could remember . . . everything, too. . . . I'm glad to put in a plug for him; you don't work for a person without knowing whether he's bona fide or not.

"Eric underneath it all had a very kind heart; I saw this. There was a young boy in prison that he wrote many letters to, because he thought he could help him—and he offered me a really big raise toward the end. He had so many children to support that I decided I couldn't take it. He didn't have to offer me that raise, and I thought if I took it, I'd have to burst myself trying to give him back full value.

"Before he entered one of his groups he would stand outside the door and . . . compose himself . . . seeming to wipe everything out of his mind. . . . He . . . worked hard over the kids on dope, and he used to come out of his group sessions as white as a sheet. He really gave them all he'd got."

It was Dr. Benjamin Weininger's opinion that "If [Berne] had been accepted by the Psychoanalytic Institute, he would never have developed TA. [Developing their own theory] happened to many persons rejected by the Analytic Society: Alfred Adler, Carl Jung, my pupil Reuben Fine, . . . and of course, Erich Fromm and Karen Horney."

Misfortune, then, actually seemed to smile on Berne, by goading him into founding his own movement. Mrs. Gene Prescott, who had regularly been present at Berne's open forum on group therapy at Mt. Zion, suggested at one point that several of her colleagues would like to participate in some of Berne's discussions if only they could be held after working hours. Berne took up the idea and started holding Tuesday evening seminars at the office in his apartment. They snowballed. Six people attended the first meeting, which was held on February 18, 1958. Thirteen came to the fourth meeting and at the end of six months more than forty people were enrolled. The meetings became a regular fixture with a regular name: "The San Francisco Social Psychiatry Seminars."

An enthusiastic little band began surrounding Berne. His dry wit, his way of turning conventional explanations for psychopathology upside down, his starting theories "which shook the ground from under one's thoughts" excited his listeners; the fact that he "had his arms open to everyone" was a major source of his appeal. "It was the first time in my psychiatric practice that I had found a psychiatrist who would take in nurses, social workers [and] probation officers and I thought, wow!" said Dr. Kenneth Everts, who attended these early meetings (and, as first president of ITAA after Berne's death, led Transactional Analysis through a period of rapid expansion). "I had grown up with doctors and they wouldn't listen to anyone but doctors." Eric,

Dr. Everts told us, "would listen to anyone, absolutely anyone. It was sort of a shocker."

In such a gathering Berne, too, must have found a kind of intimacy, the intimacy which eluded him in ordinary day-to-day contact with most other people. He appreciated the free-flowing feedback of these disciples, which allowed him to develop his ideas further and further emancipate himself from his long standing subservience to the entrenched deities of the mental health empyrean. And he must have sensed that with his discovery of Transactional Analysis he was no longer alone. He had hit upon something big.

15

Go Ahead! You Can Do It! It's Easy!

Go ahead! You can do it! It's easy!
Sara Gordon Berne
If anybody has any questions to ask, I know the answer. If nobody has any questions to ask, I still know the answer.
Eric Berne, The Happy Valley

It was a golden age. That's how Dr. Martin Groder described the decade of the sixties, when Berne conducted his Transactional Analysis seminar each Tuesday evening in his San Francisco office. "I have lived through many golden ages, and this was one of them. Eric took these people, some of them offbeat and losers, really, and he inspired them, and they did marvelous things."

"Those seminars were a high," said Claude Steiner. "They were wonderful, exciting times. Even if I'd already heard what he had to say; it was always new and exciting. Every Tuesday night was wonderful."

Most of all, it was a golden age for Eric Berne. The bright, taciturn, spindly loner of Sainte Famille Street now had his knights of the round table. His childhood dream of an "Agamemnon Club" where he, the leader, would dazzle his followers with his intellectual brilliance had come true.

No King Arthur he. He was Merlin, the magician, and his book of magic was *Transactional Analysis in Psychotherapy.*

Bob Goulding, a psychiatrist at the Veterans Hospital in Roseburg, Oregon, read the book by chance and it set him afire.

Every week he drove 600 miles down (and 600 miles back) to San Francisco to attend the seminars and to take training and supervision privately from Berne in Carmel. He had happened to borrow the book from a friend and had said to himself: Christ! I'm going to see this guy! "I was tremendously excited. It had all kinds of things that I had been looking for for years—and good psychotherapy."

Fanita English got the book from a colleague, who loaned it to her because he was mildly interested in it. She took it with her to read at a hotel where her husband was attending a publishing convention. She remembers the raised eyebrows and the bantering questions she got from other guests who saw she was reading a book from the avant garde Grove Press, which was much in the public eye at that time because of its daring and succesful publication of *Lady Chatterley's Lover*. They asked her with heavy emphasis if she were *enjoying* the book. She was, indeed, and was greatly moved by it. She was at a stage in her career where she had been considering giving up the practice of therapy. After ten years of practice, she felt stuck. Her clients didn't seem to get better, or even to change. The book was "like a detective story. I was finding the answer to this question, that question, and that question, and I just couldn't put it down." She took TA training and later became one of the major contributors to TA theory.

Pat Crossman, on her way to a beauty parlor in Oxford, England, happened to see *Transactional Analysis in Psychotherapy* in the window of a bookstore and picked it up to read under the dryer. She had been working as a psychiatric social worker for about ten years in the National Health Service in the field of mental health. National Health was a new system, and she had been busy trying to figure out what was going on: her conclusion was that "analysis equalled paralysis." She said: "I read it while I was working in my therapeutic community where all hell was breaking loose. Doctors were attacking each other, everything was in an uproar. I took my book on Transactional Analysis and began sharing it with the patients, much to the consternation of my colleagues and superiors. That's when I realized it was so powerful.

"In those days it was hard for a psychiatrist to do group

therapy, as there was the 'psychoanalytic church' and the fear of splitting the transference. I had begun to want something that was fresh, but still was consistent with the other framework. And Transactional Analysis was; it explained things and enabled patients to see what was happening on the mental health unit. The patients were playing games with the psychiatrists in training, and they jumped at it.

" . . . This book made it all so simple. The Parent, the Adult and the Child, games and scripts. It was a scholarly book and yet very unpretentious. It must have been a very nice person who wrote it, I thought. When my husband became a faculty member at Berkeley in 1964, I called Berne on the phone and told him briefly of my experiences at Oxford.

"He said, 'This is great, come on over.'" Soon Pat became one of the select "inner circle" who sat near Berne at the regular Tuesday evening seminars. Eventually she acted for a while as his co-therapist and was asked to take one of his groups while he was away traveling.

Others got wind of the phenomenon in other ways. Dr. Tom Harris, Chief of Navy Psychiatry in World War II and at the time a practicing psychiatrist in Sacramento, California, heard Berne lecture at a psychiatric conference in Los Angeles and "did a 180-degree turn. I'll never forget when I walked out from hearing that first paper. It was an experience of great emotional intensity . . . I became totally involved in reassessing everything I knew and reworking everything after that. I thought it was wonderful, the work of a genius."

Dr. John M. Dusay, then in his residency at Langley Porter Neuropsychiatric Institute of the University of California Medical School at San Francisco, happened to notice an announcement of the "San Francisco Social Psychiatry Seminars" (as the Tuesday night seminars were then called) on the bulletin board at the clinic. He dropped in one evening, was excited about what he heard, and got his supervisor, Dr. Stephen B. Karpman, who taught there, to go with him the next week.

Dusay said: "I was immediately taken by the fact that he liked to let young people who were just starting out present cases. I was able to do this the first time I attended a meeting."

Karpman told us that when he had first listened to Berne

(speaking at the Oak Knoll U.S. Naval Hospital in Oakland), he thought he was just another speaker. But after he had heard Berne talk in the seminar and compared him to others, "It was as if he had 100 IQ points more than the people around him. Just looking at him, I thought he was in a different world—completely separate from everyone else—on a space platform 100 feet high looking down with a perspective on everyone. I thought he looked like he came from another planet, or like a Martian from a television science fiction story."

Bill Collins (now a Ph.D., but at that time a social worker who was employed at the California Medical Facility at Vacaville Prison) went to the seminar one night in 1959 for the first time. He immediately got into an argument with Berne, who he found to be "very cocky and adamant" about what he was saying. "I hadn't run into anybody in the social sciences or treatment field who seemed that cocksure. I think it hooked the rebel in me . . .")

Very soon after that, however, Bill took up using TA in the prison. Later, he said, he "started preaching the doctrine in southern California. I began saying, 'Here's what Berne says' . . . and people would start yawning, and Berne said: 'Don't tell them what I say, tell them what *you* want to say, or you'll lose your audience. . . .' He was right. I had no problems thereafter.

"Originally when we were with Eric there was just a lot of joy and zest in it. There was a long time that I needed to hear things from Eric as a child from a parent, and I got a lot of permission from Eric. I could walk onto a stage, like at UCB or UCLA, or in hospitals and prisons, and social workers would come up to me and say: 'How'd you get to be able to do that—an M.S.W. and you're teaching all these psychiatrists and psychologists?

"I got it from Eric . . . I had the feeling that I really knew what I was talking about, because I'd used TA and it had worked and besides, Big Daddy Eric said: 'Go get 'em!'

"He would say: 'You just need to tell these people. You know more about it than they do, just go ahead and do it.' He gave me a lot of permission."

Clinical social work psychotherapist Mary Boulton told us: "The thing about him that was so marvelous was that he was like a stand-up comedian. He really believed that people could learn a lot while enjoying learning, having fun and laughing. Well, I was absolutely entranced by his philosophy, his manner, and his FREE-CHILD. . . . He was hilarious! And the humor was all based on our work, our problems [as therapists], and was wonderfully apt."

Also, according to Dr. Kenneth Everts, "His energy seemed unlimited. I often wondered how he got enough sleep. His seminars, particularly [taxed him] —he would fly in early Tuesday morning, work all day, and then conduct his seminar at night, and it didn't seem to matter to him how late he stayed up, even though he had to work the next day."

The seminar began to have growing pains after a few months. As Mary Boulton described it: "When I first went to the seminars . . . there was a group of very knowledgeable people who had been coming . . . since 1958—some from Mt. Zion days—and they were developing his theory and even going beyond some of his ideas and were very sharp. And then there was the group of newcomers who might have been sharp but didn't know the phraseology, and they'd say: 'What's the Adult? What's the Child?'

"I was one newcomer who always asked a lot of questions, and he said to me: 'Mary, now, don't ask one more question. Come to two meetings and don't open your mouth. Then you'll learn a lot.' I was very hurt by this. . . .[But] it was from encounters like this that the idea of teaching a class to newcomers grew. Some newcomers left the seminar when they couldn't take Eric's confrontations."

The class was called a "101" according to Boulton, because college courses up to 100 are considered elementary, whereas those above 200 are considered advanced. "After the six weeks' course, we would have a graduation ceremony, which took the form of a masquerade party. Eric loved these parties. He would wear a "Spanish outfit with a . . . hat like the flamenco dancers wear and a suede vest with self-fringe. His happy Child grinned as he asked my opinion of it the first time he wore it."

Berne recalled the first 101 in an article printed in the *Trans-*

actional Analysis Bulletin (TAB). The class had been started on the suggestion of Dr. Gordon Gritter and ran for ten weeks, beginning September 29, 1959. In response to flyers distributed widely to mental health centers, doctors and other professionals crowded in from Bay Area clinics and departments. They covered every inch of floorspace, even perching on folding canvas chairs that had been bought for the occasion.

Dusay told us he had sat in on Berne's 101 course "many, many times." Eventually he was allowed to teach part of it. "I was the first one allowed to teach it besides Berne."

A lone psychiatrist in a profession of loners, Berne had limited resources. A psychiatrist has just so many hours in a day that he can use to make money; Berne, with two families and two offices to maintain, found it very difficult to accumulate the financial resources to support a new movement. Much of his time was occupied in spreading the word about his new system.

His activities in 1961, for instance, included: five courses of six weeks each at prestigious medical school hospitals; four workshops of two days each at a prison, two hospitals, and a welfare department; three one-day workshops at two penal institutions and a hospital; and three lectures at two hospitals and a community center. (He flew from San Francisco to Berkeley by helicopter for lectures and commuted by airplane between San Francisco and Carmel every week in order to maintain his office in both places.) In addition to the above he saw an average of fifty patients a week in his private practice, and was working on books at night. In 1963 he brought out *The Structure and Dynamics of Organizations and Groups* and in 1966 *The Principles of Group Treatment*.

So without a big money backlog, the movement had to be a crusade, and it was. People donated their time and energy to the common cause.

Viola Litt Callaghan went to the first meeting of the seminars on February 18, 1958. A recent recipient of an M. A. in Psychology from San Francisco State University, she had heard Berne lecture at the university and had subsequently asked him about career opportunities. She liked his directness. "He had a system of thought you could follow, and it was quick and energetic and you didn't have to change the past to change the present."

At the first meeting he had passed around a piece of paper so people could sign their names, and afterwards Vi had said: "Do you want me to type it up? Give me a piece of carbon paper." She was alarmed at the condition of the carbon paper he handed her, however, and argued about whether it was usable. "Berne got an edge in his voice," she said. So Vi typed it up on "this delightful old-fashioned typewriter, old-style, like the second made in the world." Sure enough, the carbon paper didn't work, so Vi took the list home to type, "And from then on," she told us proudly, "I was his unpaid secretary" for the seminars.

Later Anne Morse (Garrett) offered her secretarial services to Berne to help run the Tuesday evening seminars. She became the ITAA executive secretary, circulation manager, and mail-order-sales committee-of-one for *The Transactional Analysis Bulletin* and eventually editorial assistant for the publication. Like Eric, she received no pay. For a time the address of the ITAA was "Mt. Eden" (near Hayward, California), because the Mt. Eden post office was around the corner from Anne's house.

Dave Kupfer's young wife Judy also worked as a volunteer in Carmel, doing "things she didn't know she had it in her to do," according to Edith J. Chester, "and she did them so well."

The paid help Berne was able to manage was usually furnished by students who put in a few hours now and then. Gwen McEwen, a student at Monterey Peninsula College, sometimes worked in the Carmel TA office and sometimes acted as Berne's cook between marriages. During Berne's lifetime neither the Social Psychiatry Seminars nor the ITAA ever had a full-time professional executive staff, nor was the ITAA always completely solvent. When Berne died, the ITAA balance sheet showed a net worth of $644.68.

In keeping with the spirit of the sixties, the TA "establishment" was anti-establishment, off-beat and fun. After the seminars on Tuesday evening, at which the participants were not supposed to eat or drink but to concentrate on the serious aspects of developing TA theory, everyone would go on a "field trip," usually to the Old Spaghetti Factory, a San Francisco institution—that is to say, a barnlike eatery, night spot, a North

Beach theater, bar, and watering hole, where the small talk loomed very large.

By 1963 enough people had become involved in TA that it was decided to hold an annual conference. This took place at the Asilomar Conference Grounds in Pacific Grove, California, a rustic, bare-bones center hidden amidst dunes and wind-sculptured pines on the shores of the chilly Pacific Ocean. Mary Boulton remembered that they had a little room near the entrance of the administration building about the size of an ordinary living or dining room and that "one after another, people would stand up and tell about the work they were doing, and that was the conference."

Eric and daughter Ellen would sit at a table writing down the names of people as they came in, and Eric had a little program made up which announced who was going to present and also mentioned a "Banquet." This was a joke, "because there was a cafeteria and we had the same food selection that we had had all along." And then he said, "If we ever have a *real* banquet, that will be the time to dissolve the organization."

Only a year or so later, Boulton said, the conference had grown to the extent that they had "something going on in two rooms, so you could make your choice."

Bill Collins flew up to the first conference from Los Angeles in his own plane. This seemed to delight Berne, as he mentioned it in the *Bulletin*, praising the Los Angeles members for their ability to pick innovative ways of traveling, and saying, "One member arrived by private plane and another by motorcycle."

Mary Goulding, an outstanding trainer of therapists and TA author, told us: "The thing I remember best about Eric was the summer conferences. He would walk from room to room where people were presenting, and he would stay about five minutes, maybe ten, and then he would synthesize or ask a question and just from that little piece that he heard, he had some new theory. He would know what was important and what wasn't important. He could make connections just fantastically. . . . So it was always a delight to have him walk in the room."

Although the annual conferences grew larger, they didn't lose the sense of excitement and dedication that the early ones had. Dr. Martin Groder, who didn't become connected with TA until 1965, remembers his first conference vividly, particularly the mock therapy group held at the end. Berne tagged Groder to be the "therapist" of the group, which came to be called "Dr. Grudgeon's Grueling and Grumbling Group." The mock therapy group was an institution at the conferences for a number of years. The group was made up of TA "superstars" pretending to be the most annoying patients they had ever treated or could imagine.

In this "Grudgeon" group, Bill Collins played the part of a patient with a terrible anxiety neurosis. Whatever anyone told him, he would immediately forget. Pam Levin played a hebephrenic who kept her eyes glued to Groder's crotch, "exploiting her not inconsiderable talent for disconcerting males." Vi Callaghan worked the angles of the Karpman Drama Triangle, as an alcoholic ripe for rescue. Claude Steiner, Bob Goulding, Jack Dusay, and Dave Kupfer took equally meaningful roles. Berne portrayed a paranoid chiropractor with low-back pain, or an ulcerative colitis patient who jumped up and down in his chair, yelling it was an emergency and he had to go to the bathroom urgently and could he have permission to go.

The first year Groder took his part seriously and thought the group was supposed to demonstrate that the most difficult patients could be treated effectively with TA. The result was that he was completely overwhelmed by the experience. By the time the second conference rolled around, he had concluded it was all a put-on and was able to roll with the punches. One year he arrived with an ex-con and his replacement at the Marion penitentiary, both of whom had gone through his Asklepieion program and were well-hardened to "third-degree games," but they couldn't take this group and folded almost immediately. Sometimes there was an audience of 600, all rolling in the aisles.

In later years the group was led by Michael Breen, who was called Dr. Cream.

At times it seemed as if the organization were put together with rubber bands, baling wire, and chewing gum, but it somehow held. Mary Williams, Berne's Carmel office stenographer, doubled as M.N. Williams, Circulation Manager of the Bulletin, while Gwen McEwen, an uncertain eighteen-year-old college student on one of her first jobs, was called Executive Secretary of the ITAA. At other times, however, in the not-so-confidential purlieus of the quarterly *Transactional Analysis Bulletin*, Berne would "pierce the corporate veil" and give the game away by mentioning that at the new Carmel headquarters at 4th and Junipero Streets in Carmel, the phone would be answered, when and if the secretary was around to take phone calls.

Berne didn't get any money out of the TA organization, any salary, or anything at all except the perquisite of working full steam as the *Transactional Analysis Bulletin* editor and conductor of the Tuesday night seminars. He invited the participants after the meetings to "eat anything out of the refrigerator as long as they left the Seven-up, and the two eggs on the shelf that were to be his Wednesday morning breakfast."

But how to make an impact on the thinking of other therapists, who seemed determined not to hear about the wonders of TA? Berne was bent upon ringing some sort of gong in the celestial kingdom of therapeutic orthodoxy. On October 23, 1959, Berne wrote Al Wood, a young M.D. in Philadelphia and a recent convert, that the American Group Psychotherapy Association was not including any papers on Transactional Analysis on the January 1960 program of its New York conference. He proposed that they set up a meeting of their own to run concurrently with the AGPA conference.

Berne had noted in another letter to Dr. J.C. Whitacre, II, that he had received close to a hundred letters during that year showing interest in TA, many of them from universities, such as Chicago, Oregon, and the University of Southern California.

In a second letter to Dr. Wood in November 1959, Berne wrote that the consensus of the San Francisco TA group was that their contribution to the AGPA should be in the form of a workshop, which he invited Wood to attend.

The AGPA workshop took on added emotional overtones for Berne, because the AGPA journal had recently declined to publish his second article on Transactional Analysis.

Joe Concannon, the social worker for the Veterans Administration who had been one of the first outsiders to recognize and marvel at Berne's abilities as a therapist, remembers talking to Berne about the AGPA's refusal to publish his paper. Joe said:

"The time I really liked Eric the best and the time when he was most relaxed was when I used to drive him around. His eyesight was poor and he did not like to drive. He talked very differently at those times. He wasn't the cocky kid he was when other people were around. . . . I remember he wanted to quit the AGPA one time very badly and I wouldn't let him. I said: 'You're crazy. It's the worst thing you can do.' They wouldn't accept a paper he had written—said it wasn't group therapy. Too one-on-one. He said he didn't need them—that he was tempted to quit. He told Jay Fidler: 'Some day my group's going to bury yours.' And today TA does have more members than the American Group Psychotherapy Association."

So out of his rejection by the AGPA and the setting up of this rump workshop, Berne developed a formula for making a dent in the establishment. One of the ingredients of the formula was to have a "hospitality room," particularly at conferences of the American Psychiatric Association.

The TA hospitality rooms attracted guests in increasing numbers; when the TA members played, they let out their Free Child and the effect was contagious.

Berne embroidered on this theme by hiring a sexy, platinum-blonde college girl named Pamela Blum as a part-time secretary whom he later took on business trips and to conventions to act as hostess in the hospitality rooms. This did nothing to tarnish Berne's reputation as a with-it wild-hair worthy of the Erika Jong Psychiatric Hall of Fame.

Pam told us Berne encouraged her "to look stylish and attractive" at the APA conventions. He approved of her wearing the then fashionable mini-skirts, "the shorter, the better. . . . 'Shake 'em up in New York,'" he used to tell her, referring to the traditional East Coast analysts.

Pam resembled Mary of the Peter, Paul, and Mary singing group. Although their relationship was entirely platonic, Eric flew her down from San Francisco to Monterey so she could drive up with him in his Maserati convertible. He told Pam "if ever there was a perfect person to drive with him in his silver Maserati with the top down, it was me. He was having fun acting out a fantasy."

Pam also kept things going in Berne's San Francisco office.

She chauffeured him, lunched with him, handled his phone calls with the answering service, ordered his groceries for the seminars:—"wine, beer, coffee, Stella D'Oro cookies, those were the kind he liked—he was very set on things"—opened up the seminars, sometimes dined with him at Maye's Oyster House before the seminars, and also did a little typing and filing.

Berne adopted the "good daddy" role with her at times. For example, he loaned her $600 to buy a car, having her sign a note regarding principal and interest, but when she paid it off promptly, he returned the interest to her, saying it had been an honor to be her banker and thanking her "for everything so far" —a typically Bernean way of expressing appreciation.

"A lot of people thought I was Eric's mistress, because I traveled with him, but that was not the case. I loved him and felt very protective of him, loyal to him and in awe of him all at the same time."

During most of the sixties Berne was the principal exponent of group treatment at the McAuley Neuropsychiatric Institute of St. Mary's Hospital in San Francisco. At McAuley as elsewhere he never attempted making an omelette without cracking eggs. Two of his closest associates there, Dr. Charles Berger and Jules Levaggi, told us what it was like to assist Berne in the conduct of his groups. Dr. Berger was a psychiatric resident and later remained with the institute as a staff training supervisor. Mr. Levaggi, a clinical social worker for adult and outpatient services, was assigned by Dr. Michael T. Khlentzos, McAuley's medical director, to act as liaison between Dr. Berne and professionals wanting to observe Berne's group therapy work.

Dr. Berger told us: "Berne was quite controversial, and some people didn't like him. I, however, became quite fond of him, and he had an important influence on my career. What I particularly admired was his encouragement of both trainees *and* patients to be 'bright' and realize their highest potential. Dr. Berne had great respect for people and was genuinely interested in their opinions about therapy, about themselves and about life in general.

His "inpatient group would consist of all the patients on the ward. He would sit with the inner circle of patients and the residents and other staff would be in the outer circle, and he'd go around the inner circle and ask the patients 'Who wants to be cured today?'

"After an hour the inner and outer groups would exchange places and the patients would silently listen while Dr. Berne would ask for and receive comments from those who had witnessed the therapy session. This unusual way of conducting group therapy was of immense benefit to both trainees and patients alike.

"As he went around the group he'd want everyone to say at least one sentence. There was one patient, B. He asked B if he wanted to be cured and B said, 'No.' The second time he asked B, 'What are you doing here in the group?' B didn't reply. The third time he asked him: 'What did you do on the outside that made people so nervous that they sent you to a psychiatric hospital?' B walked to the center of the group where there was a vase full of flowers sitting on the table. He picked up the vase and threw it at Berne. It missed Berne's ear by inches and hit the blackboard behind him, splattering water over him. I was sitting next to Berne and the vase narrowly missed me too. Berne got up, blotted up the water on his coat and sat down again, saying, 'I learned something today.' I asked, 'What was that?' and Berne replied, 'I learned I shouldn't have gone around three times.' "

Mr. Levaggi added: "There was another patient, who remained on the ward long after Berne had died. When Berne went around he asked him the same question, 'What did you do outside that caused people to send you to a psychiatric hospital?' The man replied, 'Well, Dr. Berne, it's a long story.' And Berne said, 'Well, just give us the last line.' We thought he was joking, but he was serious."

We suggested to Dr. Berger that perhaps people's hostility toward Berne was a result of their thinking he was wisecracking and facetious when in fact he was serious.

"Yes," Berger answered, "He was serious. The patients, too, thought he was wisecracking, but he wasn't being funny. It is amusing, but—one does have the ability to communicate something when joking. One of the things that made us comfortable with Eric Berne was that he would make a statement, and at first we might guffaw with laughter. But [after some reflection] it would [turn out to] be a profound statement, and although with this type [of remark] one would crinkle up a smile, it still was something that one pondered. . . . People misread him. That's why they didn't really like him. They thought he was being hostile, but he wasn't being hostile at all—just direct. He was really trying to be helpful."

Levaggi added, "In the group, for instance, a patient would say: 'I have to have shock therapy,' and Berne would say, 'Well, why are you going to do it?' And the patient would reply, 'It will stop me from being depressed.' And Berne would say, 'Don't let them hit you on the head with shock therapy.' The patient would then say, 'Uh, whaddya mean, doc?' [and Berne would say] 'Don't let them give you shock therapy! I don't think they should hit you on the head with shock therapy.' Then he'd leave . . . and the patient would say, 'Dr. Berne doesn't think I should have shock therapy.' And the staff had been working for weeks trying to get this patient to agree to having it. . . ."

Jules Levaggi told us it later turned out the patient he was talking about did not choose shock treatment. He progressed and adopted Berne's philosophy. By formulating a healthier lifestyle he resolved his depression.

"This was the background of the confrontation between Berne and the other doctors on the staff. . . . If you had a patient with a severe depression and minimal response to conventional treatment, with medications and other kinds of therapy, the last resort was shock. And it just got into a routine. So Eric was really before—maybe he was sort of the *father* of the patients' rights rebellion . . ."

Berger continued this line of thought. "It was an idea of being straight with people and a lot of people wouldn't or couldn't deal with that, and he alienated a lot of people in the process. Doctors were angry at him, psychiatrists were angry at him, and the year I was there, most of the residents didn't like him. Before I got there, maybe a lot of people did like him. . . ."

Levaggi said he had never seen Berne in a rage except with his colleagues. "He treated us [younger men] with great respect, because we were in the process of learning, but those who were challenging him [he didn't. . . . Dr. Khlentzos] had a lot of respect for Berne and backed him no matter what people said."

In an article in the memorial issue to Berne in the *Transactional Analysis Journal* Levaggi told of Khlentzos's speech concerning Berne to the staff:

> We are fortunate to have Eric Berne join [us]. . . . He has something to say and teach; you may not agree with him but he is to be respected as a contributor to the philosophy. Eric is a modern day Sigmund Freud, and time will acknowledge him for his efforts. If you have any gripes with him or his methods come to me about them, because I do not want to lose this man, and I will handle anyone's complaints. . . . He has something to say and it is therefore up to all who want to learn to open their minds to receive it.

Gripes and unrest did arise. Barely sixteen weeks after Berne started at McAuley, complaints made to the director resulted in his reassignment to adults' outpatient and childrens' inpatient services. (This eliminated the complaints from the physicians treating adult inpatients, many of whom objected to Berne's recommendations that were contradictory to their own.) Since Dr. Khlentzos was the treating physician on the children's ward, the source of conflict with the private physicians was eliminated.

Berne continued at McAuley until his death. He formed a late-adolescent mixed-sex outpatient group with some of his previous patients participating, which was considered to be very successful. In both inpatient and outpatient groups Berne used his inner circle-outer circle exchange with great effectiveness.

At the annual 1964 APA meeting in Los Angeles (May 4-8, 1964), Transactional Analysis began to be noticed. Berne reported in the *Transactional Analysis Bulletin(TAB)* that the TA contingent was first given a private room with a seating capacity of about twenty; however, four times that number of tickets for dinner were sold and just before starting time the TA people switched over to a room which could accommodate eighty. ITAA leaders synchronized the new arrangements as if by clockwork, and the banquet went off as smoothly as if every facet had been planned long in advance.

In their private rooms at the Biltmore they were also honored by a steady procession of outsiders who wanted to participate in their open house. Around tea time the rooms were crammed with the curious, many of whom had followed directions posted in the lobby.

As a result, it was decided that TA hospitality rooms at many of the larger conventions might not be at all a bad idea.

Once he got people's attention, Berne could put on a demonstration of power and profound insight that was capable of thrilling even the most blasé therapist. At the American Psychological Association meeting in August of 1969, he led such a demonstration group. He had sat on one of the panels and been scoffed at as he insisted on considering cases from a TA point of view. So he asked for volunteers from the professional audience to form a therapy group right then and there on the stage.

According to his third wife, Torre: "It was one of those meetings where everybody presents a demonstration group or method of therapy. Perls, Eric, and all sorts of other psychiatrists—under tremendous pressure—a tough test. Everyone in the audience is ready to knife you, and your patients are other psychologists, psychiatrists and social workers—great competitiveness. Eric gave a fantastic performance—a 'peak' demonstration. In about 20 minutes, he analyzed one girl's problems (crying inappropriately—which interfered with her work and her social life) and came up with an insight and a remedy which seemed to cure her on the spot. He was capable of doing that—not all the time, but on occasion. It was thrilling to watch him. He issued a lot of one-sentence remedies which were right on the nose. It was a virtuoso performance.

". . . Eric could walk up in a meeting or at a party and say three right words to the right person and . . . just zap . . . them. I don't think it's true that he was a great theoretician but a poor therapist . . . not at all."

Berne had hoped that *Games People Play* would make a real

contribution in the mental health field, but its popularity with the general public surprised him. In the *Bulletin* for October 1964, he remarked that his book had once or twice jumped into the best-seller category and was concerned that one book jacket had falsely proclaimed that *Games* was a self-help manual. This might have boosted its sales, but he wanted it understood that the book was intended to be read by therapists and should be taken seriously. One movie mogul had already made a bid to make a movie from it.

A year later Berne talked about the hazards of being an author. Once an author has signed the contract he has no control over the advertising. Also the individual bookseller can advertise as he sees fit and the author has no comeback. "If he wants to sell Tillich and a package of contraceptives for $1.98," Berne doubted if anyone could prevent it, unless it was actually against the law.

Three years after its publication, following much word-of-mouth praise, *Games* set a record for remaining on the best-seller list longer than any other nonfictional work in the sixties. Eventually the book sold 5,500,000 copies, outdistanced in books on psychology only by his disciples Tom and Amy Harris and their *I'm OK—You're OK*, which has sold over 10,000,000 copies, and Muriel James and Dorothy Jongward's *Born to Win*, (a combination of TA and Gestalt techniques) which has passed 8,000,000.

The *American Medical Association News* on May 23, 1966, reported: ". . . Dr. Berne finds the mass appeal of the book a little startling [however], 'I knew I had a *buster* when I wrote the book. Everyone did but my publisher,' he said with a smile. 'But I didn't think this many people would be interested in it, because I didn't realize how sensible people are. The whole experience has raised my opinion of people.' "

Grove Press had placed a full-page ad in *The New York Times Magazine* of August 15, 1965, with the headline: "The story of the psychiatrist from San Francisco who played poker—and the dark-horse bestseller of the year . . ." The ad explained how Berne had used his poker winnings to travel to mental institutions in thirty countries, described some of the games in the book, and concluded: "The publishers read the manuscript and decided to publish it. They thought it would be a valuable contribution to the psychology of human relationships. They printed 3,000 copies.

"*And then it happened!*

"All of a sudden . . . the book started to ROLL! It was all the astonished publishers could do to jump out of the way in time.

"Overnight, from coast to coast, people were talking about *Games People Play*. Those who hadn't read it had heard about it from their friends or cocktail-party acquaintances. Print another 3,000 quick! 5,000 more! We're cleaned out—let's have another 10,000! Make it 15,000 more, and keep them coming!

"By mid-July, 1965, 70,000 copies had been sold, and the book was just beginning to go strong, at the rate of 6,000 a week!"

On August 12, 1966, *Life* magazine did an article on "Dr. Berne, Winner—Psychiatrist in the Chips," noting: "Gleefully aware that his free-wheeling approach to mental well-being causes concern in the psychiatric establishment, [Berne says:] "People tell me I oversimplify . . . I tell them OK, but I have an equally valid thesis. They overcomplicate."

All in all, the serious orientation of *Games* was drowned out by its popularity. Although Berne would have preferred a greater critical acceptance by the psychiatric and psychologic media, he tried to ignore the fact that it was being sold in some department stores along with Monopoly in the games section instead of in the book department along with Erikson and Freud.

Determined to look on the bright side of it, Berne told *Newsweek*: "It might . . . reach people who want to know more about themselves and can't be reached any other way."

He did veto offers from television producers. There was also talk of making *Games* a musical comedy. Cy Feuer and Ernest Martin in collaboration with Art Buchwald worked with Berne for a while on the project before it was abandoned.

A color television interview of Berne was filmed for the National Education Network in two half-hour segments. The programs were shown nationwide on February 7 and 14, 1967, and are still being shown to TA audiences via rental film libraries. Some of the interview was conducted while Berne was driving around the 17-Mile Drive near Pebble Beach in his little Sunbeam roadster, a sound man cramped into the small trunk compartment and the cameraman astride the hood.

In all his writings up to and including *Games*, Berne did not discuss the winner-loser nexus he emphasized frequently after achieving best-sellerdom. All of his life he had been struggling to achieve, achieve, and achieve. Now he had achieved. What next?

Losers, Berne now contended, sit around replaying old poker hands and going over old mistakes, saying, "If only I'd done this." Winners, when they occasionally lose, figure out what to do so it won't happen the next time. And what do winners do if they win? Well, winners are supposed to be able to smell the flowers and hear the birds sing, and if there are too many birds singing or too many flowers to smell, Berne had the answer for that, too.

In one of his presentations to the Tuesday evening seminars he told the members about the advice he had given an incipient senior citizen, a staid businessman in his forties who had been successful at making money but also had become very bored. Berne suggested to his patient that he turn himself into an adolescent, saying that that was better than the other choices, such as turning himself into a tree and sitting around rustling his leaves, which is what happened to Philemon and Baucis in the Greek myth. Because of their virtue and good works, Zeus had let them be turned into trees at the end of their mid-life crisis.

Berne deplored this as a form of "Waiting for Santa Claus or *rigor mortis*." At any rate, he was not one to reject the American Dream when it was thrust upon him.

16

Outsider on The Inside Track

> *Winners are programmed, too. Instead of a curse, there is a blesssing: "Long life!" or "Be a great man." The injunction is adaptive instead of constricting: "Don't be "selfish!" and the come-on is "Well done!" With such benevolent controls, and all his permissions, there is still his demon to contend with, lurking in the murky caverns of his primal mind. If his demon is a friend instead of an enemy, then he will have it made.*
> Eric Berne, *What Do You Say After You Say Hello?*

Mel Boyce once asked Berne about the place of TA in the world of psychology. Berne grinned and raised high his arm: "We are like the Statue of Liberty," he said. "Send us your poor and huddled masses."

The popularity of *Games* made it easier to attract attention to Transactional Analysis. At the same time, Berne wasn't so sure that he wanted TA to grow so rapidly. Tom and Amy Harris detected a desire on the part of Berne to keep the brakes on a little. Amy has an entry in her notes of the organization's meeting at Highlands Inn, south of Carmel, in 1966: "January, 1966, was the beginning of the feeling that this thing was really going to go places—and also of certain deviationist trends."

Amy says that Berne at times seemed to resist the idea that the organization would go international. Tom remembers Berne saying: "I want to know everybody. I want to be able to pick up the phone and call so and so in Saskatchewan and to hell with a big organization."

The night before there had been what Eric used to call a "jumping up and down" party in the Harris's room, and nobody was having a problem with his or her *Verklärung*. Eric had done headstands and started up his old practice of swinging from the rafters hand over hand. "The TA members got up there and followed him along the big wooden rafters like a bunch of monkeys," said Tom. At one point in the meeting Eric referred to his creation, the Parent, Adult, and Child, in a smart-alecky way, and Tom objected, scolding him for selling himself short, saying that Eric's works were the works of a genius and not to be joked about.

But the day after, Berne was feeling nostalgic. It was more fun to have a small organization, where all disputes could be settled and ties broken by the eminently practical system of the broadjump, guaranteed to get the right results forever (unless somebody with longer legs than Eric's should show up). It was also troublesome to have to worry about by-laws for a big new nonprofit corporation. Rather than consult a lawyer, Berne borrowed the by-laws of the Harrises' flourishing Sacramento TA organization. The Harrises' lawyer had charged them $1000 for their by-laws, but getting them for free was more fun, too.

Berne was pleased that psychiatrists were among the new adherents. But at the same time, he welcomed talented and enthusiastic mental health workers, even those without credentials. Viola Litt Callaghan brought Jacqui Olson (Schiff), a case worker for a welfare agency, one Tuesday night. Jacqui had had no training as a psychotherapist and lacked even a college degree. She had been seeing welfare clients in groups for convenience but followed no particular theory and did not really expect to get results, though she sensed something positive emanating from her experience.

It was a time when Berne was looking at groups in general (from firemen to followers of spiritualistic mediums), a viewpoint he adopted in his book *The Structure and Dynamics of Organizations and Groups*.

Jacqui told us: "I was first invited to the seminar to give a presentation. I probably talked more than anyone else. Eric didn't appear to be the leader of the group; there were a number of leaders. It was a small seminar, in a living room, people sitting around in a circle. There were people taping, people managing refreshments—there didn't seem to be any one person in charge."

Her reaction to the seminar is detailed in Graham Barnes's compendium *Transactional Analysis after Eric Berne*. She soon mentally divided the seminar participants into three rough categories. The first and most attractive group was made up of the "older professionals. Many of them were psychiatrists, but other disciplines were represented." To her they seemed to possess an enormous fund of knowledge.

"The second group consisted of much younger people: mostly men, who were students or young professionals, quick-tongued, witty and very competitive. I puzzled somewhat about what might be the goal of their competitive efforts and arrived at no answer. I would have liked to be part of that group, but never experienced myself as sufficiently clever to participate in their dialogue.

"These quick-tongued, witty and competitive young professionals were also competitive about women. The attractive women (mostly social workers) involved in the movement, or brought by the young men to the meetings, were known as *dancing girls* and were hotly pursued during after-meeting social hours and on the outside. These were by and large not allowed by Berne to speak on an equal basis with the men."

In the third category were hangers-on—people who were there because of some personal interest. Of those who attended the seminars she said:

> They were not, as is commonly believed, a remarkably warm or intimate group and viewing them in the light of my present sophistication, I would see them as a group of professional dissidents, not intellectual giants, but probably representative of the range of dissatisfied therapists of that period . . . without clear goals about what they would like to see changed or how to go about it. They were not particularly comfortable with themselves or one another, and sometimes immersed themselves in a kind of frenetic playfulness which did little to bring any

of us to the kind of intimate encounters we were purported to be seeking.

Eric's genius and creativity set the tone in the seminars, but Jacqui did not see him as legend portrays him. He was not a "warm, grandfatherly humanitarian"; he was "sharp-tongued and competitive", and argued endlessly. Also he was moody and at times caustic. Nonetheless, he gave and received loyalty and affection, "and his lively curiosity, impatience with affectation and respect for intellectual accomplishment gave structure to the group."

And Jacqui told us that Eric was "very responsive to her, both in terms of personal support and also in terms of professional support. He did not seem to be an unrelated person or a distant person." He persuaded her to go to graduate school. She went to him often with cases she was working on and "his advice was very often paternal. His general manner with me was paternal."

We observed that he must have been excited about the reparenting work she was doing on schizophrenia.

"He was quite excited and he was frightened by it," Jacqui responded. "He anticipated that I was in opposition to the psychiatric establishment [conventional theory was that the parent ego stage wasn't amenable to change] and for many years he advised me not to talk about my work—and then *he* would go out and talk about it." He once introduced her to a large group at the seminar and told the interns and residents to pay close attention to her lecture because "she cures schizophrenia." He devoted an entire issue of the *Transactional Analysis Bulletin* to describing her approach and he gave her permission to think on her own.

There were three attractive and vital young men who were known as the Crown Princes or the Three Musketeers. They grouped themselves around Berne. Some of the meetings seemed to revolve almost entirely around their intramural arguments. Two of the inner group were young psychiatrists from Langley Porter, John M. Dusay and Stephen B. Karpman, but the third was Claude Steiner, whom Berne had wanted to become research director for the seminar and encouraged to take his Ph.D. degree in psychology.

Dr. Solon D. Samuels, a prominent disciple not active in the San Francisco seminars because his home base was Los Angeles, told us: "I think Berne appreciated that I, as an M.D. and a psychiatrist, was enthusiastic about TA, because he was getting a lot of flack from psychiatrists. So when he finally got that group at Langley Porter: Jack Dusay, Steve Karpman, young M.D.s, he was . . . glad to get the admiration of these young men. . . . He wanted far more doctors, more analysts to flock to his organization. TA was attracting social workers over doctors four to one."

Steiner always sat at Berne's right. He said he did this because he operated the tape recorder; others, however, attached a greater significance to the Saint Peter position than it had in actuality. Sometimes, in order to bug Steiner, people would come early to the seminar and occupy the hallowed spot.

Steiner's curly-headed flamboyance, French heritage, and far-out style seemed to symbolize for many the dynamism of the TA group, but it won him few points among some of the less volatile members, several of whom, a decade later, still seem to feel the bruises from the jousting for the inside track with the leader. Berne himself didn't give Steiner any signals of unconditional acceptance. The most tangible evidence of his affection for Claude occured one time when Steiner's father attended the seminar. Eric said to him: "He is very bright, isn't he?" with a big, affectionate smile.

Steiner said: "I feel Eric was torn between letting me shine and muscling me out of the limelight. As a writer, he was not able to collaborate. He only wanted to compete."

Steiner described himself and his fellow Musketeers as follows: "There was this team—Jack Dusay, Steve Karpman, and myself—and Eric. Eric was vicariously enjoying the three of us. We would see who could bring the most beautiful women to the seminars, and it was all encouraged by Eric. That part is embarrassing—I mean I'm embarrassed about it. It was all inside my head, but I was aware of inviting women to the seminars so that Eric would be impressed. He used to love it—and Steve and Jack and I were pretty sexy guys. Plus the women were always very friendly to Eric, not always in a sexy way, but he liked them; they liked him."

In fact, the Musketeers were so indefatigable in the pursuit of beautiful women that Eric once told Jack Dusay and Steve Karpman not to run after the women too much, because if it didn't work out the women might not come back to the seminars.

John Dusay, a personable, success-oriented young psychiatrist (who later became a president of the ITAA and authored *Egograms*), usually came late and sat in the back, lobbing shots from the rear. Karpman believed that Dusay had enough ego that he didn't need to depend on position to be noticed. Jack Kennedy-like, even to the dimple in his cheek, Dusay may have symbolized for Berne the Jurgenesque hero—effortless in his attractiveness. Dusay assessed Berne's movement as "a little ahead of the game. It was obvious that he was a step ahead of everybody." But Berne was a step behind as far as the visible signs of success were concerned.

Dusay's San Francisco surroundings were always impressive in style, so Dusay was astonished by the meagerness of Eric's quarters. For a while Dusay went every weekend to Fritz Perls's Esalen workshops at the hot springs south of Big Sur. He was attracted to the two groups in different ways. "I used to drop in at Berne's house in Carmel on the way back and forth and have a beer. Eric was living in a little blue shack, a little blue house, across from Dorothy. It had about two rooms; it would probably cost about $100,000 today, but then —." (Dorothy told us that this little "shack" is one of the oldest and most charming cottages in Carmel and now rents for $1200 a month.)

Dusay said, "I was getting a divorce at the time and was trying to see how the guru did it." He and Berne also bachelored it up a bit. They gave 101 courses at Dusay's San Francisco house partly because of the need for this instruction but also because this was a way of meeting attractive women.

When Dusay finally married, Eric acted as preacher. *San Francisco Chronicle* columnist Herb Caen described the wedding, which took place around Christmas in 1969:

> We cannot let the year run out without saluting a

man who Thinks Big. That would be Dr. John Dusay, the psychiatrist, who married TWA stewardess Kathy Mulholland in Virginia City, taking over almost the entire town for the party. The ceremony was performed in the lobby of the Silver Dollar Hotel by yet another psychiatrist, Dr. Eric Berne . . . who is also a minister of the Universal Life Church—Kathy's father, Dr. Richard Mulholland [is] also a psychiatrist and a minister of the Universal Life Church.

Occasionally the seminar would conduct experiments in an attempt to validate a theory. One was the intimacy experiment reported on at length by Jacqui Schiff in her article, "One Hundred Children." Eric tried it on her the first time she attended the seminar.

In *TAB* Berne said the purpose of the experiment was to see whether "intimacy" would result if all other means of social interaction were eliminated. The two participants were to sit with their faces "less than twenty inches apart" and were not to indulge in "withdrawal, rituals, pastimes, activities and games." The experiment was reported to have resulted in life-long friendships.

Toward the end of Jacqui's first TA meeting, she was taken to the room next to the seminar room by Viola Litt (Callaghan) and asked to sit down. She was soon joined by Eric Berne but didn't know who he was. No one had introduced them. He pulled up a stool less than twenty inches from Jacqui and began staring into her eyes.

Jacqui said: "Eric tended to intimidate people. I was not easily intimidated. My first feeling was that it was some kind of pass. (I was, I think, about twenty-seven.)

"I just sat there and waited to see what he would do next, and he just sat there and waited to see what I would do next. Vi interrupted us; otherwise, I might be there today.

"I didn't know what he was doing. He didn't tell me what he was doing. I thought it was his responsibility to define the situation."

Another experiment involved a "Stroking-Go-Round" to see what effect might be produced by the stimulation received by stroking. "Every member was supposed to stroke [i.e., compliment] every member in turn," said Steve Karpman. "When it came to Claude's turn to stroke me, he would jokingly say: 'Go to Hell!' When it came to my turn to stroke Steiner, I would say, 'I'm glad I'm able to serve as a means for you to get in touch with your anger, Claude,' and Claude would repeat: 'Go to Hell!' So then I would say: 'Expressing yourself is a valued thing, but this is supposed to be a time for stroking others, Claude.' And Claude would say: 'Go to Hell!' "

Karpman reported that Berne had trouble with strokes. "A few times he gave crooked strokes or mixed strokes, or one that had a hook in it. He didn't really relate to anyone perfectly. There was always some little hook here or there in his relationship with others." But Karpman didn't feel that Berne was "in hiding."

"I always saw him as an extremely bright person . . . I was trying to unmask him all the time. Usually he let us see what he was like and did not try to hide himself. He was stern, warm, intelligent, mischievous, and socially awkward. His Critical Parent showed, his Free Child showed with a twinkle, his Adapted Child showed with its social awkwardness, so it was certainly all there.

"If Berne didn't like what we were doing, he'd say 'We don't talk about that here,' or 'I don't know about that, but maybe we ought to go on to the next subject.' He ran things like an autocrat, just the way he wanted. Some people got hurt or didn't like it and left. Those who could take it or were sufficiently unflappable stayed on.

"Berne always asked a question of his audience to involve the Adult. It had to concern a problem that he hadn't solved yet, a real need. He didn't want a power shift where the speaker was the Parent and the people in the seminar sat there listening like passive children. He wanted a transaction going, so that the audience would give something back to the speaker.

"He emphasized the Occam's razor principle (to reduce everything down to the core). You eliminate everything except the very best idea—the law of scientific parsimony. That was another way he taught us to think.

"He played a game in the seminar which was never defined

during his lifetime. This was to ask a question of thirty-five people and allow time for only four to answer. That was the reason why everybody was so competitive and clamorous in the seminars. In the last five minutes we all tried to get our answers in, and many of the women walked away saying we were competitive. That's also why people sat in the inner circle—so we could get our answers in. When Maggie Northcott spoke she followed the principle of Occam's Razor as she asked only one question. It was always the best, and Berne listened."

Karpman never really got to know Berne well; he doubted if anybody did. Once he found himself sitting alone with Berne on some stairs at a party and thought, "We ought to say something intimate," but he couldn't think of anything.

Berne and Karpman were into puns. At the Lake Tahoe conference they started making military puns, and Berne immediately came out with: "It was a *private* idea that he talked about in *general*, but there wasn't a *colonel* of truth in it and he *rifled* through his mind and came up with a *blank*."

At the beginning of our interview with Dr. Donald Shaskan, he told us that if we wanted to know what Berne was really like, "he was a lot like Steve Karpman in that he had ten million ideas a minute. Only Steve Karpman has a more professional background, since his father was a famous psychiatrist."

Karpman did not feel comfortable with conformity; he had always been a rebel. He told us: ". . . mostly I would just hold a position and challenge Berne—or rather I would challenge the ideas. I got D's in deportment all through grammar school, acted up dreadfully in medical school. I pride myself on this . . .

"In about the last year of Berne's life, I brought up the word 'identification' which is a passive word and isn't a TA word, and then I would argue with him and he would get all upset about it. And Claude Steiner came up to me and said: 'Well, you blew it this time, Stephen.' It was after that seminar that Berne asked me to leave. He came up to me and said, 'Well, it might be better if you dropped the seminars for a while,' and I said, 'Well, gee, I thought it was just the other way around. I think everybody had the impression you were picking on me!' And Berne said, 'Oh, me? They thought it was me? Well, in that case you can keep on coming.'

"Berne ran a tight ship. There was a lot of victim, persecutor, and rescuer stuff going on in the seminars. He zapped people for getting out of line and played one against the other. If someone talked out of turn he'd tell him or her not to come back. The rules were very clear. He ran a tough seminar."

Not long before Eric died, Karpman staged a revolution. He decided to take a stand against all Berne's seminar rules and regulations. There are several versions of this incident, depending on who's telling the story, but this is Karpman's:

"Berne had quite a few rules for not doing things during meetings: No drinking, no coffee, or refreshments until . . . the [break]. I announced at one meeting that I was going to have a revolutionary meeting, a *999*, the ultimate in seminars, which would supersede the 101s, the 202s, the 606s, or whatever. Nobody knew what I was going to do."

Karpman had a beard that made him look a little like Fidel Castro. (When clean-shaven, he looks somewhat like Marcello Mastroianni.) He continued:

"I went down to the army surplus store . . . I got a fatigue outfit . . . and hat and boots up to here. I looked just like a Cuban revolutionary, and I got there early and cleared all the furniture away from the dining room and pushed it back into the living-room area. I had a couple of wine bottles with wine glasses in the middle of the floor with apples all over the place. So we all sat around the wall eating apples and drinking wine and Berne came down and he saw all this going on. And his mind went around real fast; you could almost see the wheels going clickety-click and he runs down the stairs and sits down right next to me and says: 'I'm forming a counterrevolution—anyone who wants to go with me, let's go upstairs and take off our clothes.' And all these people took off and my revolution was already over. Afterwards the nude people came down and sat against the wall and one of them said: 'Come on, Steve, take off your clothes!' But Berne never came down nude, although he was reportedly nude upstairs."

According to another source, however, he kept his shorts on.

Claude Steiner reported that soon after the "revolution," a woman was inspired to take all her clothes off at a seminar. Eric didn't like it and tried to ignore it. "He hated it. It was embarrassing," said Steiner. The lines were to be kept strictly drawn between the serious business of the seminar and the after-hours fun.

Although Berne "ran a tight ship," he could also entertain challenging ideas. "In script analysis," Berne writes in *What Do You Say After You Say Hello?*, "winners are called 'princes' and losers are called 'frogs.' The object . . . is to turn frogs into princes and princesses. . . . The patient fights being a winner because he is not in treatment for that purpose, but only to be made into a braver loser."

Mary Edwards, now Mary Goulding, read a paper at a conference panel attacking Berne's frog-prince nexus head on. It hooked his Adult, and he abstracted it for the *TA Bulletin* in a straightforward manner, saying that Edwards felt that changing frogs into princes was the fantasy operation of a conforming Child wanting to live in a storybook castle where there was no sex or anger. Edwards had said: "Only frogs want to be princes or princesses . . . people want to become human beings and the job in therapy is to get patients out of fairy tales and into life."

Mary told us Berne was in the room when she gave that paper and he later went right on talking about princes and princesses. But, she added, he "liked new ideas. He really welcomed them."

Karpman said: "I battled him. I was pretty outspoken. I would battle anybody. . . . I probably opposed Berne more openly than anybody else." Karpman occasionally tried to corner Berne, but Berne was adept at evasion. One time he very narrowly missed being cornered, however.

The two most dramatic therapies in California in the sixties were TA and Gestalt. Gestalt was dominated by colorful Fritz Perls, who had his headquarters at the Esalen hot springs south of Big Sur. Perls was bewhiskered, powerful, irascible, and terrifying. Some of his followers never quite got over being put on "the hot seat" and publicly grilled about their psychological subterfuges.

The idea of a showdown between the two great systems, with a debate between Perls and Berne, was bandied about. But

"Fritz was so sneaky, he could murder anybody. No one would want to be on a panel with Fritz," according to Mary Goulding. Nevertheless a debate was scheduled, but shortly before the performance, Berne suddenly substituted Jack Dusay as the proponent of the TA viewpoint.

Bob Goulding said Berne was "probably afraid." Karpman said this was an example of Berne's refusal to be cornered: "Berne was slippery. He sensed a corner in the Perls debate and there was no way you could corner him."

At the Vienna Conference in 1968 Berne mentioned the rival Esalen group, stressing the good rapport existing between TA and Gestalt and the interchange of ideas between the two.

Hailed as an exploration of the similarities and differences between TA and Gestalt therapy, the debate lost something in the translation. Perls thought the encounter resulted in an "impasse." Goulding, who acted as moderator, said the meeting ended up in "absurdities and obscenities." When Perls said to Dusay "Talk to this glass, Dusay, and pretend it's Fritz," Dusay replied, "Screw you, Fritz."

The meeting did nothing to merge the two groups, but neither did it alienate them. Both sides still respected each other. Dusay said he thought he won "logically, but Perls won dramatically."

Karpman thought "Dusay did very well in the debate. He wouldn't be put down. Fritz couldn't get around Dusay's Murgatroyd game."

Perls mentioned the debate in his *In and Out of the Garbage Pail,* saying: "I like Eric Berne and I especially like Bob Goulding, who was the mediator. I had a well-meaning young opponent who was no match for me. I was disappointed that Eric did not act as my counterpart."

He went on to say, "I was always impressed by Eric's emphasis on role playing, yet what I saw in my opponent was disillusioning. Not only did it look like a leaf from the Freudian approach, but like a denial of Eric Berne's own dictum that we are *playing* roles. The two roles I could observe were confined to parent and child and they were taken so darned *seriously*. The real game they play, the compulsive pigeon-holing of each sentence as belonging to either the child or the parent, remained unnamed. . . ." He added: "Yet I am envious of Eric's success.

> Yes, I am jealous I admit
> You have a perfect smeller,
> That Eric's treatise was a hit,
> A hundred weeks' best seller.

Perls then speaks of the "drabness and poverty of the two role restriction of the Bernesians." He adds: "Give me at least occasionally a prince who turns into an ugly frog."

Berne's rejoinder came in his Vienna Conference speech. There he said that TA didn't indulge in role playing. Role playing was like child's play, where one child pretends to be the mother, one plays the father, and the third the baby. All three of these roles would be acted out from the Child ego state.

Mary Goulding said: "People are writing now about how Fritz used TA—well, Fritz grossly, badly misused it to prove it wasn't good and the stories about Eric's attempting to use Gestalt are just hilarious. Eric used to bring a chair and say, 'Shall we TRY this chair technique on this patient?'" Mary added, "and of course it wouldn't work! And then Berne would say, 'Well, now, we know THAT doesn't work! So they both were kings in their own kingdoms."

Bob Goulding added that Berne and Perls nevertheless liked each other, and that Perls attended Berne's fiftieth birthday party at his house. Although the Gouldings' attempts to get Berne to incorporate Gestalt techniques into the TA menu only strained relations between Berne and the Gouldings, their efforts have since borne fruit. They and other TA practitioners now parry the attack of critics who contend that TA is useful only in scratching the surface by pointing out that, with Gestalt and similar techniques absorbed into the TA format, deep-seated and supposedly unresolvable emotional ambivalences get solved.

Earlier Bob Goulding said Berne's ducking out was "typical of Eric. . . . Eric told me many times that every time he went out to give a lecture he got 'kicked.' ["Kick Me" is a game in which the victim is really asking for it.] He'd say: 'You do it'—so I did it."

Berne's feeling that he would get "kicked" was reported by more than one person. Torre, his third wife, remembered that "Eric used to upset people very much if they'd ask him for lectures. He'd come up in front of a non-TA audience and he'd quickly go through the rudiments of TA [which he thought they knew anyway] and then he'd make a few simple comments and that was it. People would expect him to give them a show and he wouldn't . . . give them a show.

"He used to complain about [the hostile reception] afterwards, but he'd keep on doing it anyway."

Torre told us: "One time he made people in Mary Calderone's SIECUS group in New York so mad that they would have liked to have thrown him out." SIECUS had apparently invited him with the expectation that he would accommodate them with stories of how sexual misinformation harms children, "but he said the only thing he'd learned in thirty years of being a psychiatrist was that you shouldn't give frequent enemas."

Sometimes, however, he would give them a show of wit, tinged with chutzpah. At a joint meeting with the Western Society for Psychiatrists and Psychologists on September 28, 1962, Berne presented a paper comparing Transactional Analysis and Existential Analysis. After the presentation, Arthur Burton contended that patients often get better "in spite of therapy." Berne replied that they "seem to get better in spite of Transactional Analysis more quickly than in spite of other forms of treatment."

17

A Boys' Club

> Eric had his group of boys, and not too often, but sometimes, they would come to our house and have meetings and he also let me come to all their meetings—he was very good about that.
>
> Grace Berne Rose

It was a woman psychologist who had first suggested the Tuesday evening seminars, and TA luxuriated in the dimensions of its female component. A large number of women psychologists, social workers, psychiatric nurses, and other mental health professionals had been attracted to Berne's seminar—they felt liberated in the TA atmosphere where they were permitted to listen to the discussions of the mighty, contribute occasional comments, and ask intelligent questions. In contrast, a *cordon sanitaire* existed in most psychiatric establishments where the big issues were decided behind closed doors strictly by male doctors, with perhaps an occasional female psychiatrist.

However, this wasn't exactly the whole story, as the following reactions of some of their leaders verify:

VIRGINIA HILLIKER

" 'You should project yourself more.' I heard and interpreted these words of Eric Berne as an instruction to join the competitive winners' pattern.

"And there was a competitive pattern around Eric in 1966. Men competed for Eric's attention and competed with Eric. What about the women? Well, it was a boys' club—or so it seemed to me. Girls were allowed in only if they were young, beautiful, sexy, or amusing.

"Since I was no longer young, beautiful only at times, amusing less often, and not willing to 'use' my sexuality for acceptance, I did not fit the mold.

"My Child, my basic nature, rebelled against those 'project yourself' words. It has taken me a long time to realize that projecting myself means just that—being myself—neither fitting the 'winner' pattern nor rebelling against it.

"I've finally liberated myself—and that reminds me of a statement by Eric during the last conversation I had with him. He said, 'We have to liberate our women.' My objection to this remark was clearly evident on my face, although it was unspoken. 'OK, OK, you have to liberate yourselves,' he said."

MURIEL JAMES

Muriel James (an ex-president of the ITAA and author of ten books elucidating TA concepts) started attending seminars very early—in 1958. She told us:

"For about two years I felt furious at the seminars because women were expected to be "dancing girls" and not much else. I had decided I wanted to learn from Berne, whether or not I would be listened to, so I took notes for two years of all the games played by the inner circle. That was my way of keeping my Child under control and keeping my Adult active—otherwise my Child would be—"

"Enraged?" we suggested.

"Yes, and sometimes sad. However, it was interesting being around a genius in spite of the games, or maybe, because of them. Of course, everybody plays games and perhaps, knowingly or unknowingly, Berne encouraged the excitement of sibling rivalry ('I'm brighter than you') with the small group of men, because it made him feel important."

We asked Muriel if after two years she had taken a more active part.

"Not often," she replied. "I finally concluded that there were too many people at the seminars who wanted to be heard. That was one of the agendas: to be heard. (Although frequently the participants talked more than they listened!) I finally decided it wasn't necessary for me to be heard there. I was disillusioned with the process. I profited more from my supervision with Eric. Then I could talk and be heard and he could talk and be heard. I cared more about what Eric had to say about people and their transactions than about his 'boys' club' and sexism."

At first Muriel shared her clinical supervision with psychiatrist Martin Groder. When more time became available on Eric's calendar, she asked for individual supervision and received it. "Naturally," she said, "this increased the cost, which at that time was difficult for me to meet. One day, when I was no doubt playing 'Poor Me,' I told him I was going to terminate, complaining that my two-hour drive to see him and the money it cost when so little was available seemed too much. His response was, 'Muriel, if you continue your supervision, I guarantee you'll double your income shortly.' He was right. I did. In fact, I tripled it. When I happily reported this to Eric, his retort was, 'Good, now you can pay me the $50 I'm worth each session instead of the $15 you have been paying.' An avid poker player, Eric won that hand. I agreed to continue learning, and at the higher rate.

"One of my interesting memories goes back to the second time I saw Eric when the seminar group went on a so-called 'field trip' to a restaurant. Turning to me abruptly, he asked, 'Would you go to Paris with me tonight?' and I laughingly responded, 'Well, I don't have my suitcase' (joke, joke), and he said, 'I'll get you something over there.' And I said, 'I don't even have a toothbrush.' And he said, 'We could go to a drugstore and get a toothbrush and leave in the next few hours.' I laughed again, thinking it was a joke. Later on, after I got to know him better, I asked him about that conversation. He claimed it was not a joke to him."

We wondered aloud whether Berne had not thought of himself as ugly.

Muriel said, "He was."

"But don't you think that TA people began to love that face?" we asked.

" I wouldn't love a face. I'd love the person behind it," she responded.

"But after you'd known him a long time—?" we persisted.

" After I'd known him a long time I'd probably say he surely is funny looking—because of the narrow and pinched look of his face . . . ," she commented. "I was thinking in reference to your saying he might have thought of himself as ugly, that many of our conversations were where the lights were low, like at The Spaghetti Factory, another favorite 'field trip' place, or while walking to the car or in my car with only the light from the street lights. Incidentally, in the car I didn't do the talking. He did. Words often poured out of him then. Perhaps he did feel unattractive in appearance and more acceptable in dim light.

"One of our last conversations occurred in the car. He brought up his need for therapy and asked for two professional appointments. Before the appointment day came around, he had his heart attack.

"I often wondered why he wanted to see me as a therapist. Perhaps it was because of a paper I had just written titled "Curing Impotency with Transactional Analysis." I presented it at the Golden Gate Group Psychotherapy Association in San Francisco in June 1970. When it was listed on the program, several male therapists teased me for writing on the subject. I became anxious just before the presentation, so I asked Eric, who was attending the conference, to hear it and give me feedback.

"A few moments after I started reading the paper, Eric took out the tiny black book that he usually carried in his shirt pocket and started making notes. I knew then that I had said something that interested him, since he only used this little book when he was jotting down ideas to use later in his own writing. When the paper was finished, he defended it strongly in an argument with a couple of antagonistic, non-TA therapists and said to me, 'Muriel, get that published immediately and keep on writing.' This was an important directive to me, one that I treasure.

"As a kind of memorial I dedicated one of my books to him with the words of Edwin Markham:

And when he fell in whirlwind, he went down
As when a lordly cedar, green with boughs,
Goes down with a great shout upon the hill,
And leaves a lonesome place against the sky."

MARGARET NORTHCOTT AND PAM LEVIN

PAM: "When I first came to the seminars I had a lot of difficulty in establishing the role I wanted. The men and Eric spent a lot of energy trying to define for me which role I should be in. If a woman looked nice, wanted to be playful and also wanted to think and be taken seriously, that was difficult."

MAGGIE: "In some ways it was quite confusing to me because Eric was a very sexually aware man and frequently was giving recognition to the sexuality of the rest of us human beings—and that was coming across a lot to me, and I didn't know what to do with that, particularly since I was married."

PAM: "I experienced the same difficulty. I was living in the Bay Area while my husband was stationed in Vietnam. I decided what I would do with their confusion was to stick around, maintaining my playfulness and continue to expect to be taken seriously as a contributor to TA theory."

MAGGIE: "Me too, definitely."

PAM: "This was better than any other show on the road that I'd seen. They may have suspected I was making it up about having a husband. When he came back I thought it very important to bring him to the seminars. Eric courted a relationship with him. He was a 'real' doctor (M.D.), trained in immunology research. Eric was most eager to add him to the people doing research to make TA a 'real science.'

"Pat Crossman was the only woman who sat consistently in the inner circle with Steve Karpman and Claude Steiner. She came up with a lot of good insights. Pat was one of the reasons I stayed on; otherwise I would have gotten too discouraged. I often told friends I was glad the seminar met only once a week because it took me that long to recover. It was both extremely attractive and extremely uncomfortable."

MAGGIE: "To go along with what Pam was saying—I decided to ask intelligent questions and otherwise to shut up. Eric, luckily, valued the questions. It seems to me that if we start out from the premise that we will never understand Eric, then we can relax and go ahead and put the kaleidoscopic picture together.

"One of the biggest and best experiences I had through association with Eric was the realization that great leaders are ordinary, fallible human beings and never again will I stand in awe of such."

FANITA ENGLISH

One time a woman important in TA circles said "shit." Eric stopped what he was doing and sat her down. He told her that he had had a very good friend, his closest friend of many years, through marriages and divorces. Suddenly the man had said "shit" and Eric had never spoken to him nor had anything to do with him again. Eric was telling her this as a friendly warning, never again to use the word in his presence.

According to Mary Goulding, Eric would not associate with anybody who used four-letter words. In *Sex in Human Loving* he had said," . . . a respect for the power of obscenity is not a quaint relic of an antique way of thinking. Rather it is one aspect of a way of life in which the most important quality is grace. . . . For me class = grace = reticence, the avoidance of overstatement and disharmony, in speech as in ballet as in painting. . . . I believe that obscenity should not be imposed on others without their consent."

On the other hand, under the heading of "Obscenity for Fun," he says that, "There are others who agree that uninvited obscenity is in most cases an assault and therefore reprehensible." But he mentions that a friend "tells about a male acquaintance who successfully uses obscenity as a method of seduction. As soon as possible after meeting a likely female, he makes a more than ordinarily indecent proposal to her in explicit language. In this way he wins the favors of some women and loses the respect of many others, thus demonstrating both positively and negatively the unusual corruptive powers of obscene words."

Is it possible that this male acquaintance was actually Eric Berne?

At any rate, Fanita English's first hour face-to-face with Berne was not a period of grace. After reading *Transactional Analysis in Psychotherapy* with great excitement, she got Berne's Carmel telephone number and (calling him from Chicago) as if by a miracle got him right on the phone. "He told me," she said, "if I could get four other therapists together and would pay him $50 for the session and pay for his hotel room, he would spend an afternoon telling us about TA (and that was phenomenally cheap even for that time)."

Fanita was beautiful, but besides being deeply concerned about her work as a therapist, she was a decorous and rather proper young matron. When she called for him at his Chicago hotel room, he opened the door and she immediately began formally and with almost Germanic correctness: "Dr. Berne, I do so admire your work." And, she reported to us, "he came out with a remark that was so startlingly outrageous, so shocking and so free that I didn't know what to do about him." He did use a four-letter word (equally as startling as "shit") in the form of an invitation or proposal. This was in marked contrast to the gracious way he had offered to come and talk to her and her friends for so little money.

During that afternoon Mrs. English tried to keep as far away from him as possible. Now she believes that he behaved in that manner to shock her out of her conventional way of approaching him.

When it came to the workshop, Berne acted in such a "super-abrasive" manner that he turned off all five of these somewhat conservative, psychoanalytically oriented therapists. He insisted on doing his "Intimacy Experiment," which tended to paralyze audiences who weren't familiar with Transactional Analysis or Berne's concept of intimacy. These midwestern therapists became so disenchanted with this new TA approach that they didn't even ask Berne to stay on after the workshop and go out to dinner with them. They felt that the tone of the workshop had been kookie, far-out, and California-ish. Anyway, Fanita English was already totally turned off after her introduction to Berne earlier that afternoon.

Realizing that his appearance had not been successful, he told Mrs. English not to give up on TA but to attend a Bob

Goulding—Dave Kupfer workshop that was to be given in Illinois soon. She did, and after that she decided to take further TA training. In Carmel she came to know Berne as a fellow professional. "We would talk extensively and he was completely different . . . and I began to like and admire him. . . . We would have exciting times. . . . My experience with Berne while he was in Carmel was that he was super-professional, even in social contacts. If anything, I was more free in challenging him. I'd say: 'Oh, come on! Come off it!' etc., and he'd get on his high horse. I wasn't always properly respectful. . . . But we had a good relationship. He respected me and I did not find him the brusque, unapproachable person that many people did. He didn't talk down to me, except under provocation. Other women felt that he was sexist."

Fanita read part of *Eric Berne, Master Gamesman, A Transactional Biography* while we were putting it together, and commented: "When I read your book in manuscript I kept saying, 'Oh, so that's why!' I had intuition about Eric previously, but no data, and your manuscript gave me the data. You describe this crazy, clumsy kid over and over in your chapters, doing these stupid things, trying to make contact with other human beings. Now his theory makes all the more sense."

At one of the early conferences in Monterey, Berne was to give the final paper. The meeting went on and on, as the treasurer's report was voluminous. Finally, Eric began his speech while conference members crept out to catch the last plane of the day from Monterey. Eric ended up speaking to about seven people. He walked out of the hall with bowed head, crushed that his wonderful speech had been wasted. Fanita thought this behavior gamey. He could easily have made his presentation earlier in the program. It was her opinion that Eric wanted to feel bad. However, she caught up with him and complimented him effusively on his speech, only to have him turn away. When she challenged him on this he replied: "If you had told me I was handsome, I would have listened to you."

Fanita learned the technique Berne developed at McAuley of having the patients sit in an inner circle during the first part of the group's hour, and the staff sit in an outer circle behind the patients. At the end of the hour the two circles switched places so that the patients in the outer circle could listen to the staff as they discussed what had taken place during the therapeutic hour. She used this technique for a year at Elgin State Hospital in Pennsylvania and "got great results—it worked miracles! Things like these should be emphasized. . . . We were all then seen as tremendous innovators and creators and, sure, each one of us created and added to his theory, but without this man, we, his TA disciples, would never have dared. Eric in a sense continued the revolutionary tradition of Freud, and that's the spirit that has prevailed."

VIOLA LITT CALLAGHAN

Viola Litt Callaghan was a nice girl with a Jewish background who may have reminded Berne of the girl-next-door type he was familiar with while growing up in Montreal.

One time in a meeting Eric said: "If you hear one voice louder than all the others, it will be Viola."

And, from the rear of the room, Vi said: "I love you, too, Eric."

In 1970, when his health was failing, Vi started calling "Peekaboo, I love you" to Eric in the hallway of his Collins Street house. And Eric seemed to like and need this; and he would come running to play peekaboo with her like a little kid. At a 101 graduation party one time he told Jack Dusay: "Viola's the longest nonsexual relationship on record."

Vi told us, "I knew him twelve and a half whole years. My ex-husband never believed that I could have been around Eric so long and not gotten involved. I didn't want to. I didn't know all about the sexual ins and outs and never wanted to. It kept me clean. A sexual involvement wouldn't have worked because we were already in a 'Kick Me' game. [Besides] Eric didn't know how to protect women."

We agreed and said Eric had grown up in a time when there were two kinds of women, those you put on a pedestal and those you played around with.

Vi replied: "We're not out of that yet. . . " And she added:

"Game playing is the most complicated relationship you can have. One of the fun things about the seminars was, you could have all those complicated relationships. Whether you saw each other on the outside or not—most didn't—you could do all these fun things together.

"Games make things more interesting. If you didn't have games in life, it would be pretty dull, right? And intimacy, you know, is still rare. And it's not that easy just to have it."

PAT CROSSMAN

In a note in *TAB*, dated October 19, 1965, Editor Berne handed out a stroke to Pat Crossman. He reported that during the month he had been away on a trip, Claude Steiner and Pat Crossman had each acted as a therapist for his groups. The men group members had had a positive reaction to Pat, telling Berne how much they had enjoyed having a woman therapist with sex appeal for a change.

The ITAA recognized Pat's contribution of Permission and Protection to basic TA theory and awarded her the Eric Berne Memorial Scientific Award in 1976. In her acceptance speech, Mrs. Crossman said:

> *Permission and Protection* was written in 1966. . . . We based our work on a dream. The dream was about a world where the Natural child ran free, where babies did not have to die unnecessarily, and where there was an abundance of warm fuzzies. In other words, we were flagrant romantics and rebels. We were adolescents, and we gathered around a bigger adolescent, who was Eric Berne. He was also a grandfather, an enchanter, and last but not least, a country doctor . . . within the next few years [I want us to] take another look at areas still unexplored in TA . . . the functions of the right lobe of the brain. I would like to link up TA with systems and information theory and . . . myths and fairy stories, to magic and occult sciences and to the biological sciences, and to make the next few years the rediscovery of the unconscious.

For a while Pat was acting as Berne's co-therapist in one of his groups. At first their nimble minds danced a delightful tarantella together, but there came to be a tug-of-war between the two therapists. Pat was trying to get to the patients' feeling level, whereas Eric wanted group members to sit on their feelings and analyze their feelings intellectually. Finally, Eric said (in effect): "There can be only one group leader here and I will have to be it." Pat bowed out, taking part of the group with her, the sparks from their mental interaction continuing at the Tuesday evening seminars.

At one point they also had hoped to achieve more than an intertwining of intellects, but the chemistry wasn't right. Nothing jelled. This put such a strain on their association together that Pat gave up going to the seminars.

Pat feels that Eric mustn't be made out to be a womanizer; he was primarily a thinker. But he was trapped by his own personality, by his allegiance to Freud, and by his nineteenth-century background.

"It was success Eric couldn't cope with," Pat thought. "From being a loner and an outsider, he got thrown on center stage and didn't know how to handle it."

Pat did see Eric once more, shortly before his heart attack, and they had a moving reunion, this time as friends.

"My biggest excitement actually came after his death, when I discovered his books in the ITAA headquarters which had been annotated in his own handwriting. I realized that there was a secret life that went on between him and his books and I have spent a great deal of time trying to decipher the notes. TA has greatly changed since Eric was alive and I am now separated from the TA movement by theoretical as well as personal considerations."

Due to Pat's efforts, these books are now in the rare book collection of the UC Medical Center in San Francisco.

CAROLYN CRANE

Well-known TA member Ken Ernst, a teacher, therapist, and author of *Games Students Play* and *TA Stories for Kids,* worked with Carolyn when he was teaching four-year-olds the principles of TA and following through on the children to see what effect the early teaching had on their lives. He told us: "She was a warm person, competent and strong, solid, not seductive, but very attractive and handsome . . . with dark brown hair. You'd ask her to do something and she would do it. She was a person you could relax with—a good listener—a good person who radiated honesty and sincerity. I don't know anybody who didn't like Carolyn Crane."

Part Lakota Indian and "beautiful and as elusive as mercury," she had been a patient in a therapy group of Berne's in the mid-sixties. In 1969 she was in training to be a TA lay analyst with Dave Kupfer in Palo Alto, California. She attended the Tuesday evening seminars and occasionally saw Berne at other professional gatherings. One night after a seminar, Berne asked her to wait until the meeting was over because he wanted to talk with her.

"We sat stiffly on a short couch," she said. Berne told her he "was getting a divorce and would like to begin seeing her; however, [she] must promise not to tell any of the [patients] from [her] original group." Since she never saw anyone from that group anyway, this was easy to promise. "I gave the contract too little importance, not realizing the extent of his belief system and the guilt it could generate, this proximity to an ex-patient."

Carolyn had taught in Phoenix, Arizona, schools, become "burned out" on the institutional aspects of education, and gone back to teaching after Berne had encouraged her in group to do so.

She then had taught family life education in the multiracial Oakland High School during the era of the Symbionese Liberation Army and the Black Panthers. During her years there, two of her most promising girl students were murdered by a white boy high on drugs, and Foster, the black superintendent of schools, was "executed" by the SLA as part of its program of terror.

Carolyn said that during the last year of his life Eric was giving a free course at the open education exchange and beginning to learn about feminism and consciousness raising groups. Hogie Wyckoff had disbanded a therapy group because she couldn't get her own needs met while she was the leader.

Carolyn discussed with Eric the possibility that a new leaderless group model would be necessary for exclusively women's groups based on sisterhood and equality. She wanted to combine her TA training and this new outlook and talked to Berne about arranging experimental women's groups to discover what successful model might emerge. "He saw beyond his own system," she said.

"Eric and I took a trip together, socialized with his friends, and went out to dinner when he was in San Francisco, but usually I declined because I felt uncomfortable around him. We talked about getting married and having a child; he liked that idea, he said.

"But his body seemed to be contracting inward. The physical signs told me he was dying and I even talked about it with a friend, a clinical psychologist, about six months before [his death.]

"He was the grand patriarch of a patriarchal system where potency flows ever away from the authority figure to the patient/child. To his system he added a stern 'no touch the patients' prohibition. At the ITAA convention in 1969 . . . he gave the banquet speech on exactly that topic: No touching. I listened as a new TA trainee, little knowing that Berne's injunction extended to ex-patients, forever."

Berne didn't include her as a fellow colleague in TA doings. She began to feel that he was trying to hide his relationship with her. This disturbed her. There were meetings she could have attended with him with enjoyment. By this time she thought of herself as having the status of therapist rather than patient.

But there was another barrier to a fulfilling relationship between the two—an incest fantasy. She said, "What Eric used to say when we made love was 'Who do you want to be tonight, my mother or my sister?' . . . He wasn't there with me or for me. . . . He was in a totally closed-off situation. . . . It just seemed to be a self-perpetuating pattern that he had run through many times and anyone outside that pattern was not a factor."

Carolyn's reaction to this was flight. "It wasn't rewarding." She couldn't confront him about his strange request because "I was still in the transference—he was still an authority figure from the years before when I had been in one of his groups."

(The Ethics Committee of the ITAA now has a rule concerning this problem: "Members are cautioned not to have sexual relations with a former client.")

Carolyn also remembered that one evening at Dave Kupfer's house an odd party game was introduced that was supposed to develop sensory awareness. It consisted of people forming "a human rug" where some people would lie on the floor and other people would tumble on top of them. Carolyn reported: "I was one of the ones on the bottom and Eric jumped right on top of me and I almost was badly hurt. I could not breathe."

We asked where he had jumped from.

"From a stairway," she replied, describing a distance of 5 or 6 feet. "The bottom layer got really crushed, a lot of people got jumped on, but Eric was the one who jumped on me and hurt me."

She wanted to rescue Berne from his difficulties, but didn't know how to confront him. If she could have talked straight with him in Reichian terms she would have said: Your armoring seems as if it's completely got you wrapped up and I would love to reach into you and touch you and hold you and have you feel me and to have an exchange back and forth and I wonder if it's possible and if it is, I'd like so much to touch you as a human being.

They never welded a strong alliance, although it was intermittently close. The two globules of quicksilver never coalesced into one puddle.

Fanita English also told us about the human rug. She suggested that Eric didn't know how to have satisfactory body contact with others (perhaps because of factors in his childhood): so "one favorite game of his was to encourage people to throw themselves on him in a pile." Fanita remembered on one occasion at a luncheon meeting he lectured sternly about TA being a "no touch" therapy.

"And that same evening he had a party at his home where he stood in the middle of the floor and said from a different ego state: 'Remember TA is no touch!' (with a crazy grin that was supposed to be attractive, but was not necessarily so). And then everyone threw himself on him on a pile. I had a rather unpleasant reaction to this."

CONNIE CONCANNNON

Connie Concannon brought out the protective and avuncular part of Berne. She was the daughter of Joe Concannon, Veterans' Administration social worker who became enchanted with the way Berne treated patients, and in two decades of devoted adherence to the TA movement never became disenchanted with its leader. Connie was a "second-generation TA person." Both her parents were therapists. She first went to the seminars with her father when she was in high school, at about age fifteen.

She remembered two incidents from the last six months of Berne's life:

Claude Steiner gave Eric his sixtieth birthday party on May 10, 1970, two months before his death. At that party Berne asked Connie what career she was training for. Connie, who had just completed her B.A., answered that she was planning to be a therapist. Berne asked her what she thought of TA. Connie said: "I think a lot of it is bullshit." She added that she was "circled and arrowed out."

Eric laughed uproariously. The statement seemed to hook his rebellious Child. Thereafter he took a great interest in Connie and told her that after she had completed work for her M.S.W., there was a real possibility she could come and work for him in Carmel.

Connie attended the AGPA Conference as did Berne, and they went out to dinner afterwards with a large group. Connie describes herself at this period as being "twenty-two or twenty-three, a late bloomer, a little chunky, with long, dark brown hair, at that awkward stage moving from being a teenager to a young adult." She was sitting close to Berne at dinner and he caught her looking wistfully at some attractive women therapists nearby.

Eric said suddenly: "I want to tell you not to compare yourself with women like that."

Feeling as if he had been reading her mind, Connie stammered: "Why not?"

Eric said: "You have a strong, warm heart—and that is far sexier than all the rest."

When Eric was in the hospital with his heart attack, he sent Connie a communiqué through her father to "stay in school and follow the course." He wanted her to go ahead and become a therapist.

It was a positive statement, and it was received positively. At age thirty-four, Connie is co-owner and co-director of The Oasis Center in Walnut Creek, California, which employs many different methods of therapy. Five therapists work there and they have fifteen or sixteen groups, all outpatient. She feels the message Eric gave her was "to be independent and follow her own way."

18

A Maserati, a Best-Seller, And a Young Blonde Wife

> . . . there is no doubt that many older people are rejuvenated when they take a younger mate. Thus, the Fountains of Youth, so ardently sought in Florida and other exotic places, may be right under our noses (approximately 2'6" down).
>
> Eric Berne, *Sex in Human Loving*

In July 1967, Dr. Moses Margolick, Berne's old McGill Medical School classmate, got a letter from Eric telling him that in April he had married again: a lissom and zaftig young Venus who was clever, well-mannered, part-Jewish, and who liked to play poker with him and jog on Carmel Beach. As he was writing this, she was in the kitchen preparing some delicious Jewish delicacy.

Margolick was not more surprised by the news than the San Francisco TA group, for this well-mannered goddess, Torre, had come from out of nowhere as far as they were concerned. However, Dr. Solon (Sol) Samuels of Los Angeles, one of the first of the psychiatrists to line up in the TA camp, had had a long-standing friendship with Torre, who had sung in the Gateway choir run by Dr. Samuels's wife, Anne.

"She had a nice voice," Anne said, "and read music well. I relied on her a lot in the part she played in the musicales . . . [she was] lovely. To me, she was like a wild flower. She was tall—and willowy . . ."

"Maybe you could say—a gazelle?" Sol suggested.

"Just like a little wild bird," Anne said, " a wild flower, just free and light, and I loved it in her. Her hair was blonde—it's always been very blonde—it's natural in her; she had very white skin. There was an airiness about her. You'd want her to light somewhere, to stay put."

"She had a fascination for minds, brilliant minds," Sol added.

Anne continued, "When Eric came and we watched this drama unfold, we felt like her parents."

Torre's "fascination for minds" had been the reason the Samuelses had met her in the first place. She had appeared at Lake Arrowhead one summer when the University of California at Los Angeles had put on its annual summer seminars (this one on ESP) of higher learning. Torre had come up with the "kookiest bunch of young people" but had struck up with a brilliant young engineer there and had returned with him two summers later—in 1965—for the seminar in which Eric Berne was the keynote speaker. By this time the relationship with the engineer was on the wane, but they came to the conference together.

Torre was not long on formal education, but she was a member of MENSA and therefore identifiable as having an IQ that placed her in the top 2 percent of the general population. (She called MENSA a "lonely hearts' club for intellectuals," and, according to friends, joined it principally so she could meet brainy men.)

Sol, at that time medical director of the Gateway Mental Health Clinic in Los Angeles, had been asked by UCLA to recommend a speaker for this seminar and had suggested Eric Berne; but to Dr. Samuels' embarrassment, Berne didn't live up to his billing. He didn't exert himself to give the audience a good explanation "of what TA was all about . . . he put on a brief, perfunctory performance." Apparently the audience didn't inspire him. "He was very anxious to make converts among professionals, very anxious," according to Dr. Samuels, "but these were ordinary people, not professionals [so] I spent the following two days defending Eric. I had to make a lot of apologies."

The highlight of the seminar as far as Torre was concerned was a "chess duel" between Berne and her friend. It was something like the spectacle of two throat-swollen stags locking horns in a remote glen for the possession of a hind. "It was a big competition thing between my friend and Eric," said Torre. "It was all sort of fun. They were trying to out-intellectualize each other. Everyone was aware of it and that was what made it funny." Eric won the game, but that did not seem as significant to Torre as the fact that he was obviously impressed by her.

Dr. Samuels told us, "The same day he met her, Eric announced that he was going to marry her. He announced it to everyone and pursued her from then on . . . He went after her tooth and nail. And people looked down on him because here was this great professor, this renowned man, who came up to give this speech and they came to sit at his feet and he acts like a silly boy who became lovesick over this blonde beauty. We thought at first he was joking, kidding. We didn't read the signals right. He really meant it."

Anne Samuels added, "He really went after her."

Torre hadn't heard any talk of marriage directly from Berne—although the language of the eyes had seemed eloquent enough. But she didn't hear from Eric after he returned to Carmel. He had made such a bravura sally at Lake Arrowhead; had the fogs and mists of northern California cooled his ardor? The young Venus was in her late twenties when they met—only half his age. Did Berne get Jurgen-like afterthoughts to the brief encounter?

> Now came to Jurgen a gold-haired woman, clothed all in white. She was tall and lovely and tender to regard . . .
>
> "Lady of my vision," he said, and his voice broke—"there is that in you that awakens old memories . . .
>
> "I . . . am not fit to mate with your perfection. At the bottom of my heart, I no longer desire perfection. For we who are tax-payers as well as immortal souls must live by politic evasions and formulae and catchwords that fret away our lives as moths waste a garment; we fall insensibly to common sense as to a drug; and it dulls and kills whatever in us is rebellious and fine and unreasonable; and so you will find no man of my years with whom living is not a mechanism which gnaws away time unprompted.

"... I have become a creature of use and wont; I am the lackey of prudence and half-measures; and I have put my dreams upon an allowance ... for that reason, lady, I pray you begone, for your loveliness is a taunt which I find unendurable."

James Branch Cabell, *Jurgen*

After some time had passed without a sign, Torre sent Eric a letter in which she indicated she was thinking of visiting Carmel. If Eric would give her his phone number, she would call him up. She was surprised to learn that his number was in the phone book (anybody "of any fame or notoriety" in Los Angeles had an unlisted number). At any rate, Torre made her visit to Carmel, driving up with her mother, had a brief walk on the beach with Eric, and decided to move to Carmel, "which I was going to do anyway."

This was in January or February of 1966. She got a job with Control Data in Monterey, just over the hill from Carmel, and began taking her lunches at Ring's, around the corner from her office. At Ring's a placard over the cash register announced that the restaurant was "Under No Management," and a walled garden with a Spanish-colonial wrought-iron gate offered a spot where elegantly priced hamburgers could be consumed in an atmosphere of luscious iconoclasm. There local artists, writers, and stockbrokers met and argued endlessly.

"The guys at Ring's circulated around Torre like moths around a light globe on a summer night," asserted Kurt Hartman, bookstore owner and acquaintance of both Torre and Eric.

Torre remembers: "The atmosphere at Ring's was very, very special. . . . I realized at the time that that combination of people would never be repeated."

With her long, floaty blonde hair, "which she used to bounce around like a television commercial," and her statuesque height, Torre appeared a vision of Nordic loveliness. Actually, she was "half Norwegian and half Jewish."

Her maiden name had been Torre Peterson, borrowed from a step-grandfather, her grandmother's name was Knudsen, and Torre's name at this juncture had come from a previous husband. She had officially converted to Judaism when she married Rosenkrantz, an affluent and philanthropic Los Angeles realtor.

Mac Bowe, a reporter for the *San Jose Mercury* who also made the scene at Ring's, described Torre thus: "She was a striking-looking person, very striking—I don't know, you'd hardly call her beautiful—but pretty, long hair to here, and tall. . . .

"She was very proud of being part Jewish, but she was also a pacifist. We'd argue back and forth over lunches out in the garden. You know, Hawks and Doves? She was very much against war, always, anti-Vietnam war. As could be expected, the Hawks were conservatives (I was)—the Doves, liberals. Anyway, she was against war, *until* that one in the sixties between Israel and its enemies. I didn't see her for a while, then I bumped into her. She was bouncing up and down saying: 'We won! We won! We won!'

"I said, 'I thought you didn't believe in war?'

"And she said: 'Oh, but that wasn't war—we were attacked!'

"Another time we were walking down the street and Torre was kind of slumping over, and I said: 'Torre, stand up straight!' and she said, kind of wistfully: 'Well, you know, Eric's 5'11" and I'm 5'11" and he wants to be taller than I am.'

"When she was working for Control Data she'd get on the Telex, and she'd found out how to make it play "Three Blind Mice" with its bells. I told her: 'Don't do it—don't do it! You're scrambling messages all over the country, you crazy woman!"

So she was young, and lovely, and willowy, and brainy, and blonde, and zany. It was an inspired zaniness, a zaniness that was well received in the odd-ball purlieus of Ring's and also on the beaches of Carmel.

Furthermore, she was a master at telling funny stories. TA's Mary Goulding, who saw her on occasion at Ring's, said, "Torre told absolutely the funniest jokes and told them the best of anybody I've ever known. Since Eric really liked that sort of Jewish intellectual humor, I think that was one of the first things that attracted him about her."

Mac Bowe told us: "Before they were married, Torre had thirty or forty parking tickets that had finally caught up with her from Los Angeles. I stopped into Muni Court that day and the judge sentenced her to $500 or five days in jail, zap, just like that. Torre wanted me to call Eric. She didn't have any money. I didn't want to get that involved, but fortunately, Eric didn't answer. So then the judge comes out and says: 'Do you know this young lady?" I said, 'Yes.' And he said to Torre: 'Well, I'll give you till next Monday to pay the $500.' "

(Torre told us: "There were only five tickets. They were Monterey parking tickets that were being delivered to an empty house in Hermosa Beach, near Los Angeles. I went into court with the tickets in an effort to explain instead of paying the fines. The total fine was $50.")

In the spring of 1966, Berne was asked to give the Jake Gimbel lectures on the psychology of sex at the San Francisco Medical Center of the University of California and at the University of California at Santa Cruz. The lectures required considerable research, he said, contending that he didn't know much about the topic. Later these lectures were amplified and made into the book *Sex in Human Loving*.

Before a solemn audience of 600 doctors, psychologists, social workers, and students that overflowed into the aisles and jammed the auditorium, Berne equally solemnly posited the premise that the ideal wife should: (1) wear red shoes, (2) read Chaucer, and (3) be able to decipher Sanskrit—all qualifications that Torre, and few others, could meet.

The popularity and enthusiastic response to these lectures added to Berne's elation over the success of *Games People Play*. Eric professed to be very cool about this to the general public, but he allowed his Carmel friends to see his real enjoyment. Valerio Giusi recalls the pleasure Berne showed when he told Valerio *Games* had broken the record for the number of weeks a nonfiction book had stayed on the best-seller list. Giusi said it was the first time he had realized that Eric had the same emotions other people did.

With everything happening at once, Berne was too busy that spring to visit Ring's more than a few times. When he did appear, Torre "sort of fluttered around and catered to him," according to Kurt Hartman. She put on a "virtuoso performance" of wit and charm which may or may not have dazzled Berne but which definitely floored the other male patrons in the walled garden. "They were just pushovers for this gal from Los Angeles," said Hartman.

In the beginning, the San Francisco TA people saw Torre rarely. Some of the men were convinced that the Master had outpointed them all in capturing the ultimate in female gloriousness; the women weren't so sure. It wasn't necessarily that they wanted him for themselves. They were curious about the fact that such a sharp line existed between his Carmel life and his San Francisco life. They also were not at all certain that the Southern California cornucopia style which they thought they found in Torre would go with Berne's almost European professional correctness.

In December of 1966, Berne planned a trip to a psychiatric conference in Madrid. He bought a ticket for Torre and had her meet him in Milan. They traveled from there to Monte Carlo and to Austria. Later, according to Mel Boyce, Eric told TA people that he had first bumped into his bride-to-be in Spain.

Back in Carmel, Torre and Eric often showed up at the beach, jogging and doing setting-up exercises on the sand—Eric turned elaborate cartwheels. Berne's ex-wife Dorothy would sometimes be at the beach with her friends and would be embarrassed about the exercises, because Torre seemed to be taller than Eric and it appeared that Eric "couldn't make a move without her." But the pair enjoyed themselves. "She amused him. She was a very capable, smart, clever young woman . . . They had a long time together that was very good," said Judy Nordin.

Nadya Giusi told us: "Torre and Eric had a wonderful, fun-filled relationship, at least in the beginning—unstructured, not like the former ménage. With Torre, it was all based on impulse—'Let's go to the beach,' etc. Eric really enjoyed his money and fame those last years of his life." Eric had brought Torre over to Nadya and Valerio's house "for approval"—they found her "very warm, terrific, very sympathetic—a touch-oriented person."

They had a game they would play. Eric would hum something, and since he couldn't carry a tune, Torre would have to guess what it was, "and it was hard." The only song she ever identified for sure, and this was after he had sung it over and over, was "Rule Britannia."

It was about this time that Eric took up playing his eleven-year-old son's drums in a big way. Claude Steiner mentioned to us that Berne's sense of rhythm left something to be desired, but his drumming was sufficient to impress an *LA Times* reporter who talked to him in 1967. The reporter said that in mid-interview the doctor leaped up and headed for his "game room," from which "an amazing barrage of crashes, thumps, and tara-diddles" emerged. Urged on by Claude Steiner, Eric also bought himself a Maserati 3500 GT. Several people remember his saying at this juncture that he had always wanted a Maserati, a best-seller, and a young, blonde wife.

Berne said: "You don't really know somebody 'til you know what kind of fun he can have when he lets his child out. Drumming is relaxing. I'm thinking of taking lessons. I don't beat the hell out of drums to get rid of my aggressions. All three of my ego states bought the Mazeltov [Hebrew word meaning: Good Luck!] The Child wanted it, the Adult needed it, and the Parent said 'Drive carefully!' And I do."

In fact, he drove it so slowly that his friends wondered why he had bought a hot sports car at all. Kurt Hartman said the Maserati "should have been driven by Cary Grant and Grace Kelly up the winding roads of Monaco," and he added: "It was long."

A San Francisco friend wasn't too impressed with the car. He commented: "Well, that Maserati wasn't much. It had a great name, but it was at least secondhand, or maybe sixthhand. There was something humorous about it as a gesture, something tongue-in-cheek."

Berne told his TA audience at a Tuesday night seminar that Carmel was sort of a rich retirement community where many people had nothing better to do than to compare Coupe de Villes, spread rumors, and moan about teenagers. They had completed their scripts and had lots of unstructured time on their hands, so they cruised along in the slow lane at 35 or 40 mph, complaining about other people's children. Berne said he got a lot of pleasure from whizzing past them in his Maserati with the top down. He was as old as, if not older than many of them, but he could imagine them roaring: "Damn fool adolescent!"

This symptom of resurgent adolescence in Eric bothered not

a whit his TA cohorts, who were prepared for the unexpected from their mentor for the most part, but in April of 1967, they were not really prepared to read in the gossip and humor column of *San Francisco Chronicle's* Herb Caen that Eric Berne and Torre Rosenkrantz had been issued a wedding license in Salinas, California.

Pamela Blum, Berne's San Francisco executive secretary (a graduate student at UC Berkeley), quickly planned a little informal wedding reception at her own apartment to follow the next Tuesday evening seminar. She and her roommates arranged for champagne to be served in fluted champagne glasses and baked a heart-shaped wedding cake. Pam had Torre flown up to San Francisco from Carmel without Eric's knowing about it, and everyone in TA was delighted to see his surprise when Torre walked in, right behind him, just as Eric was saying: "What a shame Torre isn't here! She would love this."

Although Moses Margolick was not to get word of the wedding until July (as noted in the introductory paragraph to this chapter), the news spread rapidly through TA circles. Sol and Anne Samuels in Los Angeles didn't find out until August, but were delighted as both Torre and Eric seemed so happy.

Berne's ex-wife Dorothy made her way to Berne's new four-bedroom house, four blocks away, to greet the happy couple, her arms full of flowers. She said: "On Saturday I went over to their house. I practically bought out the florist; I went up there and rang the doorbell. They came to the door amazed to see me. I walked in and gave [Torre] a very warm greeting, [but] I kept thinking: My children have a stepmother! She seemed hostile and controlled and I just couldn't imagine her as my children's stepmother."

Torre remembers the incident this way: "Dorothy came over with a lot of flowers and tears. And what can you [tell] the woman who wants to be married to your husband and who was very hurt, especially as I was so much younger? . . . We thanked her and asked her in, but I couldn't very well say to her: 'I'm not really married to your husband.' "

Some marriages are, no doubt, made in heaven, but others are made in the leading left-hand column of the second section of the *San Francisco Chronicle*. Torre and Eric weren't married in April of 1967. All they solemnized was the twenty-mile trip to the Salinas courthouse for the license. They only pretended to be married, partly because it made Eric uncomfortable to have his children running in and out of a house where a vision of untrammeled loveliness was installed, and partly because they both "enjoyed fooling people." Also, Torre said, "I know there was something about not wanting to marry me until I was thirty."

So at last Eric had found a tall blonde goddess who enjoyed paradox and pretense. The little pirate had captured a playmate willing to participate in "Hide and Seek." Torre was a woman who related well to the essential Berne—his intellectual brilliance, his scorn, his rascality, his wit. Neither Torre nor Eric suffered fools gladly, and her energy, like his, seemed inexhaustible. Ideas and opinions crackled and flashed from her like lightning in a great prairies line squall. They were both "take-charge" personalities. A mock-marriage appealed to her as much as to him.

The stage was thus set for an eminently successful May-(or maybe June-)December romance. As Berne put it in *Sex in Human Loving:* "In an intimate relationship, each person returns to the original naive Child ego state, where he is free from . . . Parental prohibitions and Adult requirements, and can see, hear, and taste in its purest form what the world has to offer."

All signals and portents were "go." Rejuvenation via the Fountain of Youth was inevitable. Theirs would be the intimacy that would turn "the whole universe, including the sun, moon, and stars, into a golden apple for both parties to enjoy."

But it turned out to be not so easy to live "happily ever after."

For, as Richard Sheridan said in *The School For Scandal:* ". . . when an old bachelor marries a young wife, he deserves—no—the crime carries its punishment along with it."

19

Farewell to Queen Helen

> . . . the more I marry, the less I find of comprehension.
> James Branch Cabell, *Jurgen*

> I remember asking [Berne] if . . . there were ever couples who were truly happy. He thought that there were some, but that they probably lived on some island and, in any event, they never came to see him.
> Elliott Steinberg, letter

> "Why, then," says Jurgen, "I shall marry in haste, and repeat at leisure. But can one obtain a divorce here?"
> James Branch Cabell, *Jurgen*

In the August 12, 1966, issue of *Life* magazine there was a large black-and-white picture of Eric Berne doing the "TA stomp." According to Sol and Anne Samuels, this was Berne's way of "letting his Child out." Anne said: "At the first parties after the TA meetings [in '61 and '62] Berne never participated in the hi-jinks. He just sat in the corner and watched. He was an observer. He even took notes.

"But after a while, in recent years ['66 through '69] Eric decided he must let his Child out. It was part of his formula. But letting his Child out, instead of dancing or singing, meant he'd just stand and jump. Just stand and jump! In one spot! That was his Child!"

"That was when he discovered jumping to express himself," Sol added.

Anne continued, "Just jump, with such determination—not joy—in his face, that the maternal in me would come out and I'd think, 'I'm afraid he'll have a heart attack!' He was no youngster! He'd evidently think, by golly, I'm going to jump and he'd jump practically the whole evening, it seemed to me. . . . And then the others got up and jumped, too. You know in Hasidic folklore there is a song saying: 'When the rabbi sings, the hasidim sing; when the rabbi dances, the hasidim dance.' So the rabbi jumped and everybody jumped like jumping jacks."

Pam Blum also noted Berne's expression as he did the TA stomp. However, she saw on his face a little half smile, "a little mischievous look, which was very endearing."

On July 17, 1966, Jack Languth, *New York Times* reporter, asked Berne to describe himself, and Berne replied: "I'm a fifty-six-year-old teenager. I'm sort of a swinger; I like action."

Many of Eric's new companions were from Esalen and were "very wiggy," according to Eric's long-time poker-playing associate Howard Brunn. Dr. Evelyn Siris (Mrs. Levitin) attended a party at his new house in Carmel and felt disgusted with his youthful antics. His new friends "had no conception of what this guy was really like."

Mac Bowe, who also attended Eric's party, said: "It was the wildest group of people from all segments of society." Sirrah (Dale) Harris said: "It was an intellectual hippie scene that they were in—much wife and husband trading"—and Brunn expatiated: "I mean those guys were really wild—they just let it all hang out—Eric was a little bit that way, but he wasn't as wiggy as they were." (According to Torre, Eric stood apart from this, remaining essentially an observer.)

The Giusis attended one such party and were amazed to find almost everyone lying on the floor. One guru was accompanied by a girl in a fishnet blouse with her nipples pertly peeking through. "How about that!" Eric commented. When the Giusis left, Eric had joined his guests on the carpet. "Everyone was saying, 'Let's be loose. Let's relax, etc.' "

Members of the San Francisco TA circles accepted this new phase—or what little they saw of it—as part of Berne's idea of restructuring his own personality to fit the philosophy expounded in his works. They loved him as their Nurturing Parent who gave them permission to let their own Child out; they were not concerned that his own attempts at frivolity seemed a little "out of sync." Muriel James showed us the way Berne danced with a partner at TA doings; it consisted of little hops of about a half-foot in the air, interspersed with random kicking. "I hated to have to dance with him," she admitted, "but I did like watching him dance."

Jacqui Schiff mentioned that she and Eric danced together a lot.

We asked her if she enjoyed it, and she replied: "I have no sense of rhythm at all, but it didn't seem to bother Eric. . . . I think that's probably why Eric and I danced together. He seemed to have no sense of rhythm, either. We got along just fine. We danced very vigorously. It was very enjoyable. I didn't have to follow Eric and he didn't seem at all disconcerted by my lack of response to the music. I experienced his body as rigid. . . . In some sense, dancing with Eric could be like dancing with a puppet—a kind of woodenness. . . . My body is very flexible, so I noted that about Eric."

Bob Goulding said that when Berne attempted ballroom dancing it was obvious that he was counting under his breath.

For social occasions Berne had now discarded the coat and tie of earlier days and instead might appear wearing a peace symbol or beads over a turtle-neck sweater underneath a suit jacket—and at times a black felt sombrero.

Some of his friends were amazed at the decor of his new Carmel house. The living room was painted a Sunkist orange; the bed rested on its springs on the bedroom floor. Furniture was sparse. (Buddha's under the Bo tree was probably sparser.) Torre and Eric each possessed one comfortable chair. In one of the four empty bedrooms Eric had his roller-towel arrangement for continuous feeding of paper into his typewriter. In another bedroom, "the game room," Eric had his drums. In general, the exterior of uninspired bourgeois solidity did not give fair warning to the guest stepping into an interior which gave the appearance of having been recently burglarized.

The couple had a pet, Torre's cat, and although it was a "nasty, cantankerous beast," according to Torre, Eric tolerated it; and, in fact, Eric and the cat got along quite well. Eric's devoted cleaning woman, Mrs. Betty Burney, described the new place in this fashion:

"That house he had down there was nothing like with Mrs. [Dorothy] Berne; it was sort of like a hippie place. They didn't have much furniture; things were simple and plain, you know—nothing elaborate, just old stuff, and not very much of that . . . It was absolutely furnished with nothing, practically . . . It didn't seem like he could be so happy there."

Frank and Marjory Lloyd remembered that during the period of their courtship, Torre did a great deal of research on the Jewish religion, presented it to Berne, and tackled him vigorously on the subject of concealing his Jewish roots.

Berne didn't actually tell Torre what his background was until he had known her for some time—at least a year. Torre had earlier asked Berne: "What kind of name is Berne?" (He had never said anything about being Jewish, but she suspected he was.) Berne had put Torre off by answering, "Oh, I'm just a French-Canadian boy from Quebec." Later, Judy Kupfer Nordin remembers Torre saying heatedly during an argument: "I wish my name were Bernstein rather than Berne."

Torre doesn't know whether she convinced Berne, or whether he was simply ready to come to terms with his background. She did say that one of the few times she saw Eric express strong emotion was when he knelt on his parents' grave in Montreal in 1967, repeating the Kaddish. Big tears rolled down his cheeks. He was also beginning to wonder, who would say the Kaddish for him?

The new house had no little private shack out in back where Berne could do his writing. It was all very well to be warm and outgoing as a guru, but a serious writer, which Berne was, must be reclusive. ". . . good work only comes out under pressure of a bad life; . . ." Thomas Mann warned, "he who lives does not work; . . . one must die to life in order to be utterly a creator."

Writing was the core of Berne's being. In the fame and hullabaloo that followed *Games People Play* he complained that the biggest hardship was that he had been kept from his typewriter for six months. Nadya Giusi and Gerald Goodstone thought Berne was a writer before anything else.

As a boy, Eric had been incapable of coping with extraneous noise and had expressed his gratitude to his sister Grace, later on, for her cooperation in maintaining quiet. In the army, Berne had been unable to work on *The Mind in Action* in the Tacoma barracks because the walls were thin and he could hear radios and typewriters in the background. As a result of this sensitivity to sound, he needed silence when he wanted to write after supper in his new house. "He came home, had a rest, had something to eat, went into his room, and then there could be no noise or disturbance," Marjory Lloyd reported hearing. Torre saw little of him. Evenings became lonely. She took to having another woman come over to share crafts projects. Soon the Lloyds began hearing the same sort of complaints they had heard earlier from Dorothy.

Torre said: "What Eric wanted was not to have to care about anyone. Not to have to put any of himself in a relationship. And he thought that I wouldn't ask him to. For the most part I didn't. But he also thought I'd quietly fix his meals and stay out of his way. I was happy to do that for a while. I didn't mind tiptoeing around, but then I saw it was never going to end." She added: "Generally [Eric] looked on women as servants. That was one of our difficulties."

Edith Chester, who was well acquainted with Torre and Eric, said "Torre was [and is] a fabulous cook. She can leaf through a recipe book and decide to make certain things she has never tried before and will never make again and put them all together for a dinner party and it will be just perfection! The room, the setting, the dinner itself, will be just perfection!"

But Berne liked "burned lamb chops, burned to a cinder," and "cornflakes and the same things over and over."

"[Eric] had tremendous inflexibility," said Torre. "He had this inflexible routine. One of our problems was that I tried to break into his routine. Otherwise I never saw him except at meals or on the beach. But I tried to vary it by meeting him in San Francisco, or having lunch with him in Carmel—and he didn't like it. He didn't want his routine interfered with."

Claude Steiner told us: "Berne didn't want his wives coming to the seminars. He didn't want to mix the two . . . and so Torre came anyway, and she spoke [up] and he didn't like it. He didn't like it if a woman took liberties with the seminar.

"He was terrible—he was really just terrible with women all the way through," said Steiner. "In order for a woman to talk she'd have to be ten times as brilliant as a man . . . If women behaved well, they could make a very minor contribution, but if they started getting uppity, if they wanted to speak more, or if they disagreed, or if they got annoyed with him, which they very often did—lost control of their anger—then he would get very angry. He would say: 'Don't talk like that!' "

Steiner also indicated that one reason Berne didn't want his wives at the seminars was that he wanted to be free to "play the field." Torre was the first wife who was independent enough or interested enough to cause him a problem in this regard.

When Torre first attended the Tuesday evening seminars she was required to sit upstairs in the living quarters until the meeting was over, according to Pam Blum. But gradually she worked her way down and acted as hostess or dues collector, not without opposition from Eric. Pam believed that Tuesday nights, the seminar nights, were usually strictly business but knew that Wednesday nights were reserved for Berne's "lady of the moment. He was pretty discreet about this," said Pam. "In certain ways he was definitely a gentleman . . . he didn't advertise his partners. Oh, he tended to let me know, sort of, whom he was seeing when there was a regular person."

TA's Steve Karpman told us: "I don't think any of the women stated openly that they went to bed with [Berne], but I think quite a few of them did."

When Torre questioned Eric about the TA women, he admitted that one of them, at least, had been important and had meant a lot to him, but said that she was important no longer. It was Torre who mattered to him now, he said, and his air of sincerity convinced her.

Her confidence was somewhat shaken when another woman visited him in Carmel and Torre overheard them from a nearby bedroom. It appeared that not only had they been intimately involved for years, they were still intimately involved, at least emotionally. Torre remained discreetly in absentia until the visitor left.

In *What Do You Say After You Say Hello?* Berne writes about the marriage of a young woman to an older man as follows:

A common script based on the death scene is based on the marriage of a younger woman to an older man. Even if the cynics say she marries him for his bread, the script scene is equally important, and she will always be at his side in time of danger, on the good side to take care of him, but also so as not to miss the final payoff transaction. If he is intuitively aware of this, the marriage may have only a very narrow margin of safety, since it is not easy to get along with someone who is waiting for you to die.

Nor is it easy to get along with someone who believes you are waiting for him to die when you aren't. Berne's suspicions should have been allayed by a legal device. On the 29th day of December 1967, Eric and Torre entered into a (post) "nuptial agreement." For Eric and Torre did get married on September 23, 1967, and they did have a honeymoon—five months after the April mock marriage. Berne, who was vaguely thinking of retiring from the active practice of psychiatry, had his lawyer draw up an agreement so that all present, past, and future earnings from Berne's literary efforts were to be separate property, and therefore not subject to the wife's community property interests in the event of divorce or inheritance. Only his psychiatric income was to be community property. From the psychiatric income was to come alimony and child support payments before the present-day living expenses could be taken out.

Torre believed that Berne had a paranoid streak. This belief was not based on the legal document but on her memory of a time when Eric, under an anesthetic, "kept saying something like: 'They're going to get you,' and that was his attitude and he knew it. I mean he used to say about S.J. Perelman that he enjoyed his humor, but, boy, was he paranoid—and he was really saying it about himself."

Pam Blum remembers an Ortho-Psychiatric conference banquet where George Bach, author of *The Intimate Enemy*, was sitting across the table from Eric. Bach leaned over the table and said, "Every theory of personality is definitely connected to the personality of its founder—that's why your system is paranoid and mine is manic!" Berne didn't like this comment at all, but Pam also thinks Eric had a paranoid streak. One of his favorite sayings she remembers as: '"It just goes to show—you can't trust anybody!' This was said with tongue-in-cheek, however, most of the time."

Eric wanted more children of his own. He believed that if he had another child he would probably live another eighteen years because he would be committed to see it through to maturity. Rumor had it that he wouldn't marry Torre unless she was pregnant. According to Torre, this wasn't true. However, she did valiantly try to have a child by Eric, but she had a history of being unable to sustain a pregnancy.

Torre got pregnant on Eric's fifty-seventh birthday, May 10, 1967, but unfortunately lost the baby. Judy Kupfer (Nordin) visited Torre in the hospital after this miscarriage. TA's Pam Levin remembers Torre's talking to her about her problems with pregnancy and the possibility of adopting a child.

Ellen, Berne's oldest child, was surprised that Eric was so enthusiastic about producing a third family. After he and Torre had had a quarrel, Berne had complained to Ellen, who was visiting: "I'd like to have more children, but how can I, with things as they are?"

On the subject of children and family counselors, Berne explained to one of his groups in 1952 that a psychologist wasn't ipso facto the best person to give his child a feeling of being loved. He might give affection with one part of himself, but there was another part making significant observations. The child might sense this two-way relationship and long for a feeling that his parent was someone who loved him with his undivided self.

There seemed to be more than a little of the research psychologist approach in the way Berne organized his last honeymoon. On their trip to a psychiatric conference in Europe in September, Torre and Eric stopped off in Juarez, Mexico, and got married, five months after their pretended marriage. No way to make a celebration of this, as the nuptials had long since been solemnized in newsprint. The honeymoon itself was an example of the familiar formula of mixing together people likely to have at each other's throats. Who else would take on his honeymoon three children from two previous marriages?

Ellen described the adventure as follows: "I guess he just

called up and said: 'Would you like to go to Bulgaria?' They claimed they had been married a long time, but they had just gone to Mexico and got married, and in England they had to have their passports changed . . . I left the trip early—I was having an awful time. They would just fight all the time. My brother spoke German well; the rest of us didn't. My father spoke German a little bit, but until my brother joined us, we were having a hard time in the hotels, etc.

"No one in the hotels spoke anything but German and Bulgarian. My brother came to the desk and everyone just lighted up and they spoke German a long time. My brother is very charming. When he was along, he brought the whole thing together—they stopped fighting. When he wasn't along, they fought continuously.

"When I drove, Torre complained, and when Torre drove, I was sullen. My father had Gelusils [an anti-acid stomach pacifier], and he just took tons of them. Whichever of them read the map did it wrong and the other complained."

In the Bulgarian inns Eric would shout out: "Where are the dames? Bring out the dancing girls!" But he did not succeed in attracting either dames or dancing girls or in lightening the atmosphere of this grim trip.

The children witnessed various "scenes," in one of which Torre said she "was going to find herself a young man—because [Eric was] an old man." Torre remembers this incident but says: "The age thing really didn't matter to me. What mattered . . . was that he seemed so jaded. . . . He had been through it all so many times before. He really didn't want any new relationships. He just didn't want to make the effort . . . and besides, he was cold and unfeeling from the circumstances of his childhood."

In February 1968, Eric sent Torre a ring while she was visiting friends in Arkansas—a large, square-cut emerald flanked by two pear-shaped diamonds. Torre told us: "I was very impressed with this gesture." The magnificence of the gift stunned his sister and others in his family, since he had been so careful with his money in the past. Ellen said, "Eric changed after he married Torre. There was no ostentation in him at all—until he married Torre . . . You know, she wanted to spend money—'have fun and why not' was her attitude. Whenever we'd gone anywhere we'd stay in little grungy places, but with Torre, suddenly it was first class all the way. The best rental car they had, the best hotel, the best rooms . . . In Vienna we stayed in a castle. Beautiful! He said: 'Torre taught me that the way you tell a really fine hotel is that they have heated towels in the bathroom.' And, I thought, he's really changed! . . . It was much more fun being with him when he was like that."

"Berne," Groder said, "obviously married women who didn't have much in common with him. She was so very young. They got into some yucky scenes in front of the seminars and then, in his anger, Berne would turn around and take it out on some woman therapist in the audience."

Jacqui Schiff was "embarrassed for Eric. I was just sorry . . . It wasn't my business; there was no way I could deal with it, but I didn't like it. Eric asked for it, I'm sure. He got into it—he was responsible—must have walked into it with his eyes open. Eric chose to be in that position . . . I experienced that the women in Eric's life fitted into patterns. They were mostly sexual objects . . . with most women, with his three wives, his relations were predatory."

She continued: "It seemed to me that Eric had been placing himself in a position where he had been inviting that kind of treatment for a while. Getting involved with younger women— there wasn't a lot of depth to the relationships. My feeling was that he didn't treat them well. He made a point of not being [really] involved with women."

Berne had been telling his inner-circle TA colleagues that he wasn't having any sex with Torre. In *Sex in Human Loving* he later wrote:

> . . . Stomach trouble. On the man's side, many a husband knows how sex can prevent cancer. He knows that it is his wife, or rather his choice of wife, and his responses to her, that makes his stomach churn and the acid squirt. He also knows if it churns often enough and fiercely enough, he may end up with an ulcer, and that it is not a very long churn from an ulcer to cancer in serious cases. So he pops executive mints to keep the acid down, and hopes for what script analysts call an *At*

Least: for example, at least he might get high blood pressure before he gets cancer, and die a pleasanter death. But he will tell you that a good sex life would prevent the whole disaster: churning, acid, mints, and ulcer, and the cancer or stroke at the end of the line.

Again in the same book, he wrote:

> The older man is particularly sensitive about his mate. If she turns him off too often, he may begin to lose his potency and go into middle-age droop, a condition which may become progressively more severe, but is nearly always reversible if put in the hands of an enthusiastic practitioner.

In August of 1968, Sol and Anne Samuels met Eric and Torre for dinner in San Francisco. The Samuelses had come up for the TA summer conference. Torre and Eric "met, and it was just as if two strangers had bumped into each other," said Sol. "They didn't even nod to each other. It was very uncomfortable."

In the middle of the dinner, Berne, who hadn't been saying anything, got up, murmured "excuse me," and disappeared. The three ate the rest of their dinner, the check came, the Samuelses settled the bill and "waited and waited and waited."

Torre said: "Oh he probably walked out to a cigar store to get some tobacco for his pipe," but he wasn't in the cigar store and he wasn't in the men's room either. The Samuelses felt very put down when they discovered Eric was already at the TA meeting, which he had urged them to attend.

In the spring of 1969 Eric and Torre took a trip to Hawaii. Berne was on the faculty of the Young Presidents' Organization, a group which had an annual convention in the Islands. He had gone over a number of times to participate in their conventions as a featured speaker. This year he was scheduled for two lectures before this impressive group, made up of persons under forty who headed large companies and conglomerates. They were at the top of the heap in the business world and Berne fervently admired them, reporting back to his Tuesday evening seminars that these men fitted admirably with his concept of Winners.

With most people, Berne told his seminar, he felt he usually had any situation well in hand, but not with the young presidents. One had to struggle just to keep up with them.

They were unfailingly polite. They didn't talk down to their inferiors. They smiled incessantly and never brought up anything disagreeable. All week long nobody moaned about anything he should have done differently. If anything needed fixing or doing, they said: "Here's the way to fix it: one, two, three, four," and did it immediately.

They were practically all tall men. Their wives were more attractive than most. They dressed appropriately for each event. They never discussed money or lorded it over other people. They used no four-letter words in public and very few in private. Ideally, no such words would have been used.

And it also would have been ideal for Berne to have remembered to bring his prepared speech with him and not to have knocked over a microphone. He had left the speech behind in his room, causing the YPO fail-safers to spring into impeccable action. One of the staff commandeered a car back to Berne's hotel, where Torre routed out the speech and sent it on to him. Then, with the text safely in hand, he tripped as he approached the lectern, sending the microphone crashing to the floor.

At this point a peculiar universal exhalation of breath came from the audience. Berne interpreted it as: "We don't usually have people around who behave like that." (They weren't angry. They were just rather disconsolate, as if saying sadly to themselves, "Here's a guy who doesn't measure up.")

Luckily, Berne said, he retrieved the situation in the twinkling of an eye by making a hand mike out of the microphone. The TA audience laughed delightedly as he told them the story.

But the peculiar sigh, or whatever it was, held deep meaning for Berne, because he knew the young presidents probably would say no more about the incident, and if he'd made excuses they'd have listened tolerantly and murmured "Of course, we quite understand, we know it couldn't be helped," or words to that effect.

At the end of the seminar a TA member asked Berne what he expected from people anyway—absolute perfection? And Berne told him that he had missed the point.

Was the point, then, that Berne identified the "young presidents" with his parents, those two flawless beings about whom, he told Torre, he had never said a derogatory word during the course of his two lengthy analyses?

One can almost see the little boy of five, revealed to all the world as a cutter-up of yellow rubber sheets—sheets that did not belong to him—confronted by his father, the certified winner, merciful in his mercilessness, not angry, always polite, never using profanity. He doesn't laugh if little boys trip over microphone wires, and he lets out a sigh, more in sorrow than in anger, like "Oh my God, here's a guy that's sloppy, or a jerk or something—poor guy—he will never be a proper Bernstein, or a real doctor, or a genius, or worthy of Sara's full devotion."

The Bernes' behavior toward each other was becoming increasingly hostile. Bob Blaisdell "saw them playing games with each other at home and with other people at parties (especially 'NIGYSOB' or 'Now I've Got You, You Son of a Bitch!') and they would go to Carmel parties and both carry on wild flirtations with other people." (Eric still believed in the double standard, but young women of Torre's generation did not.)

Dorothy Smythe, one of Eric's Carmel patients, remembers seeing Eric and Torre at the beach shortly before the pair split up. "Torre was sitting in the lotus position; there were two young admirers, and Torre was playing up to them. Eric was looking old and wistful."

Looking back on it all now, Torre concludes: "There was a lot of unhappiness connected with Eric. When I felt all right about myself, the dominant feeling I had toward him was, I felt sorry for him. . . . What he most reminded me of was a lost and abandoned little boy. I thought that all of his callousness and coldness was to avoid being hurt—a coverup. A lot of the time I didn't feel right about myself, though . . . I still have those feelings about him or have them again, now that I've resolved the anger."

Separations and brief reunions began. Eric started to hedge his bets, renewing ties with previous women friends but seemingly unable to decide which one to single out. At the same time, some thought he had become excessively fearful of Torre's power over him.

According to some, "Eric felt he was powerless against Torre." Dorothy Berne reported that Torre upset Berne to the point where it created enormous pressures on him—he was, emotionally, extremely disturbed by her. This raises the interesting question: Was the man who was "always tremendous about cutting people off" and who contended that no one could make you angry if you did not choose to be, truly upset by this maddeningly attractive and clever young woman, or was it merely convenient to make others think so?

"In September 1969," Torre said, "Eric went away for a month and he wrote me a letter saying he didn't believe we could make it, but he'd like another try. [He] sent [me] a telegram: 'Begin the purification rites; I'm coming back.' " Why purification rites? Torre explained, "You do that before you meet the god." He returned; they had a reunion in Carmel, but nothing jelled. "When he got back it was the same," said Torre.

Soon after, Torre, the beautiful blonde Venus, moved out of Eric's Carmel house for good. On December 1, 1969, Eric and Torre pronounced themselves separated by unhappy differences and Eric filed for divorce. (It was agreed that Eric would file the suit as Torre disliked courtrooms and legal maneuverings. The divorce, however, was never concluded.) Eric stopped Torre's allowance "and so I said I wouldn't do anything behind his back, but I would start going out with other men," Torre related.

Torre and Eric quarreled about the few sticks of furniture in the Carmel house. Torre said: "I took one chair and he took the other. The last thing he said before I left for Europe was he wanted his chair back. The first thing he said when I came back . . . was: 'Where's my chair? . . .' When Eric was in the hospital with his heart attack, he made a list of things which he felt were his which he thought I had taken . . . a couple of things were news to me. It was funny—after a near-fatal heart attack, that was his concern."

Seven or eight months after Eric died, Torre sued for a share of the estate. "I started thinking about the will and went to the lawyers and they said we should contest it and it wouldn't hurt the others—especially the children—I wouldn't have done it otherwise—and if I didn't do it, more would go to the government. They persuaded me to take a lump sum—$5000. Now I know I should have held out for a percentage—5 percent of the books."

Torre is presently married to a professor of philosophy. They have a son, Joshua, born in 1971.

After Torre left, Eric seemed to his TA associates to be very much alone and withdrawn. He alarmed his disciples by referring in May to the possibility of imminent death—this was only a month before his heart attack. He talked quite casually to a group about the subject. The news spread swiftly throughout TA circles. He continued to give the impression that he was fearful that detectives had been put on his trail. (No-fault divorce had gone into effect in California on January 1, 1970, but it may have taken some time for errant spouses to realize their good fortune. Or perhaps Eric used this anxiety as an excuse for not engaging in activities he wanted to avoid?)

Jacqui Schiff told us, "When Eric visited us [around Christmas time of 1969] he was easily depressed, easily tearful. "I was worried about him," she said. "I tried to be as supportive as he would let me be . . . In January at the Winter Conference, he was really *very* depressed."

The ending of the Eric-Torre romance was strangely like the ending of Jurgen's last affair—the chapter in which Jurgen said goodbye to Queen Helen (symbolizing "woman, the eternal") and to his numerous other loves:

> And so farewell to you, Queen Helen! Your beauty has been to me as a robber that stripped my life of joy and sorrow, and I desire not ever to dream of your beauty any more. For I have been able to love nobody. . . . Hereafter I rove no more a-questing anything; instead I

potter after hearthside comforts, and play the physician with myself, and strive painstakingly to make old bones . . . and for the sake of no notion would I endanger my routine which so hideously bores me. For I am transmuted by time's handling; I have become the lackey of prudence and half-measures; and it does not seem fair, but there is no help for it . . .

"Oh, I have failed in my vision," cries Jurgen . . . I shudder at the thought of living day-in and day-out without my vision . . .Oh, all my life was a foiled quest of you, Queen Helen, and an unsatiated hungering . . . For Jurgen has loved nothing—not even you, not even Jurgen!—quite whole-heartedly.

. . . and Queen Helen vanished as a bright mist passes . . . as had departed Queen Guenevere and Queen Anaïtis; and Jurgen was alone . . . And to Jurgen the world seemed cheerless and like a house that no one has lived in for a great while.

20

Stopped Running

> . . . Who will be at your deathbed?
> . . . What will your last words be?
> . . . What will you leave behind?
> . . . What will they put on your tombstone?
> . . . What will it say on the front of your tombstone?
> . . . What will it say on the back?
> . . . What surprises will they find after you are dead?
> . . . Are you a winner or a loser?
> Eric Berne, *What Do You Say After You Say Hello?*

One Sunday evening, Eric appeared at Valerio and Nadya Giusi's Carmel house, as he often did on Sundays after he had finished his writing, and "said in his great, loud, booming voice that he had when he wanted to use it, 'Hello!' " Then he enveloped Valerio in a big hug. After which he leaned over "and almost winking at Nadya, said: 'I've been taking hugging lessons from a woman in Berkeley!' "

"It fit," Nadya said. "Even in something like that Eric would be taking lessons." After that, his hugging became "almost official." Previously he had hugged Nadya with enthusiasm ("he leaned into it") but had very definitely "pulled back" from hugging men, not even excepting effusive, friendly, outgoing men like Valerio Giusi.

He was becoming more liberated. But at the same time, "during the last two years of his life," said Nadya, "[Eric] was putting his house in order. It was very obvious that he wasn't well. He wasn't laying on the salt (she had previously been dismayed at the amount he poured on his food); he was under a doctor's care; he was mentioning his heart; when he came to eat dinner he very carefully laid out what he could and couldn't eat.

"For nearly eighteen months before he died," she said, "Eric was aware that he was failing." It was a physical condition in her opinion, and he did not "die of a broken heart."

Some of his TA friends also felt that Berne was "failing" at this time. John Dusay thought Berne had premonitions of impending death and wanted a lot more feedback than usual on his book *What Do You Say After You Say Hello?* Berne was trying desperately to get this most-difficult-to-write-of-all-his-books together before it was out of his hands. Bob Goulding thought the book should have been named: *What Do You Say before You Say Goodbye?*

TA's Viola Litt Callaghan had "believed for about a year Berne was dying;" a psychic told another TA leader that Berne would be seriously ill before the year was out. It didn't take psychic powers to see that Berne's shoulders were more hunched than ever, his hair thinner and more faded, his expression at times tired-out and woebegone.

But to Steve Karpman Berne was "such a fountain of unlimited knowledge and goodies" that he couldn't imagine Berne's output coming to an end. "I just thought it would flow on forever."

In 1963, when he had been writing *Games*, Eric had pondered about most people's lack of sensitivity to what was going on around them. He asked his readers (and himself) whether they really "saw" a coffeepot or heard the birds sing.

Just as he took hugging lessons when his Adult told him how important it was that people get close to one another, he also programmed himself for spontaneity and tried hard to be aware of what was going on around him. In the early days with Torre he had made a serious and conscientious effort to lope down to the beach on the spur of the moment, but this didn't last long; he was soon back to his heavy writing schedule. And while in the midst of the heaviest of all writing schedules—working on *What Do You Say After You Say Hello?*, *Sex in Human Loving,* and a new handbook for psychiatric interns, not to mention the beginning stages of a book on fairy tales, he wrote again, in the last year of his life, on the desirability of getting out of the parental treadmill:

> In the cities and in the country are millions of birds, and how many of you with full awareness heard one of them sing today? In the cities and in the country there are thousands of trees, and how many of you with full awareness saw one today?
> Eric Berne, *Sex in Human Loving*

He then described how he had gone to the village post office in Carmel five times a week over a period of years and noticed that he had never seen a certain tree, "because I was pre-occupied with getting to the post office to pick up my mail so I could go back to my office and answer the letters so I could go to the post office and pick up the replies to my answers so I could answer the replies so I could go to the post office and pick up more mail to answer. My time was mortgaged to a self-imposed burden that I could never pay-off. . . ." He continued by saying that he had considered this while he was in bed in a hotel room in Vienna "listening to the quiet of the night and then to the first rustles of life at dawn. . . ." He had thought about how the people who got up at six "danced out to prepare the way" for people who got up at seven, who in turn got things in order for those who arose at eight, who readied things for the nine o'clockers.

The department stores opened at ten so they could close at noon so people could have lunch so they could rush back and open up again at two so they could shut their doors at five to get ready for dinner at seven so they could be at the theater at eight so they could hurry home to be in bed by eleven so they could get in their quota of sleep and "be in good shape when they get up again in the morning at five, six, seven, or eight."

And on Sunday, he continued gloomily, a song tells us that some of them jump in the Danube, unable to take the pressure of unstructured time. "For time is not a river, but a sea that must be crossed, from the shore of bawling birth to the littered coast of death."

The late Elizabeth Palms, a social worker who for many years had known Berne as a friend as well as professionally, told us this story: Berne was in analysis during the last year of his life with a well-known Jungian who was also a good friend of his. At his final session before his fatal heart attack—just, in fact, as he was leaving the room—Berne turned and said, "You know, I've spent my whole life teaching people how to achieve intimacy, and I've never been able to get any for myself."

Ms. Palms said that should have been his epitaph.

Others noticed Berne's physical condition. In the spring of 1970 (around April) a Carmel clinical psychologist, Edward Ohanian, was walking up Junipero Street with Eric to their offices in the same building. Junipero has a mild hill, as Carmel hills go, but Berne was "huffing and puffing quite a bit." Ohanian couldn't resist saying: "When are we going to stop playing this game that it's OK for you to smoke, but the rest of us ought to curb our smoking habits?" Eric answered with slight irritation:

"Oh, but I smoke a pipe."

Ohanian then said, "I understand," and they both smiled. "But Berne was huffing and puffing so much I suggested we stop at least once and rest and look at the trees and the scenery."

The late Frank Lloyd remembered Berne's mentioning his high cholesterol count with some concern. Eric had not accepted Torre's suggestion that he substitute oil for butter and use milk instead of cream on his cornflakes, but his daughter Ellen does remember Eric conscientiously cutting out the little rounds of fat in his salami—eight or more to the piece.

There was also some indication that the do-it-yourself aspect of his activities was beginning to pall. In January 1970, he wrote Dr. Kemp of the University of Oklahoma, thanking him for an article which was to be published in the *Transactional Analysis Bulletin* and apologizing for the tardy acknowledgment, "since I do the Bulletin single-handedly along with everything else I do."

Previously he had gloried in the spin-offs from his whirling dervish act, but now he told the seminar several times he would like "to change his name to Joe Waterhouse and go live in Chinatown" so that he could start all over again. He missed the small intimate organization he had had at the start where he had known everyone on a first-name basis.

Berne began bringing his "dear friends" the Giusis little gifts, things he had heard them say they wanted. He presented them with a copy of *Games People Play* and *The Layman's Guide* in Italian, and *The Mind in Action,* which was out of print and which Nadya had always wanted. "To Nadya, one of the great people of the world, from your secret admirer," Eric wrote in her book.

The Giusis and Berne had had a warm relationship since the time back in 1957 when Valerio had first seen Eric, lying flat on his back in heavy surf, clutching his five-year-old son, his glasses having been swept away. Valerio had managed to haul them to safety onto the strand.

Valerio told us: "Eric was a star. He was a fresh breeze. Without a doubt he had one of the most exciting minds I've ever come across, although a little shocking. I've met many great people, movie stars, celebrities, nobility, but he was the greatest. You could ask him a question and anything you could conceive of as an answer would be out. He wouldn't even look at it that way, so I knew it was genius at work—a truly creative mind. . . . What I really liked was the way he cut through all the baloney."

Eric was very fond of Diana and Livia, the two Giusi daughters (girls who might have stepped from a page of Hans Christian Andersen), and liked to get his young sons together with them as often as possible. After the split with Torre, Eric felt himself at loose ends, and the Giusis created a loving environment where it was pleasant to take his boys and where he got a sense of makeshift family. He had impromptu dinners there often.

Diana Giusi told us a story of how Eric had comforted her once when a cat had maimed a field mouse.

"I was really upset, because this cat had hurt this rat—mouse; I brought it inside and wanted to nurse it back to health again, but it was pretty well dead. He sat me down and told me that it was a cat's nature and they couldn't help it and not to touch it. I wanted to touch it, but he said you could get rabies. He spent about an hour talking about life and death, and how life wasn't always fair. It made me feel good again. And, afterwards, we [Eric, too] went up and buried it."

Eric was on the first board of directors of Nadya's Montessori kindergarten school. (She is now a family therapist largely because of his influence.) He approved of the Montessori method. "It put muscle in the Adult of the child." Eric realized that the Giusis at times were short on money, as Valerio, besides being a serious painter, taught Italian to armed forces personnel and CIA and FBI people at the Defense Language Institute in Monterey. Unfortunately, work at the institute was off again, on again. In one bleak period Eric brought Nadya the manuscript of *Principles of Group Treatment* to proofread. Nadya suspects he did this just to help them out, as she could find nothing at all to correct. He gave her $50 anyway.

On December 15, 1969 Eric wrote his lawyer a letter witnessed by two people in which he recited the facts of the separation from Torre, his third wife, and indicated he wanted Dorothy to have one-fourth of his estate and Torre one-twelfth (until his divorce would become final, which it never did). He explained he was writing the letter because he was going on a long flying trip and wanted to provide for his ex-wife Dorothy for the time being.

On March 31, 1970, he wrote a holographic codicil to his will appointing Dorothy literary executor and stating that for these services she was to be paid 10 percent of the proceeds from *Sex in Human Loving* and *What Do You Say After You Say Hello?*

Time was running out for Eric's earliest disciple, Dave Kupfer, who had just completed his last term as president of the ITAA (he had held this office since 1966); Kupfer had terminal cancer. Berne would drop by Kupfer's house quite often and sit with him for a long time. Both men would read their newspapers, saying nothing. Finally, after remaining in silent communion for the duration of the visit, Eric and Dave would nod goodbye and Eric would get up and leave, still saying nothing.

In June 1970, Dorothy and Eric attended the graduation of their older son from high school. "It was a nice summer day," and Dorothy was looking particularly pretty, wearing a turquoise wool suit. Eric "just loved it." She had made a buffet supper in case friends of their son dropped over afterwards, but she and Eric started things off by having a tête-a-tête prevue snack feast at the table, and he then proposed that they remarry.

Dorothy couldn't make up her mind about the remarriage, but when Eric suggested they go on a trip together in September, she agreed to that.

"Eric immediately told the children and they began saying, 'Oh, Mom, you really are going to marry Dad, aren't you? Oh, you really will, won't you?' And I said, 'Well, I don't know.' Things had been getting along OK the way they were. I wasn't sure I wanted to get back into *that* again."

This was the first week in June. Warren Cheney, in his biographical sketch of Berne in the memorial issue of the *TA Journal*, wrote, "Strangely, Eric was telling all his friends how well he felt the two weeks before his heart attack." Berne must have been buoyed up by the thought of the September trip with Dorothy, who, loyally and over a long period, had "kept his machinery going" in sickness and in health, in marriage and divorce.

Eric's daughter Ellen told us: "A lot of things were happening that I didn't realize. . . . After he died it all fitted together. He started calling me up and saying that he should know where I was at all times. . . .

"A couple of weeks before he died [my husband] and I were in New York and about to leave for Colorado and he called and said he'd like to know where we would be staying. I couldn't understand it. He'd never wanted to know where we would be before, when we went on a trip. . . . I called him from Utah and they said he'd had a heart attack and had gone to the hospital."

Dorothy said: "It was on my birthday, Friday, June 26, that he phoned me and said he had been feeling so terrible that he'd had his secretary drive him over to the doctor's that afternoon . . . he had had an electrocardiogram. He'd had pains in his back. . . . He [suspected] that he was having a heart attack."

By Sunday Eric felt that he had largely recovered; he was preparing to go to the beach when the heavy cardiac attack struck. He was rushed to the intensive care unit of Monterey Hospital where he was kept heavily sedated for three days.

Two hours before the heart attack Eric had phoned Carolyn

Crane and invited her to spend the afternoon on the beach with him and his son. Carolyn informed us, "I had already made plans for the day but felt that he was saying to me that he wouldn't hide me any more and that made me happy.

"The conversation that Eric and I had by phone the day of the heart attack was followed by several more when he was in the hospital. I asked him if he wanted me to visit and he said no. His voice was so weak; I didn't understand why they let him answer his own phone."

The following Tuesday night, Eric called the TA seminar and told Steve Karpman he was on the mend but "he seemed to have taken a detour off the main highway and was having trouble getting back on the freeway." He looked forward to everyone's visits, and most of the inner circle came or sent flowers, "golden" (Delicious) apples, homemade cards, or loving notes.

Claude Steiner was the last of the TA group to visit Eric. Steiner had become concerned with Berne's outlook and had tried, particularly in the last years of his life, to help him recover his *élan vital*.

The visit was on Sunday, July 12, 1970. Claude brought his friend Hogie Wyckoff with him. They put up posters and banners in the room, blew up balloons, played music, attempting to "hook Eric's Child," but Hogie said she and Steiner were shocked by the look of Berne and realized that he was much worse off than they had suspected. Claude told Eric that when he got out of the hospital he would move down to Carmel for a while and stay with him.

When Dorothy phoned that evening before bringing the boys over for their usual visit, Berne suggested that she stay at home because he was beginning to feel very tired. This was a change indeed, as Mrs. Allen Williams remembered how his face lighted up when he saw one of his sons coming through the door of his hospital room.

On Monday, Dorothy was told that Eric was making progress and would soon be getting out of the hospital. On Tuesday evening, Eric's sister Grace called and was pleased to hear that he was doing well and had just about finished correcting the proofs of *Sex in Human Loving*. Eric called Rosabel Brown, whose short but intense relationship with him dated from

1944—twenty-six years earlier—and talked with her that evening.

At 4:00 A.M. Montreal time, July 15, his old McGill classmate, the renowned cardiologist Albert Lapin, was startled to be awakened from his sleep by a call from Berne, who told him he had been having some pain and asked him if the treatment he was getting for his heart attack was the right one. After talking over the situation, Lapin indicated that he thought it was.

A woman friend called Berne on the phone early on this Wednesday morning. She remembers that he made the statement: "I have stopped running." She took it to mean "running at the beach," but now wonders if there weren't also something cryptic about it.

Dr. Talcott Bates, a highly respected Monterey Peninsula pediatrician, was making his rounds at the hospital that morning and stopped by to see his old friend and ex-therapist. Bates had first stimulated the evolution of structural analysis by telling Berne the "I'm not really a 'cowpoke'; I'm just a little boy" story.

On this Wednesday morning, Bates said, Eric "was in bed with a plastic oxygen mask over his face, blowing bubbles in the mask, and I could see him writing away [correcting proofs for *Sex In Human Loving*], nonetheless. Sweat was standing out on his face . . . I had on a [crazy] green, yellow, red, and white hippie tie that I had bought. When he admired it, I took it off and gave it to him. About ten minutes later I was down the hall and heard that Berne was dead."

He went back to the room and somebody had already taken the tie.

Eric's physician and friend of long standing, Russell Williams, gave us a synopsis from the medical chart:

> Eric came into the office on a Friday . . . with a pain in his chest. Not typical angina, but angina is rarely typical at onset.
>
> Chest x-ray, cardiogram, OK. Cardiogram is usually OK at that point.
>
> He worried, or he wouldn't have come. I worried, because what was it?

Usual procedure—have him keep track of pain, try nitroglycerin if pain lasts over two minutes, stomach x-rays Monday for hiatus hernia.

[A few days later Berne] got the bad pain and into the hospital with a real heart attack. Cardiogram typical, etc.

Got through the dangerous first few days, doing well, then about day 10 developed fever, chest pains, pericarditis (an inflammation of the sac in which the heart lies) etc. . . . It does respond to steroids (cortisone) and Eric was given prednisone at this point with good results. Fever subsided, signs of pericarditis went away and he was really on the mend. So far as is known, his post-myocardial infarction syndrome had nothing to do with his death.

On the fourteenth day, the maid brought in his breakfast. When she came back to take the tray, the breakfast was finished, Eric was sitting up on his pillows, but he was dead.

He became a statistic. . . . A few people will die on the eighteenth day, the twentieth day, even the twenty-fifth. Eric was one of the unlucky ones. Dead on the fourteenth day. This is a sudden, electrical death, . . . probably due to fibrillation.

In an interview Dr. Williams said, "His arteries were all beautiful except for the one spot. He would have been a perfect candidate for a by-pass."

Unfortunately they didn't do them in those days.

If Eric had been in intensive care at the time, it is possible that his fibrillation would have been spotted and corrective measures taken so that he could have been brought back to life. But "most patients leave intensive care by day 3—5" as "the first few hours are the most dangerous for sudden death."

Half a lifetime before, when he was thirty, Eric had written in his *Maisie Atkins* manuscript, which was never published, that atheists, who haven't the comfort of the belief in the immortal soul, must be ultra-brave to face up to the reality of the disappearance of their personality, consciousness, and entire physical being. All that remains after death are their works. Everyone yearns for immortality, he wrote, but we can achieve it only by the words we leave behind.

Fortunately for us, Berne achieved the immortality he set out to attain thirty years before.

Ω

Coda

In 1979, nine years after Berne's death, Southey Swede, a recent adherent to TA, and co-editor of *The Bulletin of the Eric Berne Seminar,* wrote in that same periodical (vol. I, no. 1, March 1979):

> Eric Berne died in 1970. Those who loved him and considered him their mentor grieved for him. I myself have passed through my own grieving. I have at times denied his death—my magical child believed that he was around someplace, playing hide-and-seek with me.
>
> Southey found a "Bernean" to train with, sought out Berne's friends and "children," and became "enraged" that Eric's friends and organizations were not Eric. They didn't match the magical picture that Swede had of the father of TA: "game-free, completely OK—OK and script free." He said: "I at times bargained with fate—if I only worked hard enough, learned enough, searched enough, somehow I would be able to bring him back."
>
> Swede wrote a book on Berne's theories and tried to become a clinical member of the International Transactional Analysis Association.
>
> . . . Alas, [those things] too did not bring him back. Then I became despairing. Was he really gone forever? Would I never really meet him? Was the gold turning to lead?
>
> Slowly I began to feel that he was literally gone. At the Eric Berne Seminar I saw his chair, sitting up on a raised platform by the windows, green vinyl torn at the edge, with stuffing coming out. It has a golden plaque on

it which reads: "Dr. Eric Berne occupied this chair frequently February 10, 1958, until July 15, 1970." The chair is empty, off to a side. The seminar and ITAA business go on around an empty chair.

"Eric Berne is dead." For several weeks this year those words kept reappearing in my mind with the feeling of shock of awareness and despair. And this was followed by the release of acceptance. I was—and had always been—on my own. I had used Eric's spirit to inspire me and cure me and now I was free of him. His power with me slipped and he joined the hall of fame of great people in my head. I am on my own. We are all on our own to think and create for ourselves.

Although a latecomer to the TA movement, Swede captured in the above words the sentiments of many of the TA members, some of whom never knew the founder personally but experienced his genius through his writings.

Ω

Notes

Virtually all statements of fact in this book are derived from letters, phone conversations or taped interviews of people who had special knowledge of Berne. We have been fortunate in being able to interview so many who knew him and who have given generously of their time to help us with our project. Even though we haven't been able to use all their comments directly, they have contributed to our understanding of the subject. We thank them all and list them here with the dates of contact and their titles (some of which may not be known outside of the Mental Health field: M.S.W.=Master of Social Work; L.C.S.W.=Licensed Clinical Social Worker; L.M.F.C.=Licensed Marriage and Family Counseler). We are particularly grateful to Ken Ernst, who loaned us dozens of hard-to-find seminar tapes, and the ITAA, which made available boxes of carbon copies of Eric's correspondence, group notes, and early literary efforts.

Edith Albert, June 30, 1981; Iris Alberto, 1978; Jean Ariss, 1976; Michael Aronovitch, M.D., January 30, 1978; Rabbi Joseph Asher, September 8, 1978; Talcott Bates, M.D., April 4, 1977; Arthur Haskel Bazell, M.D., September 28, 1981; Charles Berger, M.D., September 21, 1981; Ellen Berne, October 16, 1977, June 12, 1978, June 18, 1981, and July 16, 1981; Isadore Bernstein, August 2, 1981; Peter Besag, December 27, 1977; Bob Blaisdell, January, 1978; Pamela Blum, M.A., L.C.S.W., April 19, 1980; Mary Boulton, Ph.D., June 8, 1981; J. Munroe Bourne, M.D., February 7, 1978; M. T. ("Mac") Bowe, May, 1977; Mel Boyce, Ph.D., September 12, 1979; Alice Harvey Bransom, June 12, 1978; Carol Steinbeck Brown, January 29, 1978; Rosabel Brown, M.A., March 5, 1978, March 26, 1978, April, 1978, September, 1983, and October 3, 1983; Howard Brunn, January, 1977; Betty Burney, August 3, 1979;

Viola Litt Callaghan, M.A., September 8, 1978 and February 15, 1982. Betty Capers, July 22, 1976; Hedges Capers, Ph.D., July 22, 1976; Edith J. Chester, July, 1979; Sam Colburn, 1976; Bill Collins, Ph.D., April 27, 1982; Connie Concannon, L.C.S.W., February 13, 1983; Joseph P. Concannon, M.S.W., September, 1979; Frances Cottington, M.D., August 30, 1981, November 7-9, 1981; Herbert Courland, M.A., August 1, 1981; Caroline Crane, April 3-4, 1978, March 19, 1981, and February 23, 25, 1984; Maxine Crosby, November 25, 1978; Pat Crossman, L.C.S.W., November 30, 1978, and March 3, 1980; Ernest Crown, April 17, 1979; "Dr. H," September 15, 1981; "Dr. J," September, 1983; Robert C. Drye, M.D., 1978; Katherine Dusay, M.A., September 20, 1978; John M. Dusay, M.D., September 20, 1978; Leon Edel, January 10, 1979; Fanita English, M.S.W., January 19, 1982 and August 6, 1983; Frank Ernst, M.D., February 10, 1982; Kenneth Ernst, Ph.D., September 3, 1978; Kenneth Everts, M.D., September 3, 1978; William Fassett, 1979; Norman Feitelson, D.D.S., June, 1981;

Lorne Gales, October 19, 1977; John Gamble, January 6, 1978; Annette Zang Gatterdam, July 4, 1977; Jack Geisen, April 6, 1979; Diana Giusi, May 16, 1976; Livia Giusi, May 16, 1976; Nadya Giusi, L.M.F.C., May 16, 1976; Valerio Giusi, May 16, 1976; Alta Goldner, January 23 and 24, 1983; Gerald Goodstone, M.D., November 15, 1978; Mary Goulding, M.S.W., May 31, 1976; Robert L. Goulding, M.D., May 31, 1976; Martin Groder, M.D., June 27, 1982 and January, 1983; Amy Harris, February 1, 1982; Sirrah (Dale) Harris, July, 1979; Thomas A. Harris, M.D., February 1, 1982; Kurt Hartman, July 8, 1979; Wilbur (Bill) Harvey, November 25, 1978; The Honorable S.I. Hayakawa, Summer, 1981; James Horewitz, M.D., September, 1981; Mardi Horewitz, M.D., February 21, 1983; Muriel James, Ed.D., October 24, 1979, and spring, 1980; Norman James, Ph.D., January 18, 1982; Stephen B. Karpman, M.D., September 8–9, 1978, January 18, 1982, and February 20, 1983; Jake Kenny, April, 1979; Margaret Frings Keyes, M.S.W., November 19, 1981; Leo Kohn, M.D., June, 1979;

Gus Lannestock, summer, 1977, and January 27, 1978; Albert Lapin, M.D., June 15, 1978 and June 30, 1981; Jules Levaggi, M.S.W., September 21, 1981; Pamela Levin, R.N., September 20, 1978, and August 9, 1983; Anne Levine, May 30, 1978; Rachmiel Levine, M.D., May 30, 1978; Evelyn (Siris) Levitin, M.D., September 9, 1979; Lawrence Levitin, M.D., September 9, 1979; Frank Lloyd, February 21, 1976, April 28, 1976, January 8, 1977, July 4, 1977, February 21, 1978, April 28, 1978, March 31, 1979, July 23, 1980, and spring, 1981; Marjory Lloyd, February 21, 1976, February 13, 1979, July 4, 1977, and July 20, 1980; Moses Margolick, M.D., March 12, 1978 and June 15, 1978; Gwen McEwen, July 28, 1979; Robert Michel, McGill Archives, March 28, 1980; Bruce Miller, April 19, 1981; Patricia Miller, April 19, 1981; Virginia Mitchell, L.C.S.W., May 29, 1977; August 26, 1983 and September 10, 1983; Anne Garrett Morse, October 12–15, 1979, November 10, 1979, and August 26, 1983; Vinie Need, spring, 1977; Judith Kupfer Nordin, October 12, 1977; Margaret Northcott, L.C.S.W. January and March of 1982, and September 20, 1979; Edward Ohanian, Ph.D., August 5, 1979;

Francis Palmer, Ph.D., January, 1978; Elizabeth Palms, M.S.W., Fall, 1982; Polly Parker, 1978; Don Parker, February, 1981; Ray Poindexter, M.D., April 28, 1982; Herb Rogers, 1979 and 1980; Arthur Rose, April 30, 1982 and September, 1983; Charles Rosen, M.D., May 30, 1978; Joseph Saltzer, M.D., December 13, 1978 and January 19, 1978; Anne Samuels, November 13, 1978 and April 21, 1982; Solon D. Samuels, M.D., November 13, 1978, April 26, 1982, and August 22, 1983; Jacqui Schiff, M.S.W., February 20, 1980; Katie (Martin) Schlepp, January 9, 1977, February, 1979, August 16, 1979, and August 2, 1980; Donald Shaskan, M.D., March 7, 1981; John Short, Ph.D., May 29, 1977 and August, 1977; Carol Solomon, September, 1978; Dorothy Smythe, May 5, 1976; Elliott Steinberg, April 28, 1977; Claude Steiner, Ph.D., November 24, 1979 and October, 1983; Martin Steiner, M.D., June 4, 1981; Ursula Steiner, March 21, 1981; William K. Stewart, J.D., fall, 1977, spring, 1978; June Turner, 1978; Faith Wallis, January 27, 1978; Benjamin Weininger, M.D., July 19, 1982; Kraig Weston, April 25, 1977; Neil Weston, April 25, 1977; Benjamin Bradford Whitcomb, M.D., January 11, 1978; Mary (Mrs. Allen) Williams, January 15 and 18, 1976 and May 30, 1977; Mona (Mrs. Henry) Williams, February, 1980; Russell Williams, M.D., November 10, 1977; Hogie Wyckoff, March 20, 1981; Gabriel Yelin, M.D., January 4, 1978 and February 13, 1978.

In the interest of brevity the above dates will not be repeated in the body of the notes.

It is fortunate that we began interviewing people more than eight years ago, as several of those we talked to have died in the interim. With those exceptions, all our sources have had an opportunity to review their statements before publication.

As to the organization of these notes: key phrases from the text are in boldface, sources are parenthesized; our comments are not. We have used the pseudonyms of "Elinor" and "McRae" to protect the privacy of Berne's first wife, and name codes for the wives and Berne's sister for brevity's sake.

Name Codes Used

Elinor=first wife: taped interviews on October 9, 1977, June 10-12, 1978, June 7, 1981, and letter, June 10, 1977.
Dorothy B=Dorothy De Mass Berne, second wife: taped interview May 4, 1976, and conversation, May 4, 1979, telephone conversations May 10, 1976, May 29, 1976, and several undated telephone conversations.
Torre H=Torre Houlgate-West, third wife: taped interviews October 23, 1977 and March 27, 28, 1981, also telephone conversation of July 6, 1977 and letters of March 14, 1983 and August, 1983.
Grace BR=Grace Berne Rose, Berne's sister and only sibling: taped interviews July 24, 1976, February 20, 1977, and letter November 4, 1976.

List of Title Codes

The names of frequently cited books written by Berne are given these codes:

EB=Eric Berne. **GAMES**=*Games People Play*, New York: Grove Press, 1972. **HELLO**=*What Do You Say After You Say Hello?* New York: Grove Press, 1972. **LAY/GUIDE**=*A Layman's Guide to Psychiatry and Psychoanalysis*, New York: Simon & Schuster, 1968. **ORGSNGROUPS**=*Structure and Dynamics of Organizations and Groups*, New York: Grove Press, 1963. **PGT**=*Principles of Group Treatment*, New York: Grove Press, 1966. **SEXNHL**=*Sex In Human Loving*, New York, Simon & Schuster, 1970. **TA/PSYCH**=*Transactional Analysis in Psychotherapy*, New York: Grove Press, 1961.

PREFACE

PAGE ix. **powerless in the face of beauty** (Mrs. Allen Williams, Carmel secretary to EB for 12 years). **demystification . . . cant** (Solon D. Samuels).
PAGE x. **destiny . . . striving** (EB, *HELLO*, p. 31). **great misfortune . . . deceiving world** (*Ibid.*). **Eric hiding . . . charade continuing** (Steiner later added: "When I said this I implied both good and not so good things. I hope both kinds were uncovered. For instance, I think that Eric was and thought of himself as a wizard.") **bright kind of madman** (Russell Williams).
PAGE xi. **desirable to repress . . . minds among us** (E. Lennard Bernstein,

name changed in 1943 to "Eric Berne"/Lennard Gandalac, pseud. "Dreams" *The McGilliad*, January 1931, p. 15).
PAGE xii. **behaved perversely . . . hated them** (Fanita English). **cut through him like a knife** (Mrs. Allen Williams).
PAGE xiii. **generally unattainable** (Claude Steiner, *Scripts People Live*, New York: Grove Press, 1974, p. 18).
PAGE xiv. **early days TAer . . . personal drawbacks** (Pam Levin). **loved him . . . love him still** (Amy and Thomas A. Harris).

Introduction

PAGE xvi. **really is a difference . . . books** (EB, *PGT*, pp. 216-217, 220; EB, *TA/PSYCH* pp. 4, 229, 272-273; EB, *HELLO*, pp. 399-401).
PAGE xvii. **Some professionals . . . Child** (EB, *TA/PSYCH*, pp. 16-17).
PAGES xvii-xviii. Books cited are: EB, *TA/PSYCH*, Claude Steiner, *Scripts People Live*, New York: Grove Press, 1974; Thomas A Harris, M.D., *I'm OK—You're OK*, New York: Harper and Row, 1967; Muriel James and Dorothy Jongward, *Born To Win, Transactional Analysis With Gestalt Experiments*, Reading, Mass.: Addison Wesley, 1973; Mary McClure Goulding and Robert L. Goulding, M.D., *The Power Is in the Patient*, San Francisco: The TA Press, 1978; *Changing Lives Through Redecision Therapy*, New York: Brunner-Mazel, 1979; See also John Dusay, M.D., *Egograms*, New York: Harper and Row, 1977; "Transactional Analysis," in EB, author and editor, *LAY/GUIDE*, 277-304.)

Chapter 1: Scattering Golden Apples

PAGE 1. **What to do about death?** (EB, *SEXNHL*, p. 267). **live past . . . age . . . father . . . mother died** (Nadya Giusi and Torre H).
PAGE 2. **specifically asked not to come:** Torre states that she was not specifically requested to stay away from the ceremonies, in contrast to information given us by family members. **weeping uncontrollably:** Torre H.'s recollection is that she arrived after the others, rather than before. **not personally known the deceased:** The services were conducted by Rabbi David Robbins.
PAGE 3. **wet the ground with his tears:** Steiner spent a week in seclusion going over hundreds of hours of seminar tapes and produced a memorial eight-hour tape of the best excerpts for the Eric Berne Seminar. **Perishing Republic** (Robinson Jeffers, "Shine Perishing Republic" in *Modern American and British Poetry*, New York: Harcourt Brace and Co., 1955, p. 194). **wake me up** (Kurt Hartman. Variation: Frank Lloyd, "Once Upon a Time," article, *Carmel Pine Cone*, April 22, 1976).
PAGES 3-4. **tower of the Carmelite Monastery** (Virginia Mitchell).
PAGE 5. **Barron read: awareness . . . intimacy** (from: EB, *GAMES* pp. 178-179, 180, 184).
PAGE 6. **big boys stole the plums** (EB, *ORGSNGROUPS* pp. 196–198).
PAGE 7. **tears still well up in my eyes** (Steiner, *Scripts People Live*, New York: Grove Press, 1974, pp. 19–20). **ashes . . . at . . . feet:** There wasn't room at Berne's feet; an urn containing Kupfer's ashes was buried near Berne's head at the El Carmelo Cemetery in Pacific Grove, Ca.
PAGE 10. **wheeled out the corpses** (Carolyn Crane). **magnificence there somehow** (Pat Crossman). **full-blown grief reaction** (Virginia Mitchell). **world-

beater from the beginning (Mary Goulding, quoting a remark made by another member of Berne's early seminars).
PAGE 11. **never able to love** (Frances Cottington). **kicked . . . [women therapists] out of his life** (Vi Callaghan).

Chapter 2: The Blonde Princess

Elinor, Berne's first wife, is the source for most of the statements or quotations in this chapter. Some other sources follow:
PAGE 12. **which girl to choose** (EB, *SEXNHL*, p. 262). **what is she doing for him?** (*Ibid*., p. 256).
PAGE 13. **. . . salon . . . like the one his mother had** (Grace BR).
PAGE 14. **paying no attention to his guests** (Gabriel Yelin).
PAGE 16. **couldn't carry a tune** (Torre H). **ethereal blonde . . . dark villain** (EB, "The Mythology of the Dark and Fair," *Journal of American Folklore*, date unknown, adapted from a paper read before the San Francisco Psychoanalytic Society, March 13, 1950).
PAGE 18. **ten extra ounces of energy** (Mrs. Allen Williams).
PAGE 19. **artists who sacrificed others** (Jack Languth, "Dr. Berne Plays the Celebrity Game," *New York Times Magazine*, July 17, 1966).
PAGE 20. **should have read it in 1923** (Albert Lapin).
PAGE 21. **persecutor . . . rescuer . . . victim** (Stephen B. Karpman, M.D., "Fairy Tales and Script Drama Analysis," *TAB* 7:26, April, 1968). **powerless in the face of beauty** (Mrs. Allen Williams).

Chapter 3: Moral Fibre

Elinor, Berne's first wife, is the source for most of the statements or quotations in this chapter. Some other sources follow:
PAGE 24. **How much greater is Dante** (EB, *SEXNHL*, p. 259).
PAGE 25. **stages of sexual bliss** (EB, *SEXNHL*, p. 256).
PAGE 27. **melancholy, romantic and exceedingly mild** (Edoardo Weiss, "Paul Federn," in Franz Alexander et al., ed., *Psychoanalytic Pioneers*, New York: Basic Books, 1966, p. 143).
PAGE 32. **six days of excitement . . . until further notice** (EB, *SEXNHL*, p. 256).
PAGE 33. **study about the shock treatment** (EB, letter to Dr. Clarence B. Farrar, Ed., *American Journal of Psychiatry*, April 11, 1943).
PAGE 34. **shortened his last name** (Barbara Hart and Carolyn Riley, *Contemporary Authors* vols 5–8, first revision, 1969, Detroit: Gale Research Co., pp. 106–107, places date in early 1943. EB's letters confirm this.) **changed hers to Byrne** (Letter from EB to Mr. Alan C. Collins, Curtis Brown, Ltd., on December 28, 1936, in which Eric suggests that Mr. Collins call Mrs. S.G. Byrne at EB's New York address in order to make an appointment with Eric).
PAGE 35. **Abraham Bellyache** (Mark Twain, "Concerning Jews" in *Literary Essays*, Harper and Brothers edition, New York: Colliers, 1918, pp. 263–268). **Leonard, then . . . Eric L. Bernstein** (Warren D. Cheney, M.A., M.A., "Eric Berne: Biographical Sketch," *TAJ, 1*:1 January 1971, pp. 15–16). **academic anti-Semitism** (Rachmiel Levine, M.D., May 30, 1978).
PAGE 36. **who will be for me?** (Marie Syrkin, *Golda Meir, Woman with a Cause*, New York: Putnam, 1963, p. 42). **anti-Semitism . . . blows** (Howard Brunn). **sour and blacken** (Amos Elon, *Herzl*, New York: Holt, Rinehart and

Winston, 1975, p. 115). **adroit at handling difficult situations** (Robert Goulding and Mary M. Goulding mentioned that when asked what his background was Eric would state he was Canadian).

Chapter 4: An H Marriage

Elinor, Berne's first wife, is the source for most of the statements or quotations in this chapter. Some other sources follow:
 PAGE 39. **An "H" Marriage** "An A marriage starts off as a shotgun or makeshift one. The couple are far apart, but soon they find a single common bond, perhaps the new baby. . . . As time goes on, they get closer and closer . . . An H marriage starts off the same way, but the couple never gets any closer. . ." (EB, *SEXNHL*, p. 149). . . . **all men** (Eugene Delacroix, *Journal*, New York: Crown Publishers, 1948, p. 355).
 PAGE 40. **Father William caper** (Lewis Carroll, *Alice in Wonderland*, New York: Bramhall House, 1960, p. 70).
 PAGE 41. **last morsel on his plate** (Cyprian St. Cyr, pseud., EB, "A Living Situation—Independence" *TAB*, 7:22, April 1967, p. 58) **Dancing . . . Weeping** (EB, *SEXNHL, supra,*) p. 262, a quotation from the *Bhagavant*.
 PAGE 45. **excluded and stupid one** (Maxine Crosby, Elinor's sister). **for a ride in the convertible** (Grace BR). **calmed down for a nap** (letters from EB to his sister, Grace BR, September 29, 1943; and to his mother, November 4, 1943, January 3, 1944 and January 31, 1944 [paraphrased]).
 PAGE 46. **Nellie is fine** (Letters from EB to his sister Grace, September 29, 1943; to his mother, November 4, 1943, January 3, 1944, and on January 31, 1944 [paraphrased]).
 PAGES 46–47. **minor adventures . . . shock therapy** (letters from EB to his mother, September 20, 1943; to the Superintendent, New York Psychiatric Institute, 168th St., New York City, October 28, 1943; to his cousin Miriam in Seattle, Washington, November 3, 1943; to his mother again on November 4, 1943, December 29, 1943, January 3, 1944, and March 24, 1944; and to his Seattle relatives, the Bernsteins, Uncle Arthur and Aunt Belle on March 28, 1944 [paraphrased]).

Chapter 5: The Happy Days Lie Ahead

Elinor, Berne's first wife, is the source for most of the statements or quotations in this chapter. Some other sources follow:
 PAGE 49. **half a loaf** (EB, *SEXNHL*, p. 144). **man who smokes a pipe** (EB, *The Happy Valley*, p. 7).
 PAGE 51. **Krishnamurti** (Langston Hughes, *I Wonder as I Wander*, New York: Rinehart & Co., 1956, p. 283). **McGill graduate and his wife** (Frank Lloyd).
 PAGE 52. **dislike for all he stood for** (Elinor). Elinor's sister, Maxine Crosby, however, remembers their mother reading aloud glowing letters from Elinor, describing her meeting the young psychiatrist and their first trips into New York. **precarious financial state** (Letter from EB to Grace BR, April 14, 1944, [paraphrased]).
 PAGE 53. **Dr. Berne's letters** (Wilbur Harvey said: "the usual comment was that they didn't want anything to do with a wild man like that.")
 PAGE 56. **that darned old pipe!** (Wilbur Harvey, Elinor and Ellen Berne). **never liked men much** (Maxine Crosby).

PAGE 57. **her lawyer disbarred** (Wilbur Harvey).
PAGE 58. **lump sum of $1300**: The lump sum was referred to later on in the tapes as $1700. The cost of living figure for a family of four in 1947 was $193 per month according to the Bureau of Labor Statistics. (*Historical Statistics of the United States, Part I*, US Department of Commerce, Bureau of Census, p. 176). **spending money** (*Historical Statistics of the United States, supra*, p. 176).

Chapter 6: *Forever May Last as Long as Seven Years*

Elinor, Berne's first wife, is the source for most of the statements or quotations in this chapter. Some other sources follow:
PAGE 60. **Love is a sweet trap** (EB, *SEXNHL*, p. 144). **father's smile** (EB, *HELLO*, p. 123).
PAGE 62. **skinny, energetic, with-it** (Frank Lloyd). **melting brown eyes** (Elinor).
PAGE 64. **long since dead** (Deems Taylor, *Of Men and Music*, New York: Simon and Schuster, 1937, pp. 3–8).

Chapter 7: *Prince Lennie*

PAGE 68. **haircut** (EB, *SEXNHL* p. 198). **doctors were "the ideal"** (Mordecai Richler, *The Street*, New York: The New Republic Book Co., 1969, p. 58). **the doctor's house** (H&E Jorgensen, "A Fragment from a Biography of Eric Berne," *TAJ* 8:2, April 1978, p. 177).
PAGE 69. **maid in uniform** (*Ibid.*, p. 176). Eric's Aunt Edith, 76 years old, and still living in Montreal, confirmed that her sister Sara's ten-room house was "beautiful" before Dr. Bernstein's death. Eric's Uncle Isadore Bernstein of Chicago told us that Berne's fictional description of the interior was an accurate portrayal (August 3, 1981).   **ethnic hostilities**: When Grace was 7, a French-Canadian youngster in her neighborhood called her an anti-Semitic name and made her cry (Grace BR). **certainly was a pirate** (EB, unpublished story, "The Sister" [paraphrased]).
PAGE 70. **fireplace and red carpet** (Isadore Bernstein, August 2, 1981). **daughters did all the housework.** (Edith Albert).
PAGE 72. **gentle, benign, and kind** (Gabriel Yelin). **stern disciplinarian** (Dorothy B).
PAGE 73. **take care . . . sister** (H&E Jorgensen, *TAJ* article, p. 178).
PAGE 74. **put her husband through medical school** (Edith Albert, June 30, 1981, who also told us Sara was the first Jewish teacher in Montreal). **do something else** (H&E Jorgensen, *TAJ* article, p. 179). **Ten extra ounces of energy** (Mrs. Allen Williams). **shanghaiing** (Isadore Bernstein, *supra*). **traveling optometrist** (H&E Jorgensen, *TAJ* article, p. 177 [Grace BR]).
PAGE 75. **worked in a cigar store** (Isadore Bernstein). **no easy cinch** (Grace BR). **gravedigger . . . secondhand furniture-antique store** (Isadore Bernstein and Edith Albert). **normal school** (Edith Albert). **tussling** (H&E Jorgensen, *TAJ* article, p. 178).
PAGE 76. **sight of blood** (Mrs. Allen Williams). **maybe . . . sleepwalked on purpose** (H&E Jorgensen, *TAJ* article, p. 178). **always a psychiatrist** (*Ibid.*). **intuitive, even psychic** (Edith Albert). **written every day of his life** (Gwen McEwen). **helped mother with newspaper articles** (Grace BR). **horoscopes** (Edith Albert). **but do something** (Grace BR).
PAGE 77. **excellent therapist . . . religious conversion**   (Margaret

Northcott). **walk on water . . . Bernsteins against the world** (Ernest Crown). **Caspar Milquetoast** (Frank Lloyd). **he would have been killed** (Grace BR).

PAGE 78. **tall, handsome figure** (J. Munroe Bourne). **girls of more than average good sense** (EB, *LAY/GUIDE*, p. 99).

Chapter 8: "Crazy" Lennie

PAGE 79. **excruciating sensitivity,** (National Student symposium on the Education of the Gifted and Talented, *On Being Gifted*, New York: Walker and Co., 1978, p. 38). **not waving, but drowning** (Bernard S. Miller and Merle Price, eds. *The Gifted Child and the Community*, "The British National Association for the Gifted Child," New York: Walker and Co., 1981, p. 155). **Lennard:** Berne didn't change the spelling of his name to "Lennard" until high school days, but we use the later spelling throughout this chapter for simplicity's sake.

PAGE 80. **called him a dirty Jew** (Dorothy B). **Gentiles Only** (Mordecai Richler, *The Street*, Washington D.C.: New Republic, 1969. p. 68). **all the British-Canadians . . . got out** (Dorothy B). **Where is the picture?** (Torre H).

PAGE 82. **stuck his head in all the pictures** (Frank Lloyd). **an artist in their midst** (Gerald Goodstone). **a cigarette, cigar, and pipe** (Letter from "Lennard Gandalac" [Eric Bernstein] to Bennett Cerf, July 20, 1937).

PAGE 83. **claimed that he had written it:** After researching the point thoroughly, Faith Wallis, of the McGill Archives, concluded that Lennard's authorship of the Revue "appeared to be a canard." She could find no evidence of it in any of the student publications of the period.

PAGES 83–84. **stroke hungry** (Margaret Northcott adds: "He was very much a 'left-brain person.' He knew the power and thus the danger of physical touching but did not live long enough to experience its healing effects in his own personal therapy.")

PAGE 84. **bizarre, arrogant, or self-centered:** Lorne Gales, McGill's longtime alumni official, told us that everyone at the University who knew him well had liked Lennie and admired him. We are greatly indebted to Gales for putting us in touch with so many of Berne's former classmates, which he did by publishing our need for information in an alumni newsletter. However "Lennard enjoyed being the negative target of people" in Goodstone's opinion. "He enjoyed doing things people didn't like." **Lennard the center of her existence** (Elinor).

PAGE 88. **IQ perilously close to 200:** This was a phrase Berne used to describe himself in a manuscript found among his papers. **IQ 130 or over** (Fyer, Henry, and Sparks, *General Psychology*, New York: Barnes & Noble, 1954, p. 238). **trail blazer . . . fields of psychiatry . . . love and affection** (Warren D. Cheney, M.A., M.A., "Eric Berne, 1910–1970," *TAB*, 9:35, July 1970, pp. 73–74).

PAGE 89. **level of general culture** (Ernest Jones, M.D., *Sigmund Freud, Four Centenary Addresses* New York: Basic Books, 1956, pp. 43–44). **element of "degradation" . . . ambivalence . . . great men . . . life histories** (Sigmund Freud, "The Goethe Prize Address, 1930," *Standard Edition of the Complete Psychological Works*, London: Hogarth Press, 1955, XXI, pp. 205–212). **genius as a lack . . . great in despite** (Thomas Mann, "Death in Venice," *Stories of Three Decades*, New York: Alfred Knopf, 1951, p. 384). **'real' shape of the glowworm** (*Ibid.*, "Felix Krull," p. 359).

Chapter 9: There's only Room for One

PAGE 91. **resident's gate** (H&E Jorgensen, *TAJ* article, p. 180). **the Real Depression** (Joseph Saltzer).
PAGE 93. **bounced along also** (Leo Kohn). **fourteen hours a day . . . $50 a month** (*Maisie Atkins* manuscript).
PAGE 94. **rats and frogs** (Lennard Gandalac [pseudonym for Eric Bernstein], letter to Bennett Cerf, Random House, May 31, 1937). **set sail for Istanbul** (Lennard Gandalac to Bennett Cerf, July 20, 1937). **before World War II . . . broke out** (*Maisie* manuscript [paraphrased]). **Fort Lee** (*Ibid.*) **Turkish prison** (Lawrence Levitin).
PAGE 95. **Levantine travels of 1937 and 1938** (Eric L. Bernstein, M.D., "Psychiatry in Syria," *American Journal of Psychiatry*, 95:1415–1419, 1939). **dating for six weeks** (Arthur Rose).
PAGE 97. **Ring sanitarium** (E. Lennard Bernstein, M.D., letter to B.L. Pampel, M.D., Superintendent, Montana State Hospital, Warm Springs, Montana, April 3, 1939). **Condom** (Eric L. Bernstein, M.D., "Who Was Condom?" *Human Fertility* 5: pp. 172–176, 1940).

Chapter 10: The Martian Finds a Haven

PAGE 100. **All my kidding is serious** (EB, *SEXNHL* p. 246). **cobwebs** (Frank Lloyd).
PAGE 101. **sick soldiers . . . psychiatric reconditioning** (Letter to "Helen" from Capt. Berne, December 11, 1944). **round of drinks or . . . working on a book** (Rosabel Brown).
PAGE 103. **patting a dog** (Rosabel Brown). **evicted** (Marjory Lloyd).
PAGE 105. **baleful and myopic eyes** (Talcott Bates, M.D., Professor Toro's Column, *Monterey Peninsula Herald*, Monterey, Calif., July 23, 1970). **more soda water** (Nadya and Valerio Giusi). **host's garden** (William K. Stewart). **nervous as a cat** (EB, *The Happy Valley*, New York: Grove Press, 1968, p. 11).
PAGE 106. **underlying conflicts** (EB, *Medical Tribune*, May 7–8, 1966).
PAGE 107. **female spider . . . devouring her partner** (James Branch Cabell, *Jurgen*, New York: Dover Publications, Inc., 1977, p. 139). **auction . . . for the Scottsboro boys** (Langston Hughes, *I Wonder As I Wander*, New York: Rinehart and Co., 1956, p. 283).
PAGE 108. **an anthracite blackness** (Myron Brinig, *No Marriage In Paradise*, New York: Rinehart and Co., 1949, p. 23). **leapt into his bed** (Gus Lannestock).
PAGE 109. **toast of Carmel wine** (EB, *The Mind In Action*, New York: Simon and Schuster, Inc., 1947. Also EB, *LAY/GUIDE*). **purple and pink fuschias . . . glittering dark eyes . . . great curled shells . . . three Siamese cats** (Margaret Parton, *Laughter on the Hill*, Toronto: McGraw-Hill [Embassy-Whittlesey House Publication], 1945, p. 73, 74. Information in brackets, Kraig Weston).
PAGE 110. **sharpen its claws in his back** (Neil Weston. Also, *Laughter on the Hill, supra*). **strip and sunbathe** (Marjory Lloyd). **rooster in on the doctor** (John Short). **wee, tiny thing** (Kraig Short Weston). **received a bill for $25** (Gus Lannestock).
PAGE 111. **all doctors are jerks** (Kraig Weston). Neil Weston also observed that it was one of Berne's favorite expressions.
PAGE 112. **Eric "put on his amused look"** (Katie Schlepp). **a real, royal drunk-out** (Katie Schlepp). **knocked over a tiny little woman** (Kraig Weston).

PAGE 113. **little bleatings of terror** (Neil Weston). **Off to the bushes!** (Katie Schlepp). **waltzed and whirled** (Kraig Weston). **rudimentary jungle noises** (John Short). **walked . . . on his hands** (Ibid.). **a sort of French-Canadian shuffle** (Katie Schlepp). **At last we are alone together!** (Frank Lloyd, article in *Carmel Pine Cone*, April 22, 1976). **funny, evil smile** (Katie Schlepp).

PAGE 114. **prose . . . poetry . . . Jewish dialect** (John Geisen). **mammoth thermometer** His ex-secretary, Anne Morse, pointed out that the seemingly senseless act of sticking the thermometer in the ocean was related to an experiment on the natural production of cortisone.

PAGE 115. **rainy Tacoma** (EB to "Kempler," February 4, 1946).

PAGE 116. **physical cruelty** (EB, letter to his lawyer, Mr. Davis, on July 4, 1946). **got out as scheduled** (EB to Paul Federn, M.D., July 10, 1946). **Federn and Henry Simon** (EB letter to Marie, July, 1946, to mother, July 4, 1946 [paraphrased]).

PAGE 117. **two guests** (EB, "Group Attendance: Clinical and Theoretical Considerations," *The International Journal of Group Psychotherapy*, 5:392–403, 1955, repeated in EB, *ORGSNGROUPS* p. 87). **'Peter Meter' . . . 'Whang Control'** (Neil Weston).

PAGE 118. **"Dorothy la Desirée"** (Chief heroine of *Jurgen, supra.* **retroussé nose** (description of Dorothy by Katie Schlepp). **twinkle in her eye** (Frank Lloyd).

Chapter 11: Jack in the Beanstalk Meets Cinderella

Dorothy Berne, Eric's second wife, is the source for most of the statements or quotations in this chapter. Some other sources follow:

PAGE 119. **This could be it,** (EB, *SEXNHL*, p. 255–256.)

PAGE 120. **July issue of** *Vogue* (EB, "Psychoanalysis: Five Questions Answered," *Vogue*, July 15, 1947, pp. 38–39,77, 80.)

PAGE 121. **six eggs**: Anecdote found among Berne's papers, paraphrased.) **She still does** (Frank Lloyd, April 28, 1976).

PAGE 124. **seventeen mental hospitals** (Warren D. Cheney, M.A., M.A., "EB: Biographical Sketch," *TAJ 1*:1, January 1971, p. 20).

PAGE 127. **Happiness . . . Jewish psychiatrist** (Frank Lloyd).

PAGE 128. **four yards** ("Psychiatrist in the Chips," *Life*, August 12, 1966). **keeping my machinery running smoothly** (EB, *TA/PSYCH*, p. 16.)

PAGE 131. **twenty years later** (EB, *SEXNHL*, p. 255.)

Chapter 12: Poker

PAGE 133. **winning hare** (EB, *SEXNHL*, p. 263). **have in their pockets** (EB, *SEXNHL*, p. 241). **financed trips . . . in thirty countries** (*New York Times*, August 15, 1965). **cheapskate** (Gus Lannestock) **fed off each other** (Howard Brunn).

PAGE 134. **second best** (William K. Stewart, 1977). **everybody makes mistakes—except winners** (EB, *SEXNHL*, p. 241). **a GREAT poker player** (Robert Goulding).

PAGE 135. **the Nixon of Psychology** (Francis Palmer). **bread . . . literally** (Howard Brunn). **We're here to play** (William K. Stewart).

PAGE 136. **he was transparent** (William Fassett, 1979).

Chapter 13: The Dorothy Who Did Not Understand

Dorothy Berne, Eric's second wife, is the source for most of the statements or quotations in this chapter. Some other sources follow:

PAGE 138. **The Dorothy Who Did Not Understand** (Same chapter title used for Chapter IV of James Branch Cabell's *Jurgen, supra*, p. 16). **just Santa Claus** (EB, *SEXNHL*, p. 261). **Duke of Logreus** (James Branch Cabell, *Jurgen, supra*, p. 73). **fulfilled the family recipe** (Grace BR: "We were always with the best.")

PAGE 139. **stayed within the fold** (EB, *The Mind in Action*, New York: Simon & Schuster, 1947, p. 271. Its book jacket refers to Berne as a "senior student at the San Francisco Psychonalytic Institute.")

PAGE 140. **Over 300 hours of training** (Levitin). **Berne's script . . . same as Freud's** (Mel Boyce, "Introduction" to *How To Cure: Berne Theory* by Southey Swede, booklet, Woodstock,N.Y., 1970). **an authority on hell** (EB, *HELLO*, p. 225).

PAGE 141. **committed suicide:** Federn, however, did have a son in New York.

PAGE 143. **neither father his wife** (EB, *TA/Psych* pp. 45–46).

PAGE 144. **judge awarded $3300** (Letter, EB to Grace BR, May 22, 1961). **left-wing to say the least** (Kraig Short Weston).

PAGE 145. **night sweats and grinding his teeth** (Paraphrased version of Berne's letter to Albert Lapin, M.D., April 4, 1955).

PAGE 146. **shallow . . . self-centered . . . insulting** (Robert Coles: "Doppelgänger for Freud," *New York Times Book Review*, October 8, 1967.

PAGE 147. **bound together by children** (EB, *SEXNHL*, p. 259). **hero to his wife's psychiatrist** (EB, *SEXNHL*, p. 263).

PAGE 148. **lacks proper tools:** paraphrased statement from one of two proof sheets in which Berne discussed Peter Giovacchini's article: "Characterological Aspects of Marital Interaction" for *The Psychoanalytic Forum 2:*1, spring, 1967, p. 18. The sheets were found among the papers of the late David Kupfer and were given to us by Judith Kupfer Nordin.

PAGE 149–150. **middle-class husbands . . . middle-class wives** (EB, *SEXNHL*, p. 257).

Chapter 14: The Unsinkable Dr. Berne

PAGE 152. **thoroughly misled** (James Branch Cabell, *Jurgen, supra*, p. 141). **band of brigands** (Group Notes, rephrased).

PAGE 153. **finished his training at an earlier date** (Dorothy B., Donald Shaskan, M.D., and another pyschiatrist [anonymous]).

PAGE 155. **fired first and found out why later:** No records were available from government sources under the Freedom of Information Act. *The Directory of Medical Specialists*, Chicago: Marquis Who's Who, 1972–1973, p. 1639, lists Berne as having worked for the army until 1954 and the Veterans' Administration until 1956.

PAGE 156. **curry favor with newcomer . . . inexcusable** (*Group Notes*, June 29, 1953, paraphrased).

PAGE 158. **sought out Dr. Khlentzos** (Jules Levaggi, M.S.W., co-author with Viola Litt Callaghan, M.A., and Charles Berger, M.D, of "A Living Euhemerus Never Dies" *TAJ I:* 1, January, 1971, pp. 64–70).

PAGE 159. **hegira** (EB, "The Natural History of a Spontaneous Therapy Group," *International Journal for Group Psychotherapy 4:* 1, January 1954).

NOTES

PAGE 162. **damned good therapist:** Kenneth Ernst, author of *Games Students Play* and *Pre-Scription* was five years in analysis with Berne, and also observed him with other patients. Ernst said Berne was very quiet most of the time and didn't seem to be paying much attention to what was going on. At the end of sessions, however, he would pull things in from two, three, or even five years back and show how they made a pattern. The connections he made from seemingly unrelated facts suddenly brought everything into clear focus. Ernst was convinced he was a genius.

PAGE 164. **Shook the ground** (undated proof sheet of review by R.J. Starrels, M.D., for unknown magazine, found among Berne's papers) **arms open to everyone** (Kenneth Everts).

Chapter 15: Go Ahead! You Can Do It! It's Easy!

PAGE 166. **Go ahead!** (Grace BR). **I still know the answer** (EB, *The Happy Valley*, New York: Grove Press, 1968). **Agamemnon Club** (EB, *ORGSNGROUPS,* pp. 196-198).

PAGE 171. **folding canvas chairs** (*TAB* 2:5, January, 1963, p. 45, *supra*). **to Berkeley by helicopter** (*TAB, 1:* 1, January, 1962).

PAGE 172. **net worth of $644.68** (*TAB, 9:* 35, July, 1970, p. 111).

PAGE 173. **private plane . . . motorcycle** (*TAB, 2:* 8, October, 1963, p. 98).

PAGE 174. **rolling in the aisles:** The Asklepieion program was a blend of TA and the Synanon "Game," effectively used with criminals at the U.S. Penitentiary in Marion, Illinois. See Kenneth L. Windes, "The Three 'C's' of Corrections: Cops-Cons-Counsellors" in *Transactional Analysis after Eric Berne*, Graham Barnes, ed., New York: Harper's College Press, pp. 138-145. **Dr. Cream** (Pam Levin). **rubber bands . . . chewing gum** (*TAB, 5:* 19, July, 1966, p. 164).

PAGE 175. **close to a hundred letters** (EB, Letter to J.C. Whitacre II, M.D., June 15, 1959, [paraphrased]). **left the two eggs on the shelf** (Viola Litt Callaghan, *supra*).

PAGE 180. **modern day Sigmund Freud** (Levaggi, Berger, and Callaghan, "A Living Euhemerus Never Dies," *TAJ 1:* 1, January 1971, p. 65).

PAGES 180-181. **banquet . . . TA hospitality rooms** (*TAB, 3:* 11, July, 1964, p. 143).

PAGE 181. **therapy group right then and there** ("TA at the American Psychological," *TAB* 7:28, October, 1968, p. 95).

PAGE 182. **popularity . . . surprised him** (*TAB 3:* 12, October, 1964, p. 161). **Tillich . . . contraceptives** (*TAB 4:* 16, October, 1965, p. 81).

PAGE 183. **Monopoly in the games section** (Solon D. Samuels). **can't be reached in any other way** (*Newsweek*, August 8, 1966). **Games** a musical comedy (Jack Languth, "Dr. Berne Plays the Celebrity Game", *N.Y.Times*, July 17, 1966). **television interview . . . half-hour segments** (*TAB 6:* 21, January, 1967, p. 30).

PAGE 184. **17-Mile Drive** (*TAB* 7:28, October 1968, p. 95). **Philomen and Baucis** (EB, undated seminar tape entitled "Feeling Good—Feeling Bad" [paraphrased]).

Chapter 16: The Outsider on the Inside Track

PAGE 185. **demon to contend with** (EB, *HELLO*, p. 131).
PAGE 186. **$1000 for their by-laws** (Amy Harris).

PAGES 187–188. **older professionals . . . structure to the group** (Jacqui Schiff, "One Hundred Children Generate a Lot of TA: History and Development and Activities of the Schiff Family," in Graham Barnes, *Transactional Analysis after EB*, New York: Harper's College Press, 1977, p. 55).
PAGE 190. **women might not come back** (John M. Dusay, M.D.).
PAGE 191. **less than twenty inches apart** (*TAB* 3:9, January, 1964, p. 113, [paraphrased]).
PAGE 192. **Go to Hell:** Steiner reports that this "Stroking-Go-Round" led to his development of the Stroke Economy concept. See Claude Steiner, *Scripts People Live*, New York: Grove Press, 1974, pp. 110–117. March 6, 1981.
PAGE 193. **inner circle:** Ken Ernst mentioned that at one meeting someone complained that those who sat in the back felt left out. All the CTM's (Clinical Teaching Members of the ITAA) and Inner Circle were up in front, clustered around Berne. So Berne went back while the meeting went on and sat in the rear to check this out. Ernst said: "He paid attention to every little detail."
PAGE 195. **turn frogs into princes** (EB, *HELLO*, p. 37). **only frogs want to be princes** (*TAB*, 7:38, October, 1968, "TA with Children and Adults," p. 85 [paraphrased]).
PAGE 196. **rapport . . . between TA and Gestalt** (*TAJ* 3:1, January, 1973, pp. 69–71 [paraphrased]). **absurdities and obscenities** (*TAB* 7:28, October, 1968, p. 79). **Screw you, Fritz** (Robert Goulding, M.D.).
PAGE 197. **prince who turns into an ugly frog** (Fritz Perls, *In and Out of the Garbage Pail*, Lafayette, Ca.: Real People Press, 1969 [pages unnumbered]). **TA didn't indulge in role playing** (EB, *TAJ*, 3:1, January 1973, p. 66). **THAT doesn't work:** *Try* is considered a "con" word in TA circles, the word a child will offer his parent when he doesn't really intend to perform. **Gestalt techniques into the TA menu:** See James and Jongward, *Born To Win: Transactional Analysis with Gestalt Therapy*; also Muriel James, *Breaking Free*; and Goulding and Goulding, *Changing Lives Through Redecision Therapy* and *The Power is in the Patient*.
PAGE 198. **frequent enemas** (Torre quoted Berne as saying that the other sexual traumas hadn't seemed to have caused much difficulty, except the anal attack, when the parent either takes a rectal temperature constantly or gives unnecessary enemas). **better in spite of Transactional Analysis** (*TAB* 2:1, January, 1963, p. 43).

Chapter 17: A Boys' Club

PAGE 204. **shit** (Anonymous). **class=grace=reticence** (EB, *SEXNHL*, pp. 16–17). **obscenity as a method of seduction** (*Ibid*., p. 30 and n30, p. 30).
PAGE 208. **woman therapist with sex appeal** (*TAB* 5:1, January 7, 1966, p. 91 [paraphrased]). **grandfather and enchanter . . . country doctor** (Pat Crossman, "Acceptance Speech, EB Memorial Scientific Award," *TAJ* 8:1, January, 1977, p. 104, as subsequently edited by Crossman).
PAGE 210. **elusive as mercury** (Don Parker, February, 1981).

Chapter 18: A Maserati, a Best Seller, and a Young, Blonde Wife

Torre Houlgate-West, Eric's third wife, is the source for most of the statements or quotations in this chapter. Some other sources follow:
PAGE 215. **2′ 6″ down** (EB, *SEXNHL*, pp. 228–229). **lissom and zaftig** (EB, letter, to Moses Margolick, M.D., July 6, 1967 [paraphrased]).

PAGE 216. **lonely hearts' club for intellectuals** (Mac Bowe). **brainy men** (Judith Kupfer Nordin).
PAGE 217. **mate with your perfection** (*Jurgen, supra*, p. 303, 304).
PAGE 218. **like a television commercial.** (Kurt Hartman)
PAGE 220. **didn't know much about the topic** (EB, letter to Robert A. O'Reilly, M.D., Chairman, Santa Clara Department of Medical Institutions, San Jose, Ca., February 25, 1966 [paraphrased]).
PAGE 222. **crashes, thumps and taradiddles** (*L.A. Times West*, February 12, 1967). **'Drive carefully!'** (*Life*, August 12, 1966).
PAGE 224. **taste in its purest form** (EB, *SEXNHL*, p. 141). **a golden apple** (*Ibid.*). **old bachelor** (Richard Sheridan, "The School for Scandal," *Penguin Plays: Four English Comedies*, Hammondsworth, England, and Baltimore, Md., Penguin Books, 1970, p. 333).

Chapter 19: Farewell to Queen Helen

Torre Houlgate-West, Eric's third wife, is the source for most of the statements or quotations in this chapter. Some other sources follow:
PAGE 225. **the less I find of comprehension** (James Branch Cabell, *Jurgen, supra*, p. 271). **probably lived on some island** (Elliot Steinberg, letter to Rosabel Brown, April 28, 1977). **repeat at leisure** (*Jurgen, supra*, p. 240).
PAGE 228. **concealing his Jewish roots:** Torre sometimes brought sheafs of notes on the Jewish religion to the beach and enthusiastically read them aloud to Eric and others. (Frank Lloyd). **good work . . . bad life** (Thomas Mann, *Stories of Three Decades*, New York: Alfred Knopf, 1961, "Tonio Kröger," p. 100). **biggest hardship . . . kept from typewriter** ("Dr.Berne Plays the Celebrity Game," New York Times, July 17, 1976).
PAGE 229. **unable to work . . . walls were thin** (Letter from EB to "Marie," from Tacoma, Washington, July 12, 1946).
PAGE 231. **marries him for his bread** (EB, *HELLO*, p. 195).
PAGE 232. **loved him with his undivided self** (EB, Notes, Group Proceedings, May 27, 1952 [paraphrased]).
PAGES 234–235. **stomach churn** (EB, *SEXNHL*, p 224).
PAGE 235. **middle-age droop** (*ibid.*, p. 71). **waited and waited and waited:** This happened more than once, as Katherine Dusay, M.A. (September 20, 1978), told us: "When [Eric] got tired of being around people he would walk out, go upstairs or close the door—no excuses."
PAGES 236–237. **winners . . . absolute perfection** (Tape of TA Tuesday evening seminar of May 13, 1969 [paraphrased]).
PAGE 239. **imminent death** (Ellen Berne). **detectives . . . on his trail** (Claude Steiner).
PAGES 239–240. **able to love nobody . . . unsatiated hungering:** (James Branch Cabell, *Jurgen, supra*, p. 304–306).

Chapter 20: Stopped Running

PAGE 241. **a winner or a loser?** (EB, *HELLO*, p. 432).
PAGES 243. **millions of birds . . . time is not a river** (EB, *SEXNHL*, pp. 156–157).
PAGE 244. **do the *Bulletin* single-handedly** (Letter from EB, to David E. Kemp, Ph.D., January 5, 1970). **Joe Waterhouse** (Stephen B. Karpman, M.D., and Fanita English). Two weeks before his final heart attack, Berne called his

ex-secretary, Pamela Blum, and asked her to come over and see him. "This was part of a process he was going through at this time with several people. He was tying up loose ends almost as if he knew his death was imminent. He told me how good he felt about our relationship during the three years we had worked together. . . . I was very touched that he went to the trouble to get together to say such lovely things." (Pamela Blum).

PAGE 246. **Dorothy one-fourth . . . Torre one-twelfth** (Letter from EB to his lawyer, Mr. Kopp, December 15, 1969 [paraphrased]). **silent communion** (Hedges and Betty Capers).

PAGE 247. **how well he felt . . . before his heart attack** (Warren D. Cheney, M.A., M.A., "EB, Biographical Sketch" *TAJ 1*.1, January 1971, p. 20). **"Kept his machinery going"** (EB, *TA/PSYCH* "Acknowledgements"). See also "Jack in the Beanstalk Meets Cinderella," Chapter 11.

PAGE 249. **not really a 'cowpoke' . . . just a little boy** (Talcott Bates, M.D., letter to Professor Toro, *Monterey Peninsula Herald*, Monterey, Calif., used as an obituary for EB, July 23, 1970).

PAGE 250–251. The selection from the *Maisie* manuscript has been paraphrased.

Ω

Index

Adelphi, 101
Agammemnon Club, revisited, 166
Albert, Edith, 95
American Civil Liberties Union, 144
American Group Psychotherapy Asso. 175, 213
American Journal of Psychiatry, 95
American Medical Asso. News, 182
American Psychiatric Asso., 176, 180
Anderson, Marian, 112
Aronovitch, Michael, 91
Asher, Rabbi Joseph, 6

Bach, George, 231
Barron, Gerald (Jerry), 4
Bates, Talcott, 104, 249
Bazell, Arthur Haskel, 154, 155, 158
Berger, Charles, 177–179
Berne, Dorothy, 2, 36, 118, 119–151, passim, 223, 228, 229, 246–248
Berne, Ellen ("Nellie"), 3, 32, 36–63 passim, 115, 129, 173, 232, 244, 247
Berne, Eric,
  Army career,
    beginning of service, 41
    Baxter General Hospital, Spokane, Wash., 42
    Bushnell General Hospital, Brigham City, Utah, 115
    Carlisle Barracks, 49
    Fort Ord, Monterey County, Calif., 50
    head of psychiatric reconditioning, 101
    Fort Lewis, Madigan General Hospital, Tacoma, Wash., 116
  boyhood, 68–79
  early career positions,
    Mt. Sinai, New York, clinical asst. in Psychiatry, 13
    Englewood Hospital intern, 92, 93
    Ring Sanitarium, 97
    sanitarium in Connectictut, 12, 13, 19, 33
    Yale, 93
  childhood,
    birth of sister, 70, 71
    father, death of, 73
    predisposition towards psychiatry, 75, 76
  experiments,
    greeting rituals, xi–xii
    intimacy, xii, xiii, 205
    "stroking-go-round," 191–192
  golden age, 166–198
  grandparents, 74–75
  group technique,
    'roll call," 178
    "inner-outer circle switch," 178, 206–207
    reveals own dream, 152
  loyalty hearing, 144–145
  marriage, secret, 232
  marriage, mock, 223–224
  name changes, 34, 36
  novel Maisie Atkins, 94, 97, 250
  patients, respect for, 177–179
  poker and psychiatry, 137
  shock therapy, opposition to, 179
  TA terms, first used, 159
  terminations,
    Fort Ord, 144, 155,
    Mt. Zion Hospital (group therapy class), 157
    San Francisco Psychoanalytic Institute, 153–154
    Veterans Adm., 144, 155
  therapist, as, 161, 162, 181
Berne, Eric, Jr., 126
Berne, Sara, 13, 41, 52, 73–79 passim, 83, 84, 95–97, 106
Berne, Terence, 126–127
Bernstein, Eric Leonard, or Lennard, see Berne, Eric,
Bernstein, Isadore, 75 ("put husband through med school")

269

Bernstein, Sara, *see* Berne, Sara,
Blum, Pamela, 71, 176–177, 223, 226, 231
Born To Win, xvii–xviii
Boulton, Mary, 170, 173
Bowe, M.T. ("Mac"), 219–220, 226
Boyce, Melvin (Mel), 140, 161, 185, 221
Bransom, Alice Harvey, 16, 29, 46, 48
Brazil, Judge Anthony, 148
Breen, Michael, 174
Brill, A.A., 138
Brinig, Myron, 109
Brooks, Van Wyck, 108
Brown, Carol Steinbeck, 107, 112, 117, 142, 150
Brown, Rosabel, 62, 100, 103, 105, 108, 118, 248
Brunn, Howard, 115, 118, 135, 136, 226
Bulletin of the Eric Berne Seminar (BEBS), 252
Buchwald, Art, 183
Burney, Betty, 142, 227
Burton, Arthur, 198

Cabell, James Branch, 20, 35, 86, 138, 152, 218, 225, 239–240
Caen, Herb, 190–191, 223
Cagney, James, 107
Calderone, Mary, 198
Callaghan, Viola Litt (Vi), 2, 6, 171–174 *passim*, 186, 191, 207–208, 242
Canadian Jewish Chronicle, 74
Carmel Pine Cone, 3, 4, 51, 101, 102
Changing Lives Through Redecision Therapy, xviii
Cheney, Warren, 88, 247
Chester, Edith J., 172, 229
Colburn, Sam, 109, 116
Coles, Robert, 145–146
Collins, William J. (Bill), 169, 173
Concannon, Constance (Connie), 213–214
Concannon, Joseph P. (Joe), 161, 162, 175, 176
Conlan, Louis, 5
Cottington, Frances, 10 ("unable to love"), 87
Courland, Herbert (Herb), 8
Crane, Caroline, 7, 10 ("last amour"), 209–212, 247–248
Crosby, Maxine, 45
Crossman, Patricia (Pat), 10 ("Mickey Mouse masks"), 167, 208–209

Crown, Ernest, 82

Day the Dam Broke, The, 111
Delacroix, Eugene, 39
Dr. "H," 153–154
Dr. "J.," 157
Dusay, John, 6, 7, 8, 72, 124, 142, 168, 171, 174, 188–191, 196, 207, 242
Dusay, Katherine (Mulholland), 191

Edwards, Mary, *see* Mary Goulding
Egograms, 190
ego state,
  Adult, xvi, xvii, 159, 170, 192, 195, 224
  Child, xvi, xvii, 159, 170, 192, 195, 197, 200, 213, 224, 248
  Parent, xvi, xvii, 159, 192, 197, 224,
Elinor, xiii, 12–65 *passim*, 100, 125
Elinor's mother, 17, 28, 45, 52, 53, 55, 100
Emanu-El, Temple, 6
English, Fanita, xi–xii (post office experiment), 22, 38, 136, 167, 204–207, 212–213
Erikson, Erik, 105, 124, 138, 139, 153
Ernst, Frank, 2
Ernst, Kenneth (Ken), 209
Esalen, 195
Europa, 66–67
Everts, Kenneth, 164, 170

Fassett, William, 136
Faulkner, William, 42
Federn, Paul, 26, 27, 41, 116, 139, 141
Fidler, Jay, 176
Freud, Sigmund, 17, 89, 207, 209
frogs, 195, 197

Gamble, John, 162,
games,
  Blemish, xiii
  Lucy and the Football (or, Great Expectations), 216
  Kick Me, 197–98, 205, 206, 207
  Little Red Riding Hood, 25
  Let's You and Him Fight, 13–14
  Murgatroyd, 196
  Now I've Got You, You Son-of-a-Bitch (NIGYSOB), 237
  Poor Me, 201
  Uproar, 130
Games, definition of, xvii

INDEX

Games People Play, 1, 4, 5, 9, 85, 106, 133, 146, 150, 181–185 passim, 220, 228, 242, 245
Games Students Play, 209
Garbo, Greta, 51
Garrett, Annie, see Anne Morse,
Geisen, John B. (Jack), 109
Geisen, Florence, 109
Gestalt-TA debate, 195–197
Gifted Child and the Community, The, 79
Gimbel, Jake, lectures, 220
Giusi, Diana, 245
Giusi, Livia, 245
Giusi, Nadya, 2, 9, 221, 226, 228, 241, 242, 245
Giusi, Valerio, 2, 3, 220, 221, 226, 241, 245
Golden Gate Group Psychotherapy Association, 202
Goodstone, Gerald (Gerry), 73, 79–84 passim, 125, 139, 143, 228
Goulding, Mary (Edwards), xvii, 158, 173, 195–197, 219
Goulding, Robert L. (Bob), xvii, 134, 174, 196, 197, 205–206, 227, 242
Gray, Gretchen, 109
Gritter, Gordon, 171
Groder, Martin, 3, 166, 173–174, 234
Group therapy, Mt. Zion, 157–158
Group therapy vs. psychoanalysis, 167–168
Grove Press, 167, 182

Happy Valley, The, 49, 105, 166
Harlow, Jean, 51
Harris, Amy, xiv ("love him still"), xvii (co-author of *I'm OK— You're OK*), 185, 186
Harris, Sirrah (Dale), 226
Harris, Thomas A. (Tom), xiv ("love him still"), xvii, 168, 185, 186
Hartman, Kurt, 3 ("says anything funny"), 218, 220–222
Harvey, Wilbur (Bill), 55, 56
Hayes, Roland, 112
Herzl, Theodor, 35, 36
Hillel, 35
Hilliker, Virginia, 199–200
Houlgate-West, Torre, 2, 9, 198, 215–239 passim, 242, 244–246
House and Garden, 126
Hughes, Langston, 112
Human Fertility, 97

I'm OK—You're OK, xvii, 182

In and Out of the Garbage Pail, 196
Intimacy, quest for, xii–xiii, 244
Intimate Enemy, The, 231
International Journal of Group Psychotherapy, 117
ITAA (International Transactional Analysis Association), xiii, 8, 185, 209, 246, 252, 253

Jake Gimbel lectures, 220
James, Muriel, xvii, 182, 200–203, 227
James, Norman, xiii
Jeffers, Robinson, 3, 51, 108, 112
Jeffers, Una, 108
Jones, Ernest, 89
Jongward, Dorothy, xvii–xviii, 182
Jupiter, 66–67
Jurgen, 20, 21, 37, 39, 86, 107, 138, 152, 217, 218, 225, 239, 240
Jurgenesque, 118
Jurgenism, 102

Karpman Drama Triangle, 21, 174
Karpman, Stephen B. (Steve), 8, 168, 168–169, 188–196 passim, 203, 230, 242, 248
Kenny, Jake, 109
Khlentzos, Michael, 158, 177–180
Kohn, Leo, 92, 93
Krishnamurti, 51
Kupfer, David (Dave), 7, 8, 172, 174, 206, 210, 212, 246
Kupfer, Judy, see Judith Nordin

Langley Porter Neuropsychiatric Institute, 8, 189
Languth, Jack, 226
Lannestock, Gus, 110
Lapin, Albert, 18, 76, 84, 91, 144, 145, 248
Laughter on the Hill, 109
Lawrence, Frieda, 112
Layman's Guide to Psychiatry and Psychoanalysis, The, 78, 108, 153, 245
Levaggi, Jules, 158, 177–180 passim
Levin, Pamela, J. (Pam), xiii–xiv ("discoveries . . . not in time"), 7, 174, 203–204, 232
Levine, Anne, 61
Levine, Rachmiel, 61, 85, 133, 152
Levitin (Siris), Evelyn, 144–146, 226
Levitin, Lawrence, 72, 139, 144–146
Lewis, Sinclair, 51
Life magazine, 183, 225
Litt, Viola, see Callaghan, Viola,

Lloyd, Francis, 101
Lloyd, Frank, 2, 3 ("says anything funny"), 4, 101, 102, 109, 121, 127 ("happiness . . . psychiatrist"), 142, 228, 244
Lloyd, Marjory, 4, 101, 102, 104, 109, 116, 228, 229
London, Jack, 51
Los Angeles Times, 222

Mann, Thomas, 89
Manners, Lady Diana, 51
Margolick, Moses, 17, 43, 49, 50, 81, 85, 215, 223
Markham, Edwin, 202
Mark Twain, 34
Martin, Katie, *see* Schlepp
Maserati, 222
McEwen, Gwen, 172, 174
McAuley Neuropsychiatric Clinic, 158, 177, 180
McGill Annual, 81
McGill Daily, 35, 72, 85, 86
McGilliad, The, x–xi, 35, 85, 86, 102, 108
McGill University, 20, 76, 77, 78, 84, 102
Mc Gill Medical School, 76, 78, 82, 91, 138, 215
  anti-semitic quotas, 82, 85
McRae, Ian, 12–33 *passim*, 42, 43, 60
Medical Tribune, The, 106 ("underlying conflicts")
MENSA, 216
Miller, Henry, 112
Mind in Action, The, 101, 103, 108, 116, 120, 138–139, 229, 245
Mitchell, Virginia, 3–4 ("Monastery . . mind's eye"), 36, 104, 115, 142, 159 ("care free and boyish"), 161
Monastery, Carmelite, 3–4
Monterey Peninsula Herald, The, 143
Montreal anti-semitism, 80, 81
Montreal Daily Herald, 74
Montreal High School, 4, 74, 76, 84, 101, 102
Morse, Anne, 172
Mt. Zion Hospital, 157–158
Mulholland, Richard, 191
Mulholland, Katherine, *see*, Katherine Dusay
Munroe Bourne, J., 78 ("tall, handsome figure")
Mythology of Dark and Fair, The, 16

Navarro, Ramon, 112
Newsweek, 183
New York Times, The, 120, 133, 146, 182, 226
No Marriage in Paradise, 109
Nordin, Judith (Kupfer), 172, 221, 228, 232
Northcott, Margaret, 77 ("therapist . . . conversion"), 83–84, 157, 193, 203–204

Occam's Razor, 192, 193
Ohanian, Edward, 244
On Being Gifted, 79
Orthopsychiatric Conference, 231

Palmer, Francis, 135, 136
Palms, Elizabeth, 244
Parent-Adult-Child vs. Superego-Ego-and-Id, xvi
Parton, Margaret, 109
Perls, Fritz, 7, 195–197
Poindexter, Ray, 6
Poor, Henry Varnum, 112
Prescott, Mrs. Gene, 164
princes and princesses, 195
Power Is in the Patient, The, xviii
Principles of Group Treatment, 171, 246

Rose, Arthur, 95–97
Rose, Grace Berne, 2, 31, 32, 68–77 *passim*, 80, 84, 93, 95, 96, 97, 144, 199, 228
Royal Montreal Golf Club, 84, 101
Rukeyser, Muriel, 109

SAFTAS, *see* TA, seminars, Tuesday evening
St. Mary's Hospital, 177
Saltzer, Joseph, 85, 91, 92
Samuels, Anne, 215–217, 225–226, 235
Samuels, Solon D. ix ("demystification . . . cant"), 189, 215–217, 225, 235
San Francisco Psychoanalytic Institute, 138–140, 152–154, 159, 161, 164
San Francisco Chronicle, The, 190, 223
San Francisco Social Psychiatry Seminars *see* TA, seminars, Tuesday evening

INDEX 273

San Francisco TA Seminars (SAFTAS) see TA, seminars, Tuesday evening
San Jose Mercury, 219
Schiff, Jacqui (Olson), 186–188, 191, 227, 234, 239
Schlepp, Katie (Martin), 102–114 passim, 118 ("piquant gorgeousness")
School for Scandal, The, 224
script, xvii, 159, 168, 222, 231
Scripts People Live, xvii, 2, 7
Selye, Hans, 139
seven-year group, 159
Sex Information and Education Council of the U.S. (SIECUS), 198
Sex in Human Loving, 1, 12, 24, 25, 32, 49, 60, 68, 100, 115, 119, 124, 131, 133, 134, 138, 147, 149–150, 204, 215, 220, 224, 234, 242–243, 246, 248
Shaskan, Donald, 139, 145, 193
Sheridan, Richard Brinsley, 224
Short, John, 114, 117
Short, Marie, 99, 107–116 passim, 125, 126, 130, 133, 144, 146
Simon, Henry, 116
Smith, Stevie, 79
"Smyrna Embrace, The," 17,
Smythe, Dorothy, 4, 5, 237
Steffens, Lincoln, 51, 107
Steinbeck, John, 51, 112
Steinberg, Elliott, 225
Steiner, Claude, x, xii, xvii, 2, 3, 7, 166, 174, 188–195 passim, 203, 213, 222, 229–230, 248
Stewart, W.K. (Bill), 133, 135–136
Store, The, 21
strokes, xvii, 83–84, 192
stroking-go-round, 191
Structure and Dynamics of Organizations and Groups, The, 6, 156, 171, 186
Stuart, George, 100, 103
Stuart, Kippie, 100, 103
Superego-ego-id vs. Parent-Adult-Child, xvi
Swede, Southworth (Southey), 253

TA,
    Bulletin, (TAB), 8, 41, 63, 88, 170–175, 180, 181, 188, 191, 195, 198, 208, 244
    conferences, 173–174, 235
    Crown Princes (Three Musketeers), 188–196
    hospitality rooms, 176, 180–181
    seminars, Tuesday evening, 8, 164, 168, 170, 172, 199, 210, 213, 230, 236, 237
    seminars, first, 164
Karpman Revolution, 194
TA-Gestalt debate, 195–197
Three Musketeers, see Crown Princes
TA Stories for Kids, 209
Temple Emanu-El, 6
Thomas, Dylan, 112
Torre, see Houlgate-West
Transactional Analysis After Eric Berne, 187
Transactional Analysis in Psychotherapy, xvii, 128, 142–143, 166–168, 205
Transactional Analysis Journal (TAJ), 35, 180, 208
Tuesday evening seminars, see TA, seminars

University of California at Los Angeles, Lake Arrowhead program, 216
University of California at Santa Cruz, 220
University of California at San Francisco (Medical School), 209, 220

Vienna Conference (1968), 197
Veterans Administration clinics, 139, 145, 161–162
Vogue, 120

Wagner, Richard, 15, 16, 64
Wallis, Faith, 83
Weininger, Benjamin, 156, 164
Western Society of Psychiatrists and Psychologists, 198
Weston, Edward, 51, 109
Weston, Kraig, 109–117 passim, 130
Weston, Neil, 109–117 passim
What Do You Say After You Say Hello?, xii, 1, 60, 66, 140, 185, 195, 230, 241, 242, 246
Whitacre, J.C. II, 175
Whitcomb, Benjamin Bradford, 86–87
Williams, Cynthia, 109
Williams, Henry, 98, 99
Williams, Mary (Mrs. Allen), ix and 6 ("powerless . . . beauty"), xii ("cut . . . knife"), 162–163, 174
Williams, Mona, 98, 99

Williams, Russell, x ("doctor who knew him best"), 100, 109, 123, 249–250
Winter, Ella, 51, 108
Wood, Alfred (Al), 175
Wyckoff, Hogie, 210, 248

Yale University, 93
Yelin, Gabriel, 14, 81
Young Presidents' Organization, 235–236